specialtypress

WAVE-OFF!

Robert R. "Boom" Powell,
Commander, USN (Ret.)

W0391226

A History of LSOs and Ship-Board Landings

Specialty Press
Specialty Press
838 Lake Street South
Forest Lake, MN 55025
Phone: 651-277-1400 or 800-895-4585
Fax: 651-277-1203
www.specialtypress.com

© 2017 by Robert R. Powell

All rights reserved. No part of this publication may be reproduced or utilized in any form or by any means, electronic or mechanical, including photocopying, recording, or by any information storage and retrieval system, without prior permission from the Publisher. All text, photographs, and artwork are the property of the Author unless otherwise noted or credited.

The information in this work is true and complete to the best of our knowledge. However, all information is presented without any guarantee on the part of the Author or Publisher, who also disclaim any liability incurred in connection with the use of the information and any implied warranties of merchantability or fitness for a particular purpose. Readers are responsible for taking suitable and appropriate safety measures when performing any of the operations or activities described in this work.

All trademarks, trade names, model names and numbers, and other product designations referred to herein are the property of their respective owners and are used solely for identification purposes. This work is a publication of Specialty Press, and has not been licensed, approved, sponsored, or endorsed by any other person or entity. The publisher is not associated with any product, service, or vendor mentioned in this book, and does not endorse the products or services of any vendor mentioned in this book.

Edit by Mike Machat
Layout by Monica Seiberlich

ISBN 978-1-58007-235-9
Item No. SP235

Library of Congress Cataloging-in-Publication Data

Names: Powell, Robert R., author.
Title: Wave-off! : a history of LSOs and shipboard landings / Robert R. Powell.
Other titles: Wave-off! A history of landing signal officers and shipboard landings | History of LSOs and shipboard landings
Description: Forest Lake, MN : Specialty Press, [2017] | Includes bibliographical references and index.
Identifiers: LCCN 2016032678 | ISBN 9781580072359 (alk. paper)
Subjects: LCSH: United States. Navy–Aviation–History. | United States. Navy–Officers–History.
Classification: LCC VG93 .P66 2017 | DDC 359.9/40973–dc23
LC record available at https://lccn.loc.gov/2016032678

Written, edited, and designed in the U.S.A.
Printed in China

10 9 8 7 6 5 4 3 2 1

Front Cover:
Modern LSOs observe a Boeing F/A-18 Hornet close-up and heading for the carrier's "three wire" and a perfect "OK Pass."

Front Flap:
The LSO has done his job as a Vought F-8E Crusader traps aboard a carrier during the Vietnam war.

Front End Paper:
View from jet about to trap on the USS Oriskany *(CV-34). Pilot is using the ship's wake and the LSO to line up.*

Title Page:
LSO has just given the "cut" to a North American AJ-1 Savage attack bomber on USS Midway *(CVB-41). Judging from the wire caught in the tailhook, it is an in-flight engagement.*

Table of Contents:
Carrier deck is illuminated by the afterburner plumes of an F/A-18 Hornet as 35,000 pounds of thrust augmented by a steam catapult are about to launch the jet.

Rear End Paper:
View from jet about to trap on the USS Forrestal *(CVA-59). Pilot is using the Fresnel landing system to line up.*

Rear Flap:
Author as LSO for Vigilante *squadron RVAH-6 deployed in Tonkin Gulf on USS* Kittyhawk *(CVA-63).*

Back Cover:
LSO team watches a Boeing F/A-18F Super Hornet touch down on the USS Harry S. Truman *(CVN-75). (USN photo by MC3 K. Wilson)*

Back Cover Inset:
Posed photo for navy training manual shows a 1950s-era LSO standing in the correct position and giving proper signals to a landing pilot.

Distributed in the UK and Europe by

Crécy Publishing Ltd
1a Ringway Trading Estate
Shadowmoss Road
Manchester M22 5LH England
Tel: 44 161 499 0024
Fax : 44 161 499 0298
www.crecy.co.uk
enquiries@crecy.co.uk

TABLE OF CONTENTS

DEDICATION

To my wife, Marie, and all the other wives of LSOs. Being married to a navy pilot is difficult enough, not to mention enduring nights when your husband is home, but not actually at home because he is out at the air field until midnight and beyond, then out to sea for a week, or more, for CarQuals. Marie said to me when I was a RAG Paddles, "I almost wish you were back on sea duty."

I was floored. Why?

"It takes about ten days to get the house and kids running my way. When you are deployed for six, seven, eight months, I can do that. When you're off to some carrier and home after a week, it's hard."

Yes, it was hard and we Paddles never gave all of you enough credit. So, albeit belatedly, thank you for your support and understanding over the decades of carrier aviation. May this book give you some idea of why we were proud to be Landing Signal Officers.

PREFACE

I made my first trap on 15 June 1965, in a North American T-2A Buckeye jet trainer. Less than two weeks before I had been given the only "down" I received during my U.S. Navy training. The exhilaration of one's first landing on an aircraft carrier has been described many times before, although always inadequately as there are no words for the experience. I was excited and proud to have succeeded, especially after the crushing blow of failing to even be allowed to practice carrier approaches at the field. It was a landing signal officer who got me through. From my back seat he spoke all the right words in the right tone. He noted what I did wrong. He taught me how to correct. My logbook says Ellis, but does not list his rank or service. I do know he was an LSO.

What qualities does an LSO have that enable him to train pilots in the most demanding event in aviation? What skills must an LSO have to safely and routinely guide tons of airplane coming down at him at over 100 miles an hour onto a moving ship at sea? Did I have those qualities? Could I develop those skills? I would find out.

Landing signal officers are trained in what is basically an apprentice system. Thanks to my mentors, and my contemporaries, I learned. I spent seven years waving on the platform and no pilot I trained ever broke an airplane at the ship.

There is a body of lore among LSOs. Tales passed from generation to generation. Put together, the stories form a history of this unique profession. This, in turn, becomes a history of the aircraft carrier; that instrument of war is as important to national policy today as it was in the Pacific, Korea, and Vietnam. This is that history told from a vantage point in the center of the action.

ACKNOWLEDGMENTS

For this book, my thanks go to my pal Barrett Tillman who not only knows lots about naval aviation, but also can write about it superbly as his many books prove. BT also promises that when we get a Brisfit we'll go out and strafe the Bray-Corby Road as befits our shared fascination with the Great War.

Many thanks to my photo suppliers, : Doug Siegfried at Tailhook, Tommy Tomason, Warren Thompson, Stan Piet, and Jan Jacobs. I know most of what we are using is public use with navy origins, but your efforts in collecting and maintaining good copies of photographs is admirable. I will try to give credit for the images as used.

We met only once at a symposium when I had a chance to briefly compliment Norman Polmar on his work. I'm repeating that now with emphasis for all his research and knowledge.

Thanks to my British correspondents who helped provide information difficult to acquire on this side of the Atlantic, especially Jack Thomas and David "Shorty" Hamilton down in Australia.

The entire staff at the LSO School. Without the cooperation of the Officers-in-charge, "Weeds" Wedertz, "Potso" Pothier, and "RJ" Roberts, this book would not be up to date.

INTRODUCTION

In the United States Navy, they are Landing Signal Officers (LSO) or, casually, Paddles. In the Royal Navy, Deck Landing Control Officers (DLCO) or, informally, Batsmen. I will use each of the four terms as applicable, but when referring to them in general use the simplest, LSO, rather than awkward compound constructs.

The first time a ship appears in a chapter she will have her title, full name, and designation (if there is one). Thereafter I will use only title and name and may drop titles if the name is used frequently and doing so does not cause confusion. Titles are USS (United States Ship), HMS (His Majesty's Ship, i.e., the British Navy) and IJN (Imperial Japanese Navy). Other navies will be indicated where appropriate. Ship nicknames will be in quotations. In keeping with long-standing nautical tradition, ships are feminine, with the pronoun "she" and adjective "her." Also, because the first female LSO did not appear until 1983 I have little reason not to use "he," "him," and "his" for this history.

When naval aviators get together they rarely say "aircraft carrier," but rather simply say, "carrier," so too in writing. I have no set rule when to use which. In the U.S. Navy, we will also call the carrier "the boat," as in, "Hit the boat" or "Go to the boat" for landings at sea. "Looking good around the boat" is a major point of pride. "Boat" for "carrier" is a bit too casual for this book.

The standard "ball call" consists of squadron call sign and aircraft side number (who you are), type of airplane, ball (you can see it), and fuel quantity (state) in thousands of pounds. For example, in my first squadron I would have called, "Nevada 105 (Sky)hawk, ball, 2 point 4."

Each chapter concludes with end notes that include references, attributions, and bits of related information not necessary to the narrative.

U.S. aircraft designations have the unusual problem of having two: a pre-1962 of the complex navy system and one after the system was standardized between all the American services. In cases during the transition period both designations will be shown. British aircraft lacked designations for many years and relied solely on names.

What is the difference between a sea story and a fairy tale? A fairy tale begins, "Once upon a time. . . ." A sea story begins, "This Is No S**t. . . ." These tales are sometimes called TINS. They are true, but have details wrong and maybe a bit of embellishment added. They are told in ready rooms, officers messes, hangars, bars; anywhere aviators of any nation gather. I have collected TINS tales for years and will share some in this book.

Publisher's Note: In reporting history, the images required to tell the tale will vary greatly in quality, especially by modern photographic standards. While some images in this volume are not up to those digital standards, we have included them, as we feel they are an important element in telling the story.

PROLOGUE

Eugene Ely's landing aboard USS *Pennsylvania* in January 1911 is considered the beginning of carrier aviation. It is not.

Nor is Squadron Leader Dunning's bringing a Sopwith Pup successfully aboard HMS *Furious* the beginning of carrier aviation. Both were important events, but neither marked the start of consistent flights off, and especially on, a ship specialized for aviation.

U.S. Navy Captain W. I. Chambers had considered naval use of the newfangled flying machines earlier, and Glen Curtiss' flight from Albany, New York, to New York City convinced him of their value. At an air meet near Baltimore, Chambers met Eugene Ely, who readily volunteered to try flying from a ship. Arrangements were soon made with airplane maker Glen Curtiss for an experimental demonstration using a navy ship. For Curtiss it was as much a marketing event as a demonstration of his aeroplane's capabilities. Not only was Ely a civilian but the airplane was owned by the Curtiss Company and not the military.

The takeoff was from an 84-foot-long wooden platform sloping down over the bow of the light cruiser USS *Birmingham* anchored in the Hampton Roads of Virginia. Two months later, a platform sloping slightly upward was constructed over the stern and aft turret of the armored cruiser USS *Pennsylvania,* which, for the experiment, was in San Francisco Bay. Three hooks were put under the Ely-Curtiss Pusher's keel to engage ropes laid across the 119-foot-long deck and held up by wooden rails on both sides. Lt. T. Ellyson, who had just begun training at the Curtiss school and would become U.S. Naval Aviator #1, suggested sandbags at the ends of the ropes to slow the aeroplane to a stop. A heavy canvas barrier was rigged to prevent running into the ship's superstructure. The plan was to have the cruiser underway to provide wind for landing, but weather precluded this. After landing, there was lunch in the wardroom with Mrs. Ely and the captain of the *Pennsylvania*. One hour later, the Pusher was turned around and Ely flew ashore. The experiment was successful . . . and over.

Eugene Ely being led away from his airplane. He is wearing a business suit with bicycle inner tubes wrapped around his chest. After snagging five of the ropes with duffels, he slid left on roll-out until his left main wheel skidded against the longitudinal board toward the nets rigged over the side. (U.S. Navy Historical Center)

The most widely used photograph of the event. Ely has just touched down. The weights on the rope ends are sailors' duffle bags filled with sand. The ropes are held off the deck by boards running fore and aft. (U.S. Navy Historical Center)

Dunning's first landing on HMS* Furious. *Pull-down straps are fastened to the same structure as the interplane struts, forward of the lower ailerons. Grabbing them took some courage. (Phillip Jarrett Collection)

This author is lucky to be one of the very few pilots to fly the replica 1911 Ely-Curtiss Pusher built by Bob Coolbaugh (a retired naval aviator and LSO) for the Centennial of Naval Aviation. Flying the open framework, lightly wing loaded, dynamically pitch unstable, canard controlled flying machine with primitive, sluggish ailerons for roll control, made my respect for Eugene Ely's feat go way, way up.

Unnoticed at the time was the fact that Ely made his landing while the ship was not moving. The plan was to have *Pennsylvania* underway to provide wind to slow the aeroplane's relative speed, but the captain did not feel he had enough room to maneuver and remained at anchor.[1] As the landings on *Furious'* afterdeck later showed, the turbulence caused by a ship's superstructure was a major obstacle to shipboard landings. With the limited controllability of the Ely-Curtiss Pusher, any turbulence behind the ship would likely have resulted in a crash.

The smoothness of the air behind an aircraft carrier remains an issue into modern times. LSOs learn the particular characteristics of their carrier in different wind conditions and anticipate how they will affect an aircraft during its approach. They use the terms "wind over the deck" and "burble."

Later in 1911 a successful airplane catapult was demonstrated at the Washington Navy Yard, and Captain Chambers decided this was what the U.S. Navy needed for aircraft at sea. No large landing areas were needed to interfere with ships' guns. Seaplanes could be launched on scouting and gunfire spotting missions from a catapult, land alongside, and be hoisted back on board. As a result of this thinking, development of ships as carriers for airplanes at sea stopped in the United States.

Furious

HMS *Furious* has a valid claim to being the first aircraft carrier, although which of her iterations marks the beginning depends on one's definition.

Laid down as a cruiser in 1916, her completion was delayed in order to have two huge, 18-inch guns (one gun in each turret fore and aft) installed.[2] In March 1917, orders were to complete *Furious* as a "partial aircraft carrier." The forward turret was removed and replaced with a hangar and a 228-foot flying-off deck sloping to the bow. This was the configuration when

After HMS* Furious *had a flying-on deck added over her stern, landing trials using Sopwith Pups fitted with skids were attempted. They were not successful. No provision was made to arrest the airplanes; stopping depended on friction from the skids and the sloped ramp at the end of the landing area. Even if the airplane had remained intact the problem of moving it is apparent. (Philip Jarrett Collection)

Commander E. H. Dunning managed the first landing on a moving ship on 2 August 1917.

As the senior flying officer, Dunning was frustrated because after his Sopwith Pups flew off, they had to either land ashore (if land was close enough) or ditch alongside a ship, in which case the aircraft was lost and most likely the pilot would be as well. Built as a cruiser, *Furious* was fast enough to maintain speeds above 25 knots. Slowed to just above stalling, the Pup's speed was not much more than the combined ship's speed and the surface wind. Dunning flew alongside and side-slipped onto the platform where his fellow officers rushed out and grabbed ropes attached near the ailerons to stop the aircraft. Five days later, Dunning did it again. This day the winds were stronger, and after landing, the Pup was blown back into the edge of the elevator and damaged. Dunning had another Pup warmed up and took off again. There was some confusion during this approach as to his intentions, but in an apparent attempt to go around, the engine faltered and the airplane stalled and crashed into the sea. Commander Dunning was drowned.

Frederick Rutland, who succeeded Dunning as senior officer flying, wrote in a report to the admiralty, "Landings using Dunning's technique could be made 'by any good pilot,' provided a ten-landing life expectancy was acceptable."[3] HMS *Furious* was back in the shipyard in November to have a flying-on deck added. The aft turret and gun were removed and another hangar built with a 287-foot platform above. Trackways were built on both sides of the superstructure to move aircraft from landing to takeoff deck. "In March 1918 when the *Furious* emerged from the yard she was an aircraft carrier at both ends and a monstrosity amidships; as an aircraft carrier she was a horror. The hot boiler gasses that poured from her centerline funnel affected the density of air over her stern. This coupled with the bridge structure cutting off the air streams over the landing deck and creating air eddies made landing a most difficult proposition. Almost every attempt ended in an accident of varying severity."[4]

For stopping, the landing-on deck sloped upward with cables stretched across the deck and heavy sandbags at the ends, the same arrangement used on USS *Pennsylvania*, seven years before. In addition, cables were run lengthwise to prevent the airplanes from drifting off to the side. Replacing the wheels with skids on some of the Pups was also tried. All had little effect. Rutland was himself blown over the side and barely escaped the crash. Successful landings were few. Lieutenant G. Chevalier (U.S. Naval Aviator #7) was on board as an observer.[5] "After numerous attempts, the use of the afterdeck for this purpose was abandoned as they had nine crashes. The air disturbance caused by the mast and stack made the planes practically unmanageable just at the moment of lighting."[6]

Because of these problems *Furious* was declared a "take-off only" carrier. But in July 1918 she went into the record books again when seven Sopwith Camels launched from her deck to attack the German Zeppelin sheds at Tondern in Norway. It was the first time land planes launched from a ship to attack a shore target.

Carrying two 50-pound Cooper bombs each, the Camels bombed the huge sheds and set fire to Zeppelins L-54 and L-60. Only two of the Camels returned to the ship and due to misunderstood procedures did not land aboard but ditched alongside.

Less than a month later, a Camel flew off a barge towed behind a destroyer and shot down Zeppelin L-53. Another Zeppelin was shot down by Lt B. A. Smart (later one of the pilots on the Tondern raid) in a Sopwith Pup, which had launched from the forward deck of HMS *Vindex*, for a total of four feared airships destroyed by naval airplanes. That none of the attacking aircraft were seaplanes was the impetus needed to authorize the construction of the first true aircraft carriers: *Vindictive, Argus, Eagle,* and *Hermes*.

The First Takeoff

Little known is that the first takeoff from a ship in November 1910 came close to being a disaster: Eugene Ely waited as long as he could, weathered in with squalls in Hampton Roads. His original plan was to have the cruiser USS *Birmingham* steaming for a little wind over the deck but low visibility and freezing rain squelched that plan. The *Birmingham*'s CO dropped anchor off Willoughby Spit in the Roads to await better weather. Around noon Ely finally decided to go for it during a brief, calmer spell in the weather even though it meant the takeoff would be at anchor and with absolutely no help from the wind. He said he calculated he would need to run the ramp and push the nose over to clear the tail and to gain a little more flying speed as he dropped toward the water. He later admitted that he misjudged his pull out and dipped the main wheels into the bay, getting saltwater on his goggles, throwing up rooster tails from the tires, which went back through the propeller blades, cracking the propeller and setting up a severe vibration. Ely knew he was able to fly the plane for a while, but did not know how long the propeller would hold together. Visibility was terrible and he could not see Norfolk Naval Station where he was supposed to land. He could just make out Willoughby Spit hooking out from the station, headed straight for it, and landed out near the end. At the time he considered his attempt a failure because he had wrecked the propeller and he had not made it to the naval station where the observers were waiting. He was amazed by the tumultuous reception he received when the officials arrived where he landed, congratulating him for the tremendous success. Guess he was scratching his head a bit. Better lucky than good! (Bob Coolbaugh from sources at the Glen Curtiss Museum in Hammondsport, New York)

FIRST STEPS
1918–1930

USS Saratoga *with a pair of Vought O2SUs overhead. The cruiser hull she was built on and enclosed bow give her racy lines while the wide exhaust stack and split island add a distinctive profile. Many old timers claim "Sister Sara" and "Lady Lex" were the best looking aircraft carriers ever built.*

As soon as there were airplanes there was a need to send them to sea. What naval commander would not want an observer several thousand feet in the air instead of only the highest mast? How could anyone resist being able to hop in the air from the nearby river, lake, or sea?

In the Beginning

The Wrights are credited with flying first in 1903, but the possibilities of their invention were not recognized until 1908. In 1910 in Europe, Frenchman Henri Fabré built a spindly contraption on floats and in the harbor at Nice made the first successful seaplane flight.[1] Glen Curtiss put one of his early flying machines on floats in January 1911, added retractable wheels a month later, and sold the first amphibian to the U.S. Navy.

While Curtiss and Ely performed the first takeoffs and landing on a ship with the cooperation of the U.S. Navy, further development of the capability to land on a ship languished in the United States until the 1920s. With the pride and emphasis Great Britain placed on their navy as the defender of the Island, it was no surprise that the Royal Navy pursued getting airplanes into sea battles before other nations. The commandant of the newly formed Naval Wing of the Royal Flying Corps (RFC), CDR Samson, flew off a temporary platform on the battleship *Hibernia* during the Naval Review in May of 1912. Because *Hibernia* was underway doing more than 10 knots, Samson is credited with the first takeoff from a moving ship.

In 1913 a flying-off platform, hangar, and cranes were built onto HMS *Hermes* for trials. Successful launches of both seaplanes and wheeled aircraft were made using a dolly, which then splashed into the sea. Land planes would, of course, have to land ashore or ditch alongside. After alighting, the seaplanes would water taxi alongside the ship to be hoisted on board. After these experiments all aviation equipment was removed from *Hermes*. Ironically, as this was being done, World War I began and the platform and hangar storage was ordered to be reinstalled. *Hermes* was thus the first of what was termed "seaplane carriers."[2]

With the start of the war, three cross-channel ferries were taken over by the Royal Navy for conversion to seaplane carriers with flying platforms, cranes, and hangars. *Ark Royal*, a former merchant hull, was the first ship completed in late 1914 as a seaplane carrier. Her elevated deck was originally to be used as a workspace, but later was used for launching aircraft.

The next year saw three more ships (Isle of Man steamers this time) impressed into the navy and converted. Two German ships captured in Egypt in 1914 added to the World War I British seaplane carrier fleet. As aircraft evolved, bigger ships with proper platforms and facilities were needed. HMS *Campania* was converted from a passenger liner and had a 200-foot-long flight deck. *Campania* was in use by August 1915. HMS *Nirvana* and *Pegasus* were the same basic design and at sea by February 1917.

Of the 57 countries that fought in World War I, 14 had naval air arms of some sort; with Great Britain, France, Germany, Russia, and Japan having seaplane carriers.[3] They saw varying degrees of action, but in all cases were limited by the number of aircraft carried and the time it took to set up, launch, and recover those airplanes.

Zeppelin Motivation

Zeppelins were feared in England out of proportion to their effectiveness. The Royal Navy was particularly concerned because the Zeppelins could cover wide areas of ocean. A Sopwith Pup, which had taken off from a platform built on the turret of a light cruiser, shot one down over the North Sea. A year later airplanes that had taken off from *Furious* raided Tondern and destroyed two zeppelins with two of their massive storage sheds. Only a month later a Camel from an ingenious barge towed behind a destroyer bagged another Zeppelin.

These destructions of Zeppelins by airplanes launched from the sea provided a popular and official impetus to continue carrier development. By late 1918 *Furious* was operating, *Argus* and *Vindictive* were complete, and HMS *Eagle* was launched.[4]

Vindictive's career as an aircraft carrier was brief. Originally a light cruiser her design was similar to *Furious*' with flight decks forward and aft on top of hangar spaces with trackways on both sides around the superstructure sticking up in the middle of the ship. *Vindictive* saw little action during the war. Her most significant action was transporting aircraft to the mostly forgotten British Expeditionary Force supporting the White Russians against the Bolsheviks in 1919. *Vindictive* was converted back to a cruiser in 1923.

HMS *Furious*: The True First Carrier, Eventually

A trio of light cruisers was laid down in 1915: *Glorious*, *Courageous*, and *Furious*. *Glorious* and *Courageous* (both became carriers in the 1920s) were completed with torpedo tubes and 15-inch guns in late 1916. *Furious* was delayed by her new, and eccentric, main armament of two huge, 18-inch guns. She was almost complete (the forward turret gun was not yet installed, the one aft was) when orders came to add a flying-off deck with a hangar underneath where the forward turret was to have been. The deck was 228 feet long and 50 feet wide. Flight operations were to have been the same as on the seaplane carriers; takeoff from the platform, land ashore or alongside to be hoisted on board. With a cruiser hull and engines *Furious* was fast enough, 31 knots, to stay with the battle fleet, a big advantage. *Furious* joined the fleet in July 1917.

Dunning Does It

The senior flying officer in *Furious* was Squadron Leader E. H. Dunning. Dunning reasoned that if the ship was moving at 30 knots and there was a wind of 20 knots there would be little relative motion if a Sopwith Pup flew alongside at a speed just above the airplane's stall speed. On 2 August 1917 he tried this daring experiment. After taking off he flew alongside *Furious,* and when beside the platform he used rudder to skid the Pup over the center of the narrow deck. Fellow officers ran out and grabbed rope loops on the wings to hold him down on deck. The first landing on a moving ship had been done.

Rotary Engines

What makes Dunning's landing, and the others that followed, all the more amazing is that their airplanes were powered by rotary engines. Because the propeller and cylinders are rigidly connected and spin together, rotary engines cannot have exhaust pipes, oil sumps or, most important, a normal carburetor, so only limited throttling is possible. A fuel-air mixture control adjusts the engine to get full power, "max revs" as the Royal Flying Corps pilots used to say. To avoid upsetting the mixture and ending up with a lean or rich cut that could cause the engine to die at the most inopportune time, pilots pressed a button that switched off the ignition to slow for landing. As long as the button was held down the engine was not developing power. However, fuel and air continued to fill the cylinders. If the ignition was off for too long the gas would build up and when the spark plugs fired again a cylinder or two would sometimes blow off. Consequently, the technique for landing was to press the button intermittently; it became known as the "blip switch."

The idea of blipping an engine while moving normal flight controls while flying alongside a moving ship a few miles an hour above stall speed while side-slipping onto a tiny area of deck seems impossible to modern pilots.

Five days later Dunning did it again. This time the wind over the deck got the better of the handlers; the Pup blew back into the superstructure and was wrecked. A second Pup was readied and Dunning took off again. On the next approach, he felt he was moving sideways too rapidly and tried to go around. The engine faltered and the airplane fell over the side. Dunning drowned.

The landing experiments were halted.

The Landing-on Deck

To address initial concerns about airplanes swerving to the side on early carriers, wires were arranged longitudinally, fore and aft. On *Furious* the arrestor wires were held 9 inches above the deck by two ramps[6] sloping upward. Arrowhead-shaped hooks were installed between the airplanes' wheels or skids, which engaged the wires and kept the airplane on the deck and going straight. As the wire and ramp at the end came together the airplane was brought to a stop. The first arrangement also had ropes across the wires with sandbags attached at each end to halt the forward motion. Experience showed that stopping was not difficult with the slow speed of the aircraft, and the transverse ropes were taken off. A rope barrier was erected forward of the wires to prevent aircraft that failed to engage the wires from crashing into the superstructure.

Axle hooks engaged the fore and aft wires to, it was hoped, keep aircraft straight before all navies with carriers realized the longitudinal wires were ineffective and probably caused more accidents than they prevented.

Landing safely on the new deck proved to be almost impossible. Of the 13 Pups that tried, 10 were heavily damaged. The skids were rigid wood and broke with the shock of landing. The hooks not only stopped the airplane but frequently flipped it up on its nose. However, the main problem was air turbulence caused by the superstructure, bridge, and hot gasses from the funnel.[7]

The landing experiments were halted. In July, Camels took off from the forward deck to raid Tondern with no expectation of landing back on board. With the Armistice, *Furious* was laid up while decisions about deck layout were made. She returned in a very different form in 1925.

Developments and Dead Ends

Having four aircraft carriers in work at the same time turned out to be an advantage, although it did not seem so at the time. All were, in a sense, experimental. Ideas were put forward for one, tried, and changes made to another. Concepts and equipment went back and forth between them; sometimes overlapping, sometimes in series.

Experience with *Furious* identified issues to be resolved for future aircraft carriers:

- Landing: how to keep aircraft on deck and bring them to a halt
- Deck handling: the need was for expeditious launches and recoveries. The fore and aft wires and hooks were exceedingly slow. Once clear of the arresting mechanism, how best to position aircraft on deck or into hangars.
- Airflow over the deck: a flat deck could be a solution to turbulence but ship handlers need an elevated bridge. A higher vantage point also enables control of the flight deck. The location of the funnels exhausting engine gasses was a major factor as well.
- Ship speed: higher ship speeds mean faster aircraft can fly aboard. High speed is tactically important because carriers are expected to keep up with the main battle fleet.
- Vulnerability: what is the best way to protect a carrier in battle: armor, guns, or fighter aircraft?

HMS *Argus*

In 1916 an uncompleted Italian ocean liner in a British shipyard was purchased for conversion to an aircraft carrier. The original plan called for an island on each side of the ship. Aircraft on deck would move between them![8] A model was tested in a wind tunnel and wind patterns proved unacceptable, but a redesign was not ordered until after *Furious'* sea trials with its frequent landing crashes. As a flush deck carrier *Argus'* bridge was under the front of the flight deck with a pilot house in the center, which was raised when there was no flying. Engine exhaust was routed from amidships under the flight deck and at the top of the hangar to the stern. At times the smoke

A Parnall Panther landing on HMS Furious. *The wires are longitudinal only and held up by ramps at the ends. The Panther was a two-seat airplane with a raised cockpit to increase landing visibility. In addition to axle hooks, a hydrovane on the landing gear was designed to prevent the Panther from flipping over in case of a water landing. The wings did not fold, but the fuselage did. Indicative of the RAF attitude toward carrier aviation, the 1917 design served until 1926.*

made the ship look like it was rocket powered. Commissioned in September 1918 *Argus* went to sea for deck landing trials the following month. Initial landings were made on a bare deck.

In a further test a canvas and wood dummy island was erected on the starboard side with a fire box making visible smoke. Pilots reported no problems with landing approaches and liked having a vertical object to help judge height.

After the dummy island was removed, the arresting gear from the laid-up *Furious* was installed. The first location was judged too far forward and the longitudinal wires were moved back over the aft elevator. The 60 x 18–foot elevator was fixed 18 inches below the flight deck with ramps at the front and rear edges. This "wire well" kept the airplanes equipped with a row of landing hooks to straighten the airplanes and bring them to a stop. The system worked (the pilots must have been skillful to drop airplanes into such a spot), but getting the airplanes clear of the wires and out of the well was a slow process, and that section of deck unusable for anything besides landings. In early 1919 the elevator was made flush and the wires raised by powered ramps at the ends.

Argus (nicknamed the "Flat Iron" or the "Hatbox") continued with various modifications and had a long career. She had duty on the China Station before being laid-up for most of the 1930s. The exigencies of war had her partially modernized and back in service in July 1938. *Argus* saw much use as a training carrier and for ferrying aircraft but also saw combat on Malta convoys and during Operation Torch. She survived the war and was scrapped in 1947.

HMS *Eagle*

HMS *Eagle* was based on the almost complete battleship *Almirante Cochrane*.[9] Purchased from Chile, the conversion began about the same time as the keel was laid for HMS *Hermes*. Both ships were in the same shipyard and work started and stopped as priorities changed. Together with an exchange of ideas and solutions was a competition for manpower and material.

Eagle had a long but narrow (15 feet wide) island, which had the bridge, two funnels, and a tripod mast that carried the fire-control directors for the 12 6-inch guns. The starboard placement of the island is apocryphal. The gyroscopic effect of the rotary engines on early airplanes pitched the nose up on a left turn, down on a right turn, so pilots preferred to turn left in the event of a go-around. Or, it may have been simply arbitrary, as one of the ship's designers later claimed. When later carriers did have an island, placing it on the starboard side became the norm. (The exceptions were two Japanese carriers, *Akagi* and *Hiryu*.)

Although launched in June 1916, work slowed with the end of the war and was completely suspended until *Eagle* was needed for trials. In April 1920 she went to sea with only two operable boilers and her elevators covered with steel plates. Aircraft flew over and around the ship investigating wind patterns. Starting in June there were 143 landings on board with only a dozen minor accidents. Modifications in 1921 included (1) forward flight deck faired into the bow for better airflow, (2) 9,700-gallon tank for aircraft fuel replacing the thousands of 2-gallon cans stowed on the forecastle, (3) shape and size of island changed in view of wind tunnel tests, (4) steel curtains installed in the hangars to isolate fires, and (5) landing wires expanded to 328 feet, which covered the entire length of the deck between the elevators. Aircraft capacity was up to 30. When finally commissioned in February 1924, *Eagle* was the largest aircraft carrier in the world.

HMS** Hermes **in her final configuration. The aft end of the flight deck has been extended and sloped down in an attempt to reduce turbulence.

In addition to the above changes, *Eagle* was the first carrier to include the following features that were incorporated into subsequent carriers: (1) a flight deck of 1-inch steel, which formed a main supporting structure, (2) two-level hangar storage, and (3) rounded aft deck to control airflow.

HMS *Hermes*

Hermes and Japan's *Hosho* have both been claimed as the first ships to be designed and built as aircraft carriers. The answer lies in parsing the definition. HMS *Hermes* had her keel laid first, but due to delays, IJN *Hosho* was launched and completed first.

In appearance *Hermes* was a smaller *Eagle*: half the displacement weight, shorter, and narrower. Construction began in January 1918 and she was launched in September of 1919, but work was then suspended pending trials with *Argus* and *Eagle*. At one point the builder was forbidden to do any work above the hangar deck without specific approval because the final configuration was undecided.

Hermes was commissioned in February 1924 and spent time in the Mediterranean and Far East, including a brief spurt of combat.[10] Her wartime career was varied. In April 1942, sailing in convoy from Ceylon without airplanes on board, *Hermes* was attacked by waves of dive bombers from the Japanese carriers *Akagi, Hiryu,* and *Soryu*, which sank her and also a destroyer, corvette, and two tankers southeast of Trincomalee.

Japan's *Hosho*

During World War II American propaganda insisted the Japanese created nothing original, but only copied from the West. By the late 1930s this was untrue, but 50 years earlier the new Meiji government made a deliberate effort to modernize Japan and had sent an investigative delegation on an around-the-world tour to discover what was worth adopting from the West. For an army the Japanese requested assistance from the French. (That was until the Franco-Prussian War when they switched to the German victors as their model.) They noted their similarities with the island nation of Great Britain and so received training and assistance from the Royal Navy.

Japan sent observers to the war zones in Europe, including an officer who was on HMS *Furious* in 1918. That their navy had lagged behind in the 10 years since their victory over the Russians was obvious. In 1920, after some diplomatic quibbling, an unofficial, civilian mission was approved. An RAF pilot, who had experience

IJN Hosho *in 1922, after completion. The flight deck is narrow over the bow and slopes down to help airplanes taking off. The three exhaust stacks swiveled to the side during flying.*

The shape of IJN Hosho*'s forward deck is apparent as she steams on a calm day. Her maximum speed was 25 knots. Almost completely unarmored,* Hosho*'s normal capacity was 15 aircraft stored on two hangar decks.*

During modifications, IJN Hosho's island, tripod mast, and aircraft crane were removed. The forward part of the flight deck was made horizontal and a hydraulically operated barrier that could be erected in 3 seconds was installed.

in many naval aircraft, and a team of technical experts brought 100 aircraft to Japan the following year.

IJN *Hosho* (Flying Phoenix) was closely modeled on HMS *Hermes* and also designed with a cruiser hull. Commissioned in December 1922, the first landings and takeoffs were made by an ex-RNAS (Royal Navy Air Service) pilot working for the Mitsubishi Company, which was building three types of carrier airplanes designed by a former Sopwith engineer. Soon after, the cadre of Japanese pilots that had been trained by the British mission operated on the *Hosho*.

The longitudinal wires proved unsatisfactory after a series of nose-overs and were removed. Built with a small island to minimize wind problems, the island's size proved too small for navigation, flying, or gunnery control, plus the pilots thought it an obstruction so it was removed in 1924 and *Hosho* became a flush-deck carrier. Through the 1920s she was used to develop procedures and equipment with two notable innovations. *Hosho* had a heavy net as a crash barrier, which could be raised and lowered hydraulically in a few seconds. The barrier kept landing airplanes from going into the elevator well when it was lowered or interfering with aircraft taking off on the forward part of the deck. The Japanese also developed an optical landing device to assist pilots in flying a correct approach. An arrangement of overlapping, colored lights, the system worked well enough that the equivalent of an LSO was not needed. The mirror/lens system used a different principle when it was developed some 30 years later. (More on the Japanese landing system and pilot training in a later chapter.)

Like HMS *Argus*, IJN *Hosho* survived World War II. Ironically, not only was she Japan's first aircraft carrier, but also its last. Until 1933 she was a frontline warship even though she was considered experimental when the Washington Treaty came into effect. *Hosho* was a training carrier from 1933 until 1938, but as the war with China intensified she went into combat. During World War II she was primarily a training carrier with some exceptions; during the Pearl Harbor attack she was back with the main group of battleships, a role she repeated during the Battle of Midway. After the surrender, *Hosho* made nine trips to Pacific islands and China bringing Japanese servicemen home. *Hosho* was scrapped in 1947.

The Forgotten French

FS *Béarn* (a French province) was started as a battleship, but construction stopped during World War I. What there was of the ship was launched in early 1920 in order to clear the slipway for other construction. Officials from the French Navy toured HMS *Argus* and on their recommendation, *Béarn* was converted to a CV. Later, details of *Eagle*'s conversion were made available to France (with enthusiasm according to some sources; somewhat grudgingly according to others).[11] Even before her completion, aircraft performed tests on a temporary deck built on the bare hull. The full conversion was completed in May 1927.

Béarn was distinguished by her island structure that extended away from the hull, leaving the entire width of the flight deck usable. Another unique feature was her massive elevator doors. French thinking (and English) stressed the importance of getting as many airplanes into the hangar as rapidly as possible. The designers of the *Béarn* realized that when an elevator was lowered the open well became unusable space; to remedy the void they built the doors large and strong enough to allow aircraft to move across them. The difficulty was the time it took for the doors to swing open or closed. When the doors were anything but flush with the deck, landings or takeoffs were impossible. A French report in 1937 cited the following recovery times:

- FS *Béarn*: Recover 15 aircraft in 68 minutes
- HMS *Glorious*: 32 aircraft in 42 minutes
- USS *Saratoga*: 40 aircraft in 11 minutes 20 seconds

Béarn never launched aircraft into combat; she was considered an experimental ship and her planned replacements never happened. Although her elevator design may have been a failure, *Béarn* was the first to have transverse arresting gear installed, use inert gas in gasoline storage, and operate a two-engine airplane. When World War II began *Béarn* was pressed into frontline service. In late 1939 she was part of the Allied effort to hunt down the Nazi battle cruiser *Graf Spee*. When France was invaded, *Béarn* went into Toulon and loaded Bank of France gold bullion, which was transported to Canada. The aircraft carrier then loaded 102 aircraft, which had been ordered from American manufacturers. Partway across the Atlantic, when France surrendered to Germany *Béarn* went to Martinique and was interned to prevent her from going to the German navy. The airplanes were off-loaded and in time became unserviceable. Assumed by the Free French Navy, *Béarn* went to the United States for refit and optimization as an aircraft transport. Immediately after the end of World War II she carried airplanes and military equipment, including large amphibious vehicles, to Indo-China. Back in France *Béarn* ingloriously became a barracks ship until sold for scrap in 1967.

USS *Langley*

After Ely demonstrated that landing an airplane on a ship was possible the United States Navy did nothing about developing an aircraft carrier for eight years. U.S. Naval Aviation emphasized seaplanes throughout the First World War. Senior officers, including John Towers (Naval Aviator 3#) who had been a naval attaché in London in 1916 and been aboard HMS *Furious*, spoke against the concept of a CV. Finally, in 1919, when the British had four aircraft carriers in operation, the decision to convert two ships was made. However, the United States Congress allowed funding for only one.

What type of ship to convert then became an issue. A British naval constructor had brought the preliminary design for HMS *Hermes* and had been advising the U.S. Navy's Bureau of Construction since 1917.

Poor Comic Ship [12]

USS *Jupiter* was a logical choice. She was a collier with updated engines and her role as a coal ship had disappeared with the U.S. Navy's transition to oil for ships' fuel. Her large holds were easy to make into gasoline and ammunition storage and hangars. A 534 x 64–foot flight deck was erected on girders above the main deck. The hangars were only large enough for storage and maintenance. Complete assembly was done on what had been the collier's

An Aeromarine VE-7 landing on USS* Langley *(CV-1). Both the transverse arresting wires and the many longitudinal wires are apparent.

Nine days after the first takeoff, LCDR Godfrey Chevalier made the first American trap in October 1922. The Aeromarine 39B nosed over in the complex set of axial and longitudinal wires held off the deck by foldable supports.

A Vought VE-7 being hoisted aboard. VE-7s equipped the U.S. Navy's first two fighter squadrons and were on Langley *until 1927. The first takeoff was made in a VE-7.*

USS Langley *transiting the Panama Canal on a 1920s postcard.*

USS* Langley *(CV-1) in Pearl Harbor, May 1928, with 34 aircraft on the flight deck. The structure on the fantail began as a pigeon coop, but was converted into the executive officer's cabin. (Navy Historical Center via Thomason)

main deck. The airplanes were then put on the single elevator by overhead traveling cranes to be lifted up to the flight deck. (The lowered elevator was 8 feet above the deck and moving airplanes on and off took a great deal of time.) Upon commissioning in 1922 she was named USS *Langley* and designated CV-1, the first of over 200 American ships that were, and are, carriers. Because of the appearance of her raised deck she was smilingly called the "Covered Wagon,"[12] which was later taken for the ship's insignia. Considered experimental, *Langley* overcame her liabilities and developed devices and techniques that, despite its late start, made the United States Navy the leader in aircraft carrier operations.

The question of what equipment was best needed to land wheeled aircraft was approached scientifically. A navy reservist, LT A. M. Pride was put in charge of the project. A large rotatable platform that could be faced into the wind was built at the Norfolk, Virginia, air station and different systems tested. The result, which was put on CV-1, was longitudinal wires for alignment and transverse wires connected to weights to stop the aircraft. Experience showed that the action of the cross-deck cable as it pulled out tended to keep the airplanes centered, and the longitudinal wires were eventually removed.

The Mark 1 arresting gear was an adjustable stack of weights connected to a sheave (multiple grooved pulleys) that was lifted when an airplane's tailhook caught a cross-deck pennant (cable). The weights and sheaves were in pairs of towers on the flight deck. Because the towers were in the way they were soon removed and the weights suspended in the hold.

Admiral Joseph Reeves was instrumental in the development of American carrier aviation. Although his early career included command of several battleships (he was also the first CO of USS *Jupiter*), after attending the Naval War College he chose to become part of naval aviation and qualified as a Naval Aviation Observer at the age of 53.[13] His first assignment was Commander, Aircraft Squadron, Battle Fleet. And his flagship was USS *Langley*, the former *Jupiter*.

Convinced of the need to launch attacks with as many aircraft as possible, Reeves knew that the dozen airplanes *Langley* was designed for was inadequate and drove the changes that doubled, then tripled, the airplanes on board until, finally, she could operate 42. This was possible because of new equipment, the crash barrier, and new procedures, what today are called cyclic operations.

Other carriers had barriers to stop aircraft that went past the landing area, but they were more or less permanently in place. The new crash barrier was a set of wires held a couple of feet over the deck by movable stanchions, which could be quickly lowered pneumatically. If an airplane went into the barrier, there was usually little damage and it did not continue forward into the pack of airplanes parked forward. If the airplane arrested normally, the barrier was lowered and the airplane could taxi forward to its parking spot.

Earlier thinking made getting aircraft off the flight deck the goal. *Langley*'s awkward elevator (it took a quarter of an hour to get an airplane off the 8-foot-high platform onto the main deck) may have forced the new procedure: an airplane landed and its tailhook engaged the arresting wires, the hook was cleared of the wires, the barrier lowered, and the airplane taxied forward and parked. After all the aircraft were onboard, they were pushed back to the aft part of the flight deck to be refueled and rearmed. When ready they took off using the open deck in front of them, flew the mission, and landed back aboard, repeating the cycle.

Crowded conditions and rapid movement are inherently hazardous and the pilots expressed their reservations. Reeves overruled them. Because the United States Navy did not have to put up with an ambiguous chain-of-command as the British did with their RN/RAF arrangement, fast tempo and effective cyclic ops became normal on American carriers.

USS** Langley **with stacks swung to the side. The appearance of the flight deck raised by supports from the main deck gave her the name "Covered Wagon." (Navy Historical Center via Thompson)

Langley ***pier-side in 1924 at what became NAS North Island. The city of San Diego is on the other side of the harbor. Airplanes landed at the airfield and taxied up the access road to be hoisted aboard.***

NAS San Diego was established in 1917. The north side was Army Air Corps until 1937. In 1945 the Spanish Bight was filled in, connecting the city of Coronado (left of the picture) and the air station. The area on San Diego Harbor became a wharf large enough for aircraft carriers and remains in use today. (See a picture of the same area in the epilogue.)

For the first 18 months each pilot flew his approach unaided for the *Covered Wagon*'s first 200 or so landings. Then at some time in early 1923 occurred a seminal event.

The First LSO

There are many stories on how the LSO came to be; some apocryphal, some embellished. The most accurate comes from J. R. Tate, who was in the first squadron assigned to the *Langley*:

Commander Kenneth Whiting, the exec and the senior aviator, always watched the landings from the stern of the flight deck, on the port side. He developed a type of backseat driving and talked out loud and made appropriate motions. "He's too low, now he's too high, now he's okay." Lt. A. M. "Mel" Pride, who was just about the hottest pilot on board and whose piloting was precision plus, had developed a dragging nose-high approach with power, which eventually became the standard type approach. He came in for a landing in a TS-2 fighter.

On deck afterward, while discussing the landing with Whiting and "Squash" Griffin, Pride remarked to Whiting, "You were wrong on my being too low on the approach. I was over the stern by 10 feet and caught the #2 wire." Whiting looked at him in surprise and asked, "Did you see me?" Pride laughed, "We all watched you waving, too high, too low, and OK." Whiting called a meeting of all pilots and set up a plan to station an experienced pilot on the port-side stern of the flight deck, who used a pair of semaphore flags to monitor each approach. At first, Whiting supplied the comments and the flag waving was done by one of the junior aviators. We used only three signals: OK, too high. And too low. Later we added the cut. When *Lexington* and *Saratoga* came into the picture, additional signals were added and the cut became a mandatory order.[14]

A Loening OL-3 coming in for a landing on USS **Langley** ***circa 1924. LCDR Kenneth Whiting (Naval Aviator 16#) Langley's XO, may be the LSO (although the term had not yet been coined). He is wearing a safety belt with two lanyards holding him against the wind on the narrow platform. For some reason, the left flag and lanyard were scratched out on the negative.***

A VE-7 being shown a "high" signal coming aboard **Langley**. ***A special platform for the nascent LSO has not yet been built. A safety net surrounds both sides of the flight deck. The net can be swung up to be a safety barrier. A very large net extends from the aft edge of the flight deck (when the term "ramp" came into use is unknown), with the idea it that would protect the ship if the airplane flew into the stern!***

This VE-7 is equipped with a complex tailhook: an A-frame to a shaft allowing lateral motion, a hydro-vane in case of ditching, and a row of T-hooks on the axle between the wheels. The rectangular pieces hold up the fore and aft wires while the larger pieces with a rounded side move the transverse arresting wires (pennants) above the deck. Both folded down, allowing airplanes to move over them. Getting an airplane clear was slow and much like removing a bug from a spider's web.

LSO Jake Gorton had earned his wings in 1918 and set records in seaplanes. In January of 1925, *Langley* was considered ready to join the fleet. She steamed from Norfolk to the West Coast, where she trained carrier squadrons and participated in war games. *Langley*'s air operations officer was CDR Charles Mason. Enroute to the Pacific Fleet, he had the only man aboard who had made a carrier landing, LT D. L. Conley, act as LSO while pilots flew touch-and-go landings without the arresting gear rigged until he felt sure Gorton and LT Leo Compo knew what they were doing. "How Charlie Mason arrived at that decision I never knew," says Gorton, "but Compo and I were the first LSOs on an operational carrier." Mason decided Gorton would be the senior LSO and Compo would relieve him when Gorton flew.

Gorton and Compo discovered that they could tell better than the approaching pilots if it would be a safe landing. But as Gorton tells it, "We had a helluva time convincing the squadron pilots this was so. Mason had to tell the CO of some squadrons that if they did not obey the LSO, they would get a wave-off and never make a landing." He adds, "Of course, in those early days, I was learning, too, and there were times when I would make errors and bring them in out of the groove or too fast. But as time went on, I was damned sure when I gave a pilot a 'cut the gun' he was in the gear and not the barrier."

LSOs remained a feature of United States Navy aircraft carriers from then on. A decade later the Royal Navy recognized their value and created Deck Landing Control Officers (DLCO). All other navies with carriers except the Japanese also used LSOs.

The U.S. Navy's first three aircraft carriers in the Puget Sound Navy Yard in 1929. From top: USS* Lexington *(CV-2), USS* Saratoga *(CV-3), and USS* Langley. Saratoga *has a vertical black stripe on her funnel while* Lexington's *horizontal stripe is less apparent. Both have large white circles painted in the landing area to give pilots an aiming point for the flare.

USS* Langley *on display. If there was a launch, all the airplanes would be arranged as far aft as possible to maximize the takeoff run. Here, there are 11 airplanes on deck. Admiral Reeves worked out procedures so there would be 42 using hangar and deck parking.

USS Lexington *and USS* Saratoga *were the most heavily armed carriers. Because of uncertainty as to what an aircraft carrier's role in combat should be, both had four turrets with a pair of 8-inch guns as well as 12 5-inch guns on single mounts, with three on sponsons defending each ship's quarter. Both the wide forward elevator and the smaller one aft are lowered.*

Second Generation

A disarmament conference in Washington, DC, resulted in the most powerful warships built to that time, the second generation of aircraft carriers. Called because of a worldwide desire for peace following the devastation of the 1914–1918 "war to end all wars," the conference resulted in treaties on a variety of subjects. Five nations agreed to limit the numbers of the dominant warship of the day, the battleship, to prevent another armament race like the one that had preceded World War I. For Japan and the United States, which had begun building new and expensive warships, and Great Britain, which was facing replacement of its obsolescent fleet, the limits were a welcome economy measure. (The United States scrapped 15 old battleships, 2 new ones, and 13 other warships still under construction.) Aircraft carriers were something of an unknown factor. Nevertheless, new carriers were allowed in order to enable the conversion of cruisers already building. A 135,000-ton limit was agreed to for the United States and Great Britain with Japan allowed 81,000 tons. Individual ship displacement was restricted to 23,000 tons (the size of HMS *Furious* and HMS *Eagle*) but an exception was made so the United States and Japan could each convert two special cruisers.

Two Vought observation planes and a Grumman fighter without wings triced into the hangar deck overhead. The track for a traveling hoist is in the center.

A Christmas card from VF-5 for 1930 showing the track of Saratoga at sea and squadron movement over the United States. The "Problems" refer to Fleet Exercise Problems. Many humorous details can be found, including sites of crashes and delivery of new airplanes.

Lexington *and* Saratoga, *the Big Ones*

A series of heavy cruisers were authorized in 1916 but work was suspended until after the war. Construction began because Britain and Japan were competing with warship projects of their own. This arms race was one of the reasons for the Washington Conference. After the Naval Treaty was signed in 1922, four of the cruisers were scrapped[15] and *Lexington* (CV-2) and *Saratoga* (CV-3) made into the largest and most powerful warships in the world.

Steam turbine–electric drive had been selected for these ships as reduction gearing to handle the turbine's power output was not available. Already proven efficient in the colliers *Jason* and *Jupiter* (now the *Langley*) the turbine-electric equipment was heavy, complex, and difficult to maintain. However, it did generate more than 20,000 shaft horsepower during trials and gave the two ships speeds over 33 knots. The solution to exhaust gas from 16 oil-fired boilers was a single large funnel aft of the island.[16]

The flight deck was a strength deck as on the British carriers, so the hangar bays were enclosed, which meant refueling or running engines was not possible in the unventilated spaces. The hangars did have high overheads, allowing the development of tricing (a nautical term meaning to haul up with a rope) to hang aircraft fuselages, wings, and other parts under the flight deck.

The two elevators were small and barely adequate even with a section of deck that opened for airplanes too long for the elevator. U.S. Navy fleet carriers after this would have three elevators. With the long flight deck, cyclic flight operations,

HMS* Furious *before revisions in 1939, which added a small island and razed the no-longer-used hangar flying-off deck. After a varied 30-year career she was declared obsolescent and laid up in 1944.

HMS* Courageous *in Alexandria Harbor during temporary attachment to the Mediterranean Fleet in 1935. Her two-story hangar carried 48 aircraft compared to the 36 carried by the same size HMS* Furious*. The upper hangar level opened onto a short flying-off deck.

which had been developed on *Langley*, were possible. Planned for a 72-aircraft complement, Admiral Reeves insisted, as he had done on the *Langley*, that more were possible and 90 airplanes, sometimes more, were on board.

Both *Lexington* and *Saratoga* had longitudinal wires at the start. When they were removed the number of landing accidents went down. At the same time the importance of being on center when engaging the arresting gear became critical. LSOs proved invaluable in getting airplanes lined up.

Because the carriers were twins, telling them apart was not always easy. Although *Sara* and *Lex* were painted on the aft flight deck, the large letters were not always seen. Landing on the wrong ship was merely embarrassing. Sinking, even theoretically, your own ship, as happened during one exercise, would be disastrous. As a solution *Saratoga* had a wide, black, vertical stripe painted on her stack and *Lexington* a horizontal stripe at the top of hers.

For the next decade *Lexington* and *Saratoga* were what the public pictured as aircraft carriers. Both operated effectively and were instrumental in developing carrier tactics and strategy in the years between the wars. *Lexington* went down in the Coral Sea in May 1942. *Saratoga* survived two torpedo hits and a kamikaze attack to become the first aircraft carrier specializing in night operations. She was sunk during atomic bomb tests at Bikini.[17]

HMS* Glorious *had a high flight deck and bulges on the hull for torpedo protection and to stabilize top weight. On her last refit two hydraulic accelerators (catapults) were installed on her upper flight deck, which was extended aft.

The Hush Ships: Courageous *and* Glorious

During the Royal Navy buildup before World War I the First Sea Lord proposed three battle cruisers with high speed, heavy weapons, and a shallow draft named *Furious*, *Courageous*, and *Glorious*.

IJN Akagi on sea trials in June 1927 with her original three flight decks and no island. The downward angled stacks show normal exhaust; the heavy, dark smoke is unexplained. Her sleek hull shows her battle cruiser origins within the terms of the Washington Naval Conference.

IJN Kaga *flight deck in 1937. Nakajima A2N fighters are in the foreground, Aichi D1A dive bombers are in the middle, and the heavier Mitsubishi B2M torpedo bombers are far aft.*

Kaga *and* Akagi *were the only carriers designed and built with three flight decks. The arresting gear was the transverse system used on the French aircraft carrier* Béarn*. During reconstruction* Kaga*'s two lower flight decks were converted into hangars, the main flight deck was extended, and the bow was enclosed.*

(Smilingly called the "Hush" ships after the last syllable of their name.) *Furious* became the first aircraft carrier, but her sisters had their construction postponed. The Washington Conference limits meant that the Royal Navy was behind. Their existing three carriers combined operated less aircraft than any one of the new Japanese (*Akagi, Kaga*) or American (*Lexington, Saratoga*) CVs. *Furious* gained a second hangar and flying-off deck to increase her numbers. *Courageous* and *Glorious* were completed with double decks that enabled the slim ships to carry 48 aircraft.

Both ships' combat careers were brief. Only 14 days after the war began *Courageous* was torpedoed by U-boat while on anti-submarine patrol. *Glorious*, after action during the Norwegian Campaign and the miraculous save of RAF Hurricanes during the Narvik evacuation (see Chapter Four), was caught by the German battle cruisers *Scharnhorst* and *Gneisenau*. *Courageous* was the only fleet carrier sunk by gunfire.

Earthquake, Akagi *and* Kaga

As a result of an exception to the Naval Treaty, Japan was allowed to build two large aircraft carriers. A pair of cruiser hulls already on the ways were selected. *Akagi* was modeled on HMS *Furious* but had an innovative downward sloping funnel, which sprayed water into the exhaust gas to make it heavier so it did not rise up to the flight deck. *Akagi* went *Furious* one better by having three flight decks. The lower two opened directly into hangars and there was a third, smaller one below them. The middle flying-off deck was only 60 feet long. Although considered adequate for lighter airplanes of the time, it soon proved unworkable, as did the lower deck.

The second cruiser selected for conversion was sister ship to *Akagi*, *Amagi*. However, the 1923 massive earthquake that devastated Tokyo (100,000 died and most of the city was destroyed by fire) and the surrounding region wrecked the *Amagi*'s hull beyond repair. An incomplete battleship, *Kaga*, was selected as a replacement. Similar to *Agaki* with three flight decks and her original long funnel replaced by a down slanted one, she was shorter and wider.

Unlike the British trio, *Akagi* and *Kaga* were converted in the 1930s to a single flight deck and the hangars expanded to carry 90 airplanes.

Japanese Aircraft Carrier Names [18]

"Transliteration of the names of Japanese aircraft carriers into American equivalents is a pretty risky business," said Mr. Roger Pineau, a frequently published writer on the Japanese Navy after World War II. "It becomes misleading. The names should be treated as such and should not be taken too literally. For instance, when we speak of astronaut Carpenter, we don't visualize a man walking around with hammer and saw in hand."

Mr. Chris Beilstein, another expert on Japanese aircraft carriers, concurs. "The *Shōkaku* becomes 'Flying Crane,' for that is the closest we can translate the original Japanese. The first Japanese carriers carried names of mountains and provinces. These, in turn, were frequently named after mythological characters. *Shōkaku*, for example, could have been a flying crane in an age-old story, a crane that was named *Shōkaku*. This is very much like our real life Misty, the wild horse. Certainly, to translate 'Misty' to literal Japanese would be meaningless to them, or at best, misleading. It would be more accurate to translate it 'Wild Horse.' Thus, 'Misty,' to the Japanese, would mean 'Wild Horse,' just as we would erroneously translate *Shōkaku* as 'Flying Crane.'

"Think of the problem in transliterating Shangri La into Japanese," said Mr. Pineau. "To paint the picture accurately, it would be necessary to describe Hilton's book and then go into President Roosevelt's fascination with it. That would be rather difficult to do in one or two words. Perhaps the closest would be 'Paradise of the Ageless' and this would, in the Japanese mind, seem a pretty silly thing to name an aircraft carrier.

"But transliteration has a very real value, especially to those who have difficulty in pronouncing Japanese words. Many competent researchers don't even speak the language. The transliteration is a handy reference point, but should not be taken seriously, at face value."

Here is a list of the major IJN carriers and generally accepted transliterations:

Akagi	Red Castle (volcano near Tokyo)
Hiryu	Flying Dragon
Hiyo	Flying Falcon
Hosho	Flying Phoenix
Junyo	Peregrine Falcon
Kaga	Province of Japan
Ryuho	Dragon Phoenix
Ryujo	Heavenly Dragon
Shinano	Japanese Province
Shoho	Happy Phoenix
Shōkaku	Flying Crane
Soryu	Deep Blue Dragon
Taiho	Great Phoenix
Unryu	Heaven-bound Dragon
Zuiho	Lucky Phoenix
Zuikaku	Lucky Crane

Chapter 2

FLYING AT SEA

A Grumman TF/C-1 assigned to USS* Constellation *flying over its "Mother" ship. The S-2/C-1/E-1 series all had complex A-frame hooks to clear the tailwheel. The small tailwheel was primarily a bumper for tail-down landings, but led to the quip that they were the only four-wheeled airplane in the navy.

Going into the 1930s the general pattern for aircraft carriers was set. Normal was a long, single flight deck with an island on the starboard side, multiple elevators to the hangar decks, and transverse arresting wires. The speed of the ships was high both to assist in landings and takeoffs as well as to allow the carriers to keep up with the main battle fleet. Airplanes with tailhooks and folding wings were coming into use to maximize the number that could be carried. The United States, United Kingdom, and Japan followed this general pattern with each having its own variations and exceptions.

Folding Wings

The need for folding wings aboard aircraft carriers is obvious; many more airplanes can be carried. However, a folding wing is heavier and structurally complex. Only if the wings were too long to fit on elevators were early aircraft's wings made foldable. Although patented by Horace Short for his S-41 seaplane in 1912, fighter-type airplanes did not get foldable wings until combat proved that more fighters and dive bombers were vital. The FAA Skua was first in February 1937. Early model F4F Wildcats were stiff winged. When faced with how to fold the wings on the F4F Wildcat, Leroy Grumman was supposedly fiddling with a bent paperclip when he came up with the idea of wings that twisted back and lay alongside the fuselage. All 1,168 F4F-4 Wildcats, F6F Hellcats, and TBF Avengers reduced their wingspan this way. There has been a Grumman model with fold-back wings ever since: AF Guardian, E-1 Tracer, and the E-2 Hawkeyes and C-2 Greyhounds currently flying off U.S. Navy carrier decks.

The Douglas Dauntless kept stiff wings throughout its career. The Dauntless replacement, the Curtiss SB2C Helldiver, had conventional folding wings.

Most airplanes fold their wings by raising the outer section up to the vertical or canted inward. There were variations besides Grumman's:

IJN Akagi *in October 1934. A temporary island is on the starboard side while the lowest flight deck is visible at the bow. During her refit in 1937 the island was moved to the port side, the main flight deck extended, and the two lower decks covered over. A wind barrier is rigged up on the forward upper deck and the stern ramp painted in red and white stripes.*

Air Group 10 aboard the second Yorktown *(CV-10) in 1943. Hellcats are in front, Avengers are behind, both with Grumman hydraulically powered folding wings. At the aft end are stiff-wing Dauntlesses. Forty airplanes are in the picture, and there may be more, all with engines turning.*

The hangar deck of Yorktown *(in the previous photo). Space is cleared for crew to watch the evening movie while ordnance men work on bombs.*

- Because it only needed to fold a foot of wing the Japanese Zero of World War II and the 1950s F11F Tiger simply moved their tips upward (zero) or downward (F11F). Before flight the plane captain pushed the tips level and manually locked them in place.
- The F-14 Tomcat's wings did not fold, but went into "over-sweep" on the deck.
- The famous A-4 Skyhawk was the only U.S. Navy carrier aircraft since World War II with a short enough wingspan not to need folding wings.
- Several British aeroplanes had wings with a double fold to save space overhead as well as to the sides.

A corollary of Murphy's Law says that if an airplane's wings can be folded then someone will try to take off with them that way. Earlier airplanes did not have the engine power to take off without all of their wing, although there were probably attempts. Since a 1951 fiasco where an AD Skyraider got airborne with its wings folded, and crashed (fortunately, the crew was not injured), U.S. Navy aircraft (including those flown by Marines) have gotten airborne with wings folded a couple dozen times; some landed, some crashed. With only a single pilot, swept wings mounted well aft, and the added complication of a wing that raises, Chance-Vought's F-8 Crusader is the wings-folded-takeoff champion.

The crowded hangar bay of HMS Victorious *in 1942. British carriers had less overhead clearance than American carriers. The big biplane Fairey Swordfish had foldable wings from the start. The Fairey Fulmars needed a section of wing lifted up to enable them to fold all the way back.*

The F4F-4 model of the Grumman Wildcat was the first with foldable wings. Two are on a partly lowered elevator. Only one of the earlier models fit on the elevator. A bar from the tail fin to the tip holds the wing steady while folded.

The Grumman S2F/S-2 Tracker presents another solution to folding long wings: the hinge lines are angled so that when the wings fold they are offset. The escape hatch for the two crewmen in back could not be opened in flight, but the individual ones for the pilots could be and were routinely kept open when landing and taking off at sea.

F4F-4 having wings spread. The operation was purely manual. While one man could do the job, on the carrier the wind over the deck made extra hands necessary. Landing gear retraction on all models of the Wildcat was also manual with the pilot turning a crank 37 times with his right hand to retract the wheels.

A Forrestal class flight deck in the 1960s. The air wing composition is typical of the variety LSOs had to be familiar with. Planes on deck include two types of AD Skyraiders (attack and electronic warfare), F3H Demon and F11F fighters, Skyhawks, photo versions of F9F Cougars, and the large bomber A3D Skywarriors. Not in the picture: two-engine Grumman WF early warning and TF CODs.

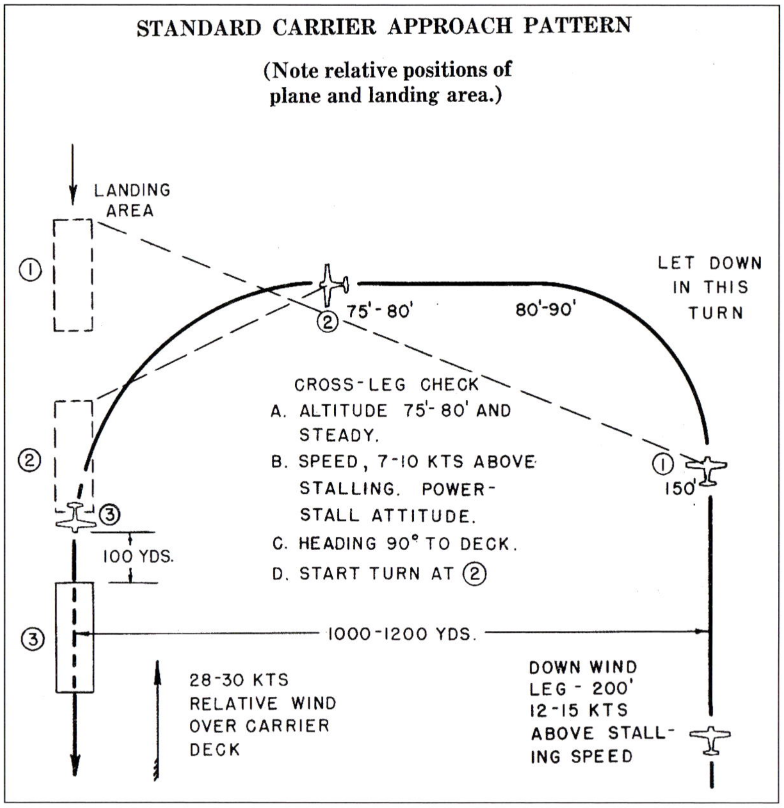

A 1944 U.S. Navy Training Manual diagram of a carrier approach. The altitudes are low to enable a flat pass. The airplane was in a turn until in close to keep the LSO in sight until the cut.

American Paddles

The image of the LSO waving airplanes aboard was firmly set in the between-wars period. Hollywood did its share with films such as *Helldivers* (1937), *Flight Command* (1940), *Dive Bomber* (1941), and *The Flying Fleet* (1929), about which a reviewer wrote, "There are some splendid sequences devoted to an airplane carrier, with its marvelous deck space and the gull-like machines gliding from the vessel and swooping back home." How was it really done?

Two Block Fox

You know it is time to land when the ship hoists the white flag with a red diamond, the Fox flag.[1] You fly alongside the starboard side of the ship (in echelon if part of a formation) at 200 feet. Past the bow break left until flying opposite the ship's heading. Lower wheels, flaps, and tailhook. Descend slightly to 150 feet (the tip of the mast on the horizon is a visual cue). Abeam the ramp (if wind over the deck is high, turn sooner) begin a smooth, descending 180-degree turn to be over the ship's wake. About halfway through the turn, "the 90," at 100 feet look for the LSO. Follow his signals for speed, height, and line-up. When he gives you the cut, chop the throttle to idle; the airplane's nose will drop. Look at the deck and judge easing back on the stick in order to hit the deck with all three wheels, a three-pointer. After the plane comes to an abrupt stop, pause, and the arresting gear will pull you backward. On the director's signal, put on the brakes and the wire will clear the hook, assisted if necessary by the hook runner. When signaled, raise your tailhook and advance the throttle to taxi briskly forward. Reach down and unlock the wings and start them folding. The barriers were lowered when the operator saw you were safely arrested. As soon as you have taxied over them, they will be raised and the deck ready for the next aircraft less than a minute behind. Follow directors' signals up the deck to park inches away from other airplanes in the pack on the bow.

LSO Signals

Primary signals are for height and line-up, which can, must, be responded to quickly. Airspeed adjustments take a bit longer so are given earlier in the approach. Incorrect configuration (landing gear, flaps, hook not down) have to be signaled at the very start of the approach. There is little time for more than three or four corrections on a pass.

Even with the rapidity of signals a good LSO communicates with a high degree of body English, not just the position of his paddles, but speed of motion, how far his arms move, and what his body is doing: leans, stance, and the position of feet, legs, torso, and head. A good LSO silently communicates as well as a mime or ballet dancer. Although any LSO can adequately wave any pilot, a true rapport comes only after working together for a long time, hours of Field Carrier Landing Practice (FCLP), and many, many passes. Workups on the carrier in good conditions, followed by months of operational flying develop a special trust, an awareness of each other's

View from a jet to USS Oriskany *(CV-34): (top left) The 90-degree position. (top right) Turning to line up using the wake as a guide. (middle left) Lined up and following the Paddle's signals. The groove is longer than it would be for a propeller airplane with a long nose. (middle right) Prior to the cut. The LSO has his arms straight out, indicating a Roger, at the correct height. (bottom) After the cut. Besides the low barriers, the tall barricade is raised, indicating the landing airplane had a problem.*

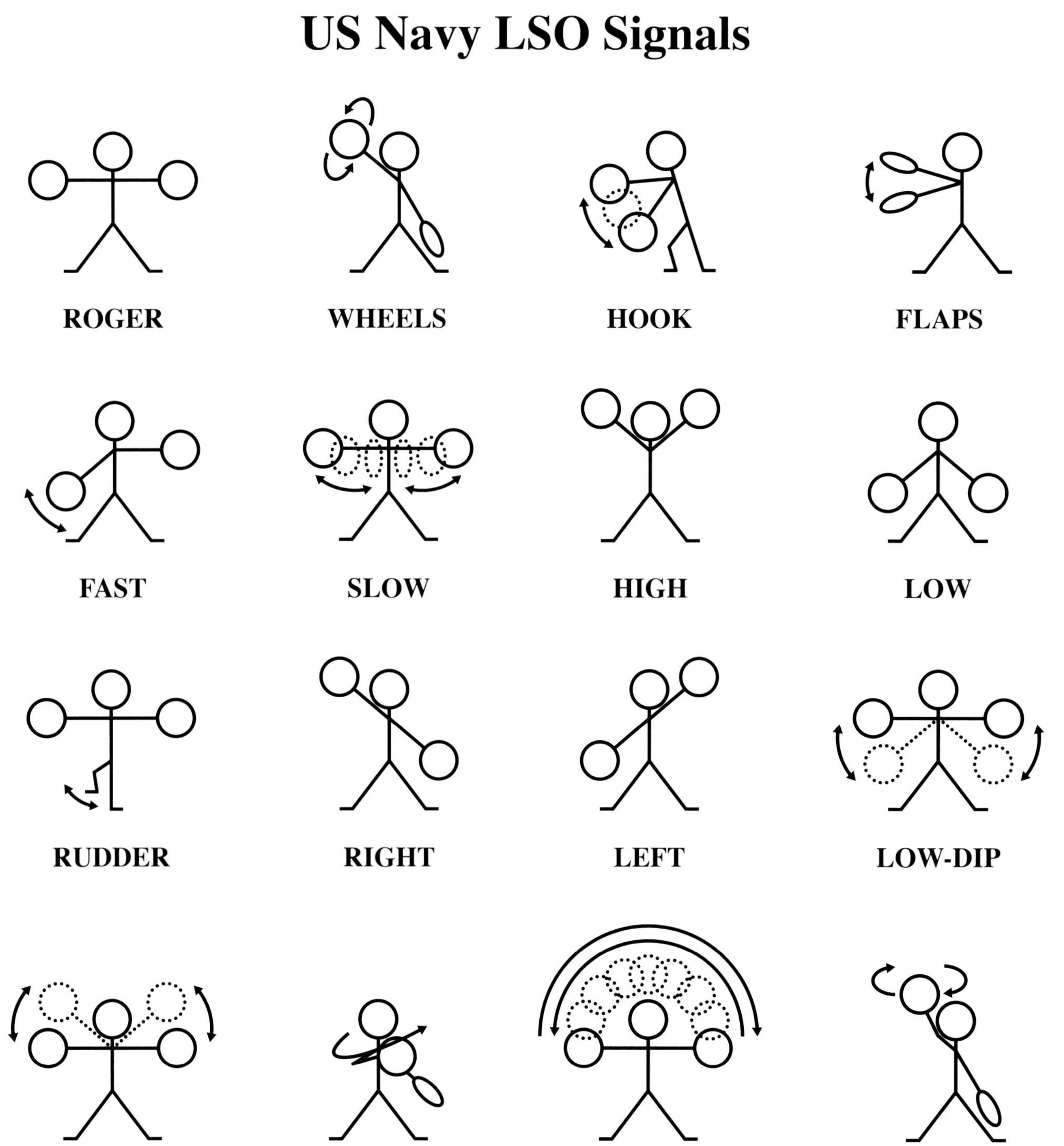

A graphic display of U.S. Navy Paddles' signals. They are shown in the approximate order in which they were given if needed. Wheels, hook, and flaps took time to correct. Right and Left indicate which way the wings should bank. The Dips are a small, quick correction just before the cut. (Jacob Powell)

Paddles at play for the camera man; simultaneous High, Low, and Roger signals. A pilot's comment on the photo, "Looks like one of my passes; some of everything."

LSOs showing U.S. Navy signals: Low (top left), high (bottom), and cut (top right). Although the carrier is at sea, the pictures look posed because the demonstrating LSOs are simply standing there. For the Cut, especially, any Paddles worth his salt would be closer to the flight deck, moving and waving with flair.

The joke is, LSO Toby Tobin (see Chapter Six) is giving the slow-flying helo a Fast signal. Helicopters did not use an LSO to land. The carrier is in a turn, which means the recovery is complete.

techniques and subtleties that can save aircraft and lives when the going gets tough.

Semaphore

Researchers found a claim that paddle signals derived from semaphore. That explanation probably came about because semaphore flags were used first, before someone realized that flapping in the wind, flags were not that visible. Flat paddles then came into use. A couple of signals probably are related to semaphore. *Roger* means affirmative, although it is also logical for "wings level" and "correct height." Back in the days pilots knew both Morse and semaphore, *Hotel/How* for "hook" and *Fox* for "fast" make sense. Of the other LSO signals, that "come left" is *Love/Lima* is probably a coincidence. "High" is *Uniform/Uncle*, "low" is *November/Nan*, and "come right" means cancel.

Arresting Gear

The first arresting gear was transverse ropes; later, wire cables fastened to weights to stop landing aircraft. The longitudinal (fore

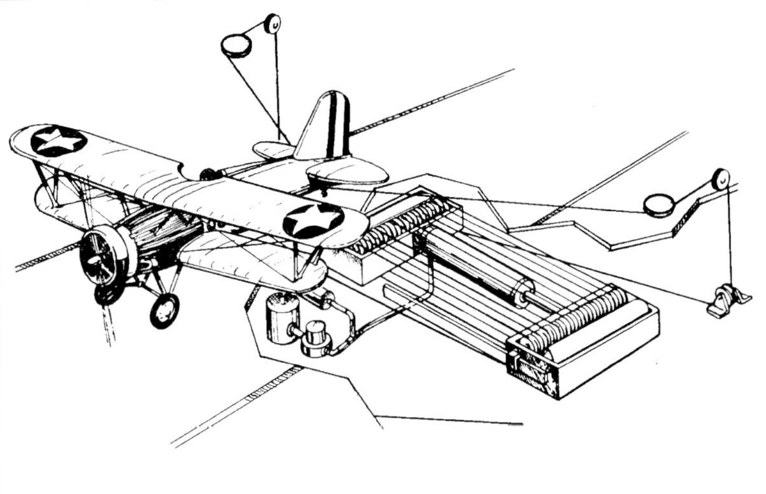

Figure 1-3. Mark 3 Arresting Gear

The Mark 3 arresting gear metered hydraulic pressure from the force of landing to bring airplanes to a stop. The same double sheave arrangement with modifications and improvements continues in use. Mk 3 arresting gear was installed on carriers CV-3 to CV-8. (History of Shipboard Arresting Gear, NAEC Lakehurst. 1-25)

and aft) wires were for guidance and to hold aircraft on deck with stopping only incidental. Although the longitudinal wires were used on all the early aircraft carriers they proved to be unnecessary and in the U.S. Navy were gone by 1931. The Mark 1 (Mk 1) system using suspended weights was used only on USS *Langley*. The towers with the weights on deck were obstructions and the system was soon revised to have the weights hung down into the ship's hold. The Mark 2 consisted of a hydraulically braked cylinder at each end of the Cross Deck Pennant (CDP), around which the cable wrapped. The hydraulic pressure was generated by the cylinder's rotation as the cable payed out. The faster the cable unwound, i.e., the faster the airplane's engagement speed, the more pressure was generated, resulting in more braking force. A disadvantage was that if the engagement was off center, the cable on the short side generated more braking force that pulled the airplane even farther to that side. The Mk 2 was put on *Langley* and *Lexington*, which kept longitudinal wires until the Mk 3 came into use.

Mark 3 arresting gear was first installed on *Ranger* (CVA-61) during her construction in 1934, added to *Lexington* and *Saratoga*, and was put on the next four carriers. The Mark 3 set the pattern for arresting gear for the future. With improvements and modifications the double sheave acting on a hydraulic cylinder with pressure accumulator continues to this day. The Mk 3 is a single engine for each cable and allows equal cable runout, improved cable tensioning, and rapid resetting. The number of CDPs and associated engines varied from as many as 12 to 16.

Some 1,000 Mark 4 arresting gear engines were built and became the work horses of World War II. The Mk 4 worked on the same principle as the Mk 3 but was capable of arresting 11,000-pound aircraft. Many were also double sheaved, meaning that two CDPs or a CDP and a barrier were fastened to one engine.

The barrier was a wire standing approximately 3 feet above the deck and connected to an arresting gear engine. The barrier was suspended from stanchions on both sides of the deck, which enabled it to be raised or lowered rapidly. A sailor stationed at the flight deck edge controlled the barrier with a lever. The barrier's function was to keep airplanes that missed a wire from crashing into the pack parked on the bow. Originally the idea was that the wire would snare the wheels to stop the airplane, but in practice it was the propeller that hit first. Fast-moving aircraft also tended to nose over on hitting the barrier. Although damaged airplanes are not good, they are far better than a catastrophic smash into many airplanes. It was possible to hook a wire and, if it was a late one, still contact the barrier. Sharp operators saw the airplane was safely arrested and lowered the barrier to prevent this. It became customary for pilots saved by this to reward the operator with a box of cigars.

An oddity that was in use for several years was arresting gear on the bow; airplanes landed with the ship backing down. The bow arresting gear provided an alternative if battle damage prevented the use of the normal wires aft. As the war progressed the utility of the gear became questionable (it was rarely used except for practice) and the bow wires were removed.

Tailhook Development

Once it was realized that a device was needed to stop aircraft, tailhooks (although some were more accurately fuselage hooks) were

A barrier engagement by an F6F Hellcat, illustrating the problem with barriers. Although they may have prevented airplanes that floated over the wires from colliding with the pack of airplanes parked forward, the set of raised wires more often tripped the airplane, with damage to the propeller, or more.

The tailhook on this Vought VE-7 has a complex arrangement of cables to do all the functions a tailhook needs: to be lowered, retracted, held up, held down (snubbed), move side to side (not too much), padded to protect fuselage, and engage the cross-deck cable.

F4B with a straight-shaft tailhook looking like it will get an in-flight engagement. An IFE is when the tailhook catches the CDP but none of the airplane's wheels are on deck. The result is a slam-down, sometimes damaging the airplane and always teeth-rattling. The jet F-4 crash through the smoke in Chapter 10 is a classic in-flight engagement.

English airplanes tended to have A-frame tailhooks. The Blackburn Shark was the Royal Navy's torpedo bomber from 1935 to 1937, when it was replaced by the Fairey Swordfish. The aircraft carrier is HMS **Courageous.**

An early version of the Vought F4U-1 Corsair with the "greenhouse" canopy. Early problems with the Corsair's shipboard landings were solved by modifying the tailwheel oleos and extending the tailwheel. The tailhook is part of the tailwheel assembly and could not be lowered until the landing gear was extended.

Bell Aircraft Company's XFL Airbonita, an attempt to navalize their P-39 Airacobra, pitching over during trials. The XFL never did land on a ship. The test arresting gear is mounted on a rotatable ramp, which could be turned to make available surface wind into a head wind to better simulate landing at sea.

The final version of the Seafire, an Mk 47, on a wave-off, circa 1950. By then the Spitfire design had evolved into a capable carrier airplane. The hook in a fairing had been moved all the way to the tip of the tail. This is the best location for keeping the airplane's roll-out straight.

This E-2 Hawkeye has arrested, rolled back, and is raising its A-frame hook before taxiing forward. The green shirt is the "Hook runner," whose sometimes-hazardous job is to knock the cable free if it has not fallen off by itself.

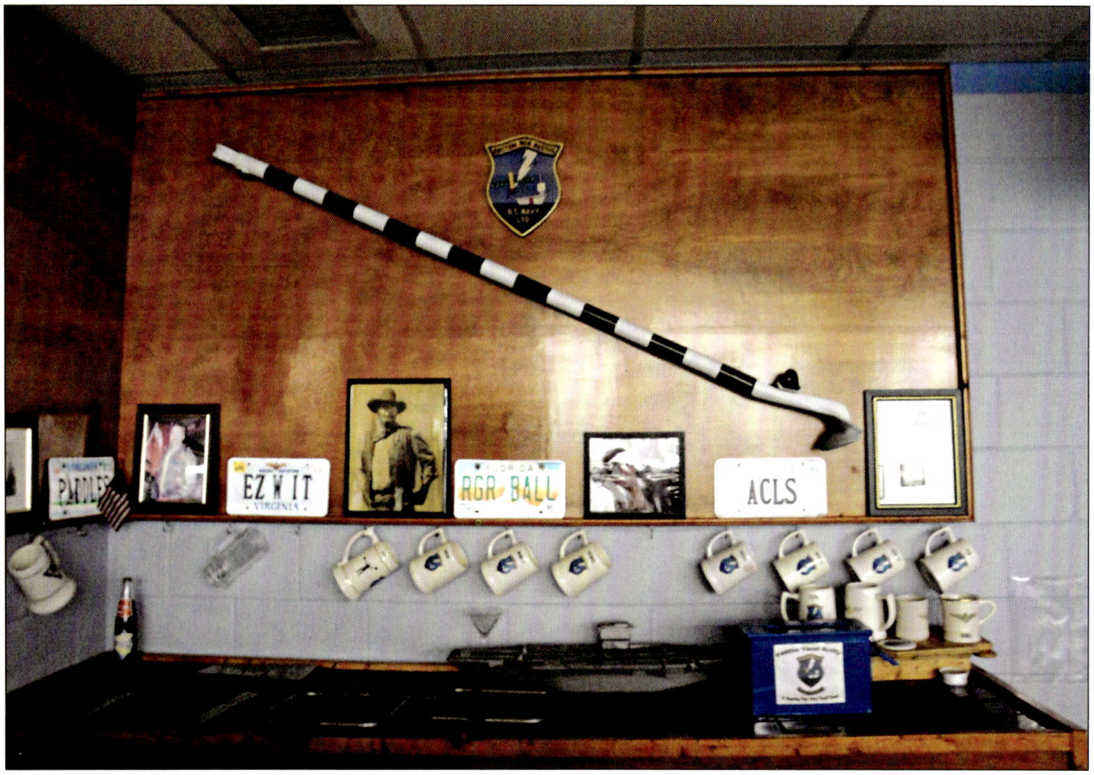

Tailhook, originally from a Skyhawk, appropriately displayed in the lounge of the LSO School at NAS Oceana. The license plates reflect LSOs' pride in their work. Left to right are "Paddles"; "Easy with it," a call to an erratic pilot; "Roger Ball"; and "Automatic Carrier Landing System." The moneybox says it is for the "Paddles Seeing Eye Dog Fund." The LSO's vision was, and is, a continuing source of frivolity.

developed to work with transverse cable arresting gear. As longitudinal wires were discovered to be unnecessary as well as cumbersome, the method of slowing an airplane by squeezing the clearance between wheels and wires with fittings on the axles (never very efficient) went away as well.

Putting a hook on aircraft is not as simple as it might seem. First there is the question of where to attach it in such a way that the airplane's structure can stand the strain of arrestment. The hook must be behind the CG (Center of Gravity), the farther the better, to hold the aircraft straight. The hook needs to be held up while in flight and lowered for landing. It should be retractable to speed clearing the landing area. The hook needs a spring or snubber to minimize bounce when it hits the deck. The shape of the hook itself must be pointed enough to pick up a wire but not so pointed that it damaged the cable. Finally, the hook must be strong enough to stop the airplane. As planes got heavier with higher landing speeds, tailhooks became thicker and heavier.

"An aircraft arresting hook is no thing of beauty. Fashioned of high-strength steel, painted in a pattern of black and white, it is cold, hard, lifeless. But, when attached to the after end of a carrier-based aircraft, the tailhook is more than hardware. It becomes the tie that links aircraft to ocean-going ships, and is the unique emblem of the carrier aviator. By this, he is set apart from his land-based fellows." (Will Hilbrink, North American Aviation Corp, 1959)

The tailhook on an F/A-18 Hornet, discolored by proximity to the afterburner exhaust nozzles. Hooks grew in size as aircraft weights and landing speeds increased. The shaft is not solid but a tube.

Takeoff

A typical flight began with all aircraft positioned at the aft end of the flight deck. After starting engines and completing checks, the airplanes taxied to the center of the deck if not there already. The launch officer used a flag to signal the pilot to go to full power while holding the brakes. If the sea was rough, the launch officer timed his release signal so that the deck was down and moving up. Once airborne, the airplane proceeded on its mission.

Initially, LSOs launched airplanes in addition to guiding them in for landing. They were the experts on flying on and off the ship. Henry Miller, the USS *Hornet*'s LSO, trained Doolittle's B-25 pilots ashore in taking off from an aircraft carrier. Later, specialized officers managed the flight deck and launched the aircraft.

The first successful shipboard catapults were developed by the USN. Through World War I the emphasis was on seaplanes; flying boats and floatplanes for scouting and spotting launched by catapult from capital ships. The acceptance of the aircraft carrier was slow in America. However, once the carriers were in operation, the catapults were adapted to flight decks. Catapult launches are slower than deck runs, but have two advantages: many more airplanes can be on deck for a mission and if there is not enough length for the first ones to deck run they can be catapulted until the rest have enough deck. The second advantage, of course, is that aircraft too heavy for a deck run can be safely fired into the air. Catapults were powered by gunpowder (adapted from artillery), pneumatics (air pressure), or hydraulic pressure. Carriers used the last until steam-powered catapults came into use in the 1960s.

Catapults firing out the side of the hangar were installed with the same idea as bow arresting gear (AG); if battle damage put the bow cats out of action or the forward flight deck was out of use, airplanes could still be launched out the side. However, they could not add the ship's forward speed to help with the takeoff, took up valuable hangar

Boeing F3Bs on a take-off run on USS* Lexington*. Planes of the time were typically airborne in 300 feet, and less than that when there was a good wind over the deck.

A VE-7 flown by Lieutenant Virgil C. Griffin made the first takeoff from an American aircraft carrier from the deck of the newly commissioned* Langley*. As* Langley *pilot Jackson R. Tate later recalled, "This was not so simple as it sounds. Because planes had no brakes, it was necessary to develop a device consisting of a bomb release attached to a wire about 5 feet long to allow a plane to turn up to full power and start its deck run. The bomb release was hooked to a ring on the landing gear and the end of the wire to a hold-down fitting on deck. A cord led from the bomb-release trigger to an operator on deck, who could release the plane on signal."

A McDonnell F2H Banshee on USS* Kearsarge *(CV-33) in 1953 getting ready to catapult. The deck crew is fastening a holdback fitting with a breakable link under the exhausts and the catapult bridle behind the nose wheel. The red and yellow jet blast deflector extends up from the deck. Later jet blast deflectors (JBD) are much larger and have sea water pumped through for cooling.

deck space, and had a short run as well as low clearance overhead and from the sea. Pilots did not like them. Also, like bow AG, experience showed they were seldom used and they were eventually removed.

British Bats

The Royal Navy took some years before settling in to what is considered standard aircraft carrier configuration and operation. HMS *Courageous*, 1928, and HMS *Glorious*, 1930, are representative of British carriers until World War II. They had armored flight decks and enclosed hangars, which later became significant in combat. The main idea for flight operations was to get aircraft down into the hangars as soon as possible, unlike American deck parking and cyclic operations on the flight deck. Forward elevators were T-shaped so that airplanes could be put below with their wings spread. Getting the elevator platform back to the flight deck determined how rapidly aircraft could be recovered. Longitudinal wires were gone from the earlier Royal Navy aircraft carriers by 1927 and the ships had no arresting gear. The aircraft of the day were light and slow enough to land without tailhooks. *Courageous* and *Glorious* even had the forward part of their flight decks sloped up to assist in stopping. Aft portions were humped where the longitudinal wires were once seated as the slope aft was thought to lessen air turbulence.

It was not until 1933 that the development of larger aircraft forced the Royal Navy to install arresting gear and put hooks on airplanes. In the interim, the major concern was aircraft going over the side, so palisades were built on the sides of the flight deck. These contraptions of metal beams and rope nets were raised when landing airplanes to catch them should they err to the deck edge.

The three "Hush" ships, *Furious, Courageous,* and *Glorious*, had multiple flying-off decks, which they kept for their entire careers, although after mid-1930 the short, lower deck could no longer be used because aircraft needed longer takeoff runs. *Furious* never did get an island, nor did little *Argus*.

DLCO is waving ADDLs at a snow-covered airfield for a Grumman Martlet (U.S. designation F6F). The signal is for practice ashore; crossed bats mean cut and are usually dropped low, but when above the head, it means cut and make this a full-stop landing.

Fleet Air Arm as Stepchild

To the fliers in the Royal Navy, 1 April 1918 will always be a foolish, if not a Fool's Day. When the RAF was created from the RFC and the not inconsiderable assets[2] of the Royal Naval Air Service the decree was, from henceforth all military flying (no matter if that flying was float planes catapulted from battleships and cruisers, flying boats on long ocean patrols, or airplanes based on the developing carriers) must be controlled by the RAF. Like Cinderella, British naval aviation was an unwanted stepchild. Aircraft for the carriers were low on the RAF's budget. Most were RAF machines adapted for carrier work, and there were never enough of them.

Command relationships aboard aviation ships, especially the new aircraft carriers, were strange. A navy captain ran the ship and her crew, but an RAF officer owned the aircraft, the maintenance men, and the pilots. Pilots acquired dual ranks as officers in the Royal Navy and RAF, not always of equivalent status. An added quirk was that all observers had to be naval officers. Career paths were convoluted as well. This dichotomy of command discouraged the type of innovations that emerged when CAPT Reeves of USS *Langley* forced the capacity of that carrier to go from the designed 14 aircraft to 41. Although his pilots considered so many airplanes moving on deck, the deck park, close landing intervals, and a rapid tempo to be hazardous, they had no choice but to follow orders. That CAPT Reeves was a fellow aviator and they were all trained naval officers did help smooth the operation.

Conversely, the captain of a Royal Navy carrier was not a pilot and had little comprehension of aviation's role in war at sea. (This split led to the tragic loss of HMS *Glorious* off Norway.) The pilots were trained as fliers and, with the exception of those who began as naval officers, understood little of ship operation and tactics. They could not be ordered to step up the pace. If the weather was less than perfect, Commander Flying (RAF) simply did not launch his airplanes. Flight operations were conservative and leisurely. If the RAF ashore was a gent's flying club in the 1930s, being on a carrier was a flying club with yachting privileges. This changed with the Inskip Award.

Lord Thomas Inskip was Minister of Defense and had lectured parliament on the "parlous state" of naval aviation under RAF control. With the European situation becoming threatening the government recognized the need for a reorganization. The result in 1937 was the Inskip Award, which placed control of naval aviation (less the long-range patrol planes of Coastal Command) firmly in Royal Navy hands. Pilots were no longer required to also be RAF officers. The navy was given two years to implement the change. Building of the *Ark Royal* was begun and the six sister ships that formed the Illustrious class were authorized. By May of 1939 the Fleet Air Arm (officially the Air Branch of the Royal Navy) was wholly navy with 20 squadrons and 340 aircraft.

Is it a coincidence that the Royal Navy began using LSOs in 1939? The British carrier accident rate had been less than that of the United States Navy[3] so why create DLCOs? Part of the answer is that because aircraft were heavier and faster, allowing pilots to land on their own was no longer satisfactory. The integrated command structure, navy ordering navy, pushed for an increased operational tempo and this, in turn, meant an improvement in technique along with specialized jobs and equipment.

A Batman aboard HMS* Illustrious *in 1944 signaling a pilot to fly up because he is below glide path. Dressed for the tropics, he is using night lamps instead of paddles. A third bulb and reflector are on his chest. Interpreting only three dots of light at night was even more difficult than the stick-lines of the American night lights.

Flags, Paddles, Arm-Waving, DLCO, LSO, Conflicts and Confusion

Much has been made over British signals being opposite American ones, but in fact only one is. Fast, slow, and some minor ones are different but not opposite. The one that is opposite and has, on occasion, confused pilots is glide slope; that is, high or low on approach. An LSO's arms raised tells the pilot he is too high. A DLCO's arms raised tells the pilot to fly up because he is too low. Advisory versus instructional. The British system is more logical because if line-up signals are telling the pilot what to do, the glide slope signals should also. Instead, the U.S. Navy requires two mental steps in responding; I'm high, therefore I must go down.

The variation between Royal Navy and U.S. Navy signals goes back to their origins. The first used on *Langley* were telling the pilot he was below, on, or above the glide slope. Line-up signals came later and they followed logically from the arms outstretched on glide slope signal matching an airplane's wings. By tilting his arms the LSO could indicate which way the pilot should bank to return to the center line. Left and right were not a consideration as the correct direction was obvious to both pilot and paddles. (When optical landing aids come into use, the radio had to be used for line-up corrections and saying "left" or "right" was necessary with the LSO having to think backward.) When the FAA instituted DLCOs in 1939, the reasoning was, if the line-up signals tell the pilot what to do, the high and low should as well. Hence a Batsman's arm held up means "fly up" while a Paddles' in that position says, "you are high, fly down." No LSO/DLCO signals are advisory in the literal sense of the word. Ignore landing signals at your peril, at least a wave-off, at worst a crash.

Differences of the other two primary, and mandatory, signals are matters of style: the Brit crossed bats down at the knees with a bit of a curtsey means "time to land the aeroplane," and the more vivid Yankee arm slash across the throat means the same thing, even though it is identical to the "cut your engine" signal. The wave-off for Americans is a frantic waving of both arms while the more genteel one bat waved in a circle over the DLCO's head requests, "take her around again, old chap."

Takeoffs

Once DLCOs were in use the "L" in the title represented both Land and Launch; Deck included movement between takeoff and landing. DLCOs were trained in ranging, moving airplanes about the deck. They were directors for teams dealing with crashes, fighting fires, rescuing crews, and clearing wreckage.

A DLCO described his actions, "During a typical takeoff I used two small flags, one red one green (or at night two red and green glowing Lucite wands) to signal to the pilot. The sea conditions governed the timing of the takeoff. On ensuring that the pilot was ready and holding the aircraft on his brakes at full throttle, I'd check the affirmative signal from the bridge, look at the swell-pattern of the Atlantic rollers and try to time things exactly. I'd sweep the green flag down to start the aircraft rolling as the ship's bow was going down to help with the acceleration, and then as the aircraft reached the end of the flight deck the rising bows gave a 'ski-jump' effect."

Without catapults (*accelerators* in Royal Navy terms), rocket bottles were used to boost heavier aircraft. There was a flag at a precomputed spot at which the bottles were fired. In theory, if they did not ignite there was enough deck remaining for the pilot to chop power and brake to a stop before going off the bow.

Japanese Lights

IJN *Kaga* and IJN *Akagi* did for the Imperial Japanese Navy what USS *Lexington* and USS *Saratoga* did for the U.S. Navy and HMS *Courageous* and HMS *Glorious* did for the Royal Navy. Those large carriers set the pattern for the ships that followed.

Japanese aircraft carriers had enclosed hangars like the British versions with unarmored flight decks like the Americans versions. The combination was unfortunate because bombs penetrated to the hangar where the explosive effects were magnified by being contained.

Like the Brit aircraft carriers, *Kaga* and *Akagi* began with multiple levels of flight deck, but after the initial experimental years went to a single ship-long flight deck. Longitudinal wires were replaced by a transverse system with a crash barrier well forward.

Akagi[4] started with a flush deck, but like the later *Hiryu*, had a small island built on the port side. The intention was that carriers would operate in pairs, side by side, with opposite traffic patterns for clearance. This was the formation of *Akagi/Kaga* and *Hiryu/Soryu* at the start of the Battle of Midway.

For the first years, Japanese naval pilots landed without assistance, relying on their rigorous training. In order to enable night flying the Kasumigaura Naval Station in 1932 developed a system of red and green lights to provide flight path indication. The *chakkan shidoto* (landing guidance light) proved useful in the daytime as well as at night and became standard on all Japanese carriers. Each unit consisted of a 1-kw bulb, a colored filter, and a refracting mirror to narrow the beam. The light intensity was varied to match conditions. The units were installed on both sides of the deck with the red lights 30 feet aft of the green. The lights were angled slightly inboard and the flight path angle could be varied by changing the height of the units. A pilot flew behind the aircraft carrier until he could see both pairs of lights, which meant he was on the

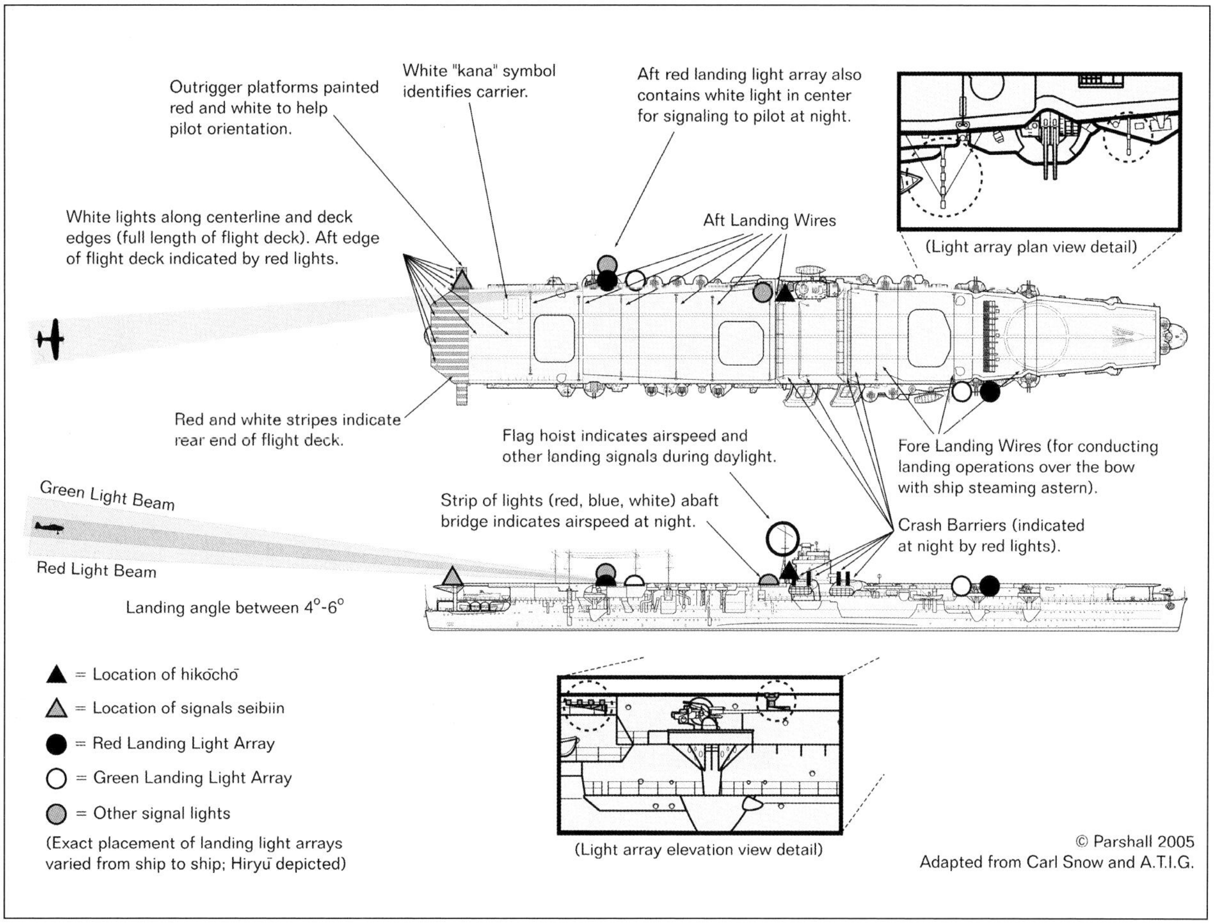

Diagram of the chakkan shidoto (landing guidance lights) on IJN Hiryu. The Hik ch was the Air Operations Officer who was stationed on the bridge and used flags to signal takeoffs and that the deck was open for landings. The Seibiin was a crewman who relayed the signals from the Hik ch . He was positioned far aft where the pilots could see him as he waved flags. The red and white stripes on the ramp helped pilots to judge their landings. (This diagram was created by Carl Snow and was first published in The Hook. Jonathan Parshall adapted it for Shattered Sword)

centerline. Seeing only red meant he was low, only green he was high, red and green he was at the correct height. Because the lights were offset, they disappeared close to the ramp; then the pilot chopped the power, made a quick line-up correction, and set a landing attitude as pilots did after getting cut by an LSO. A go-around was signaled by a crewman waving a red flag. The limitation with the *chakkan shidoto* was that it could not correct for the ship's motion. In heavy weather the beams of light moved as the aircraft carrier pitched and rolled. LSOs could provide a stable approach and anticipate the ship's movement to get a safe trap.

Training

By 1941 the pilots of the Japanese Navy were the finest carrier aviators in the world. Their selection and training were thorough and rigorous. Into the 1930s only 100 naval pilots were being produced per year! In 1937, Japanese ace Saburo Sakai was 1 of the 70 pilots accepted from a pool of 1,500 applicants (in three categories: NCO (Non-commissioned Officers [Sakai was one]), officers from the Ita Jima Naval Academy, and high school cadets). In his biography he lists some of the extreme requirements, which resulted in 45 of the 70 being eliminated 10 months into training:

- Elimination by last-man-standing wrestling matches
- Swim 50 meters in 30 seconds and remain underwater for a minimum of 90 seconds (Gasp)
- Catch flies by hand
- Shinny up a metal pole and hang on one handed for 10 minutes
- Dive off a platform, do a flip, and land on the ground (Acrobatics were heavily emphasized.)
- Find stars in the daytime

Flaws in this system included the fact that the process took time and even superb pilots are at the mercy of fate. Fate in the form of engine failures; crashes as a passenger; ship sinkings; or the Silver Bullet, the lucky shot that kills. After the battles of Coral Sea and Midway the IJN was running short of pilots. Training was shortened and the rate of completion increased, but it was too little, too late. The quality of the Japanese aircraft carrier pilots deteriorated and never caught up with the demand.

Japanese carrier doctrine stressed that carriers and their pilots must train as a single unit. With two carriers having islands on the left and one with no island this made sense. However, it made filling a carrier's complement difficult as opposed to the Allies moving entire squadrons as needed. (A shortage of flight crews was the reason IJN *Zuikaku* was not at Midway.)

Takeoffs

The IJN considered catapult launches too slow and never put them on its carriers. All takeoffs were deck runs with the lighter fighters first followed by bombers and torpedo planes.

French Ring

The one aircraft carrier the French Navy had in this early period did not have an impact on future operations, but is illustrative of imaginative ideas all the navies were trying. The massive, and slow moving, elevator doors worked but would have been eliminated when the need for speed became obvious in combat, which the *Bearn* never was in.

For a height guide, the French came up with a loop atop a post on the centerline of the landing area, which the pilot would look through to his landing spot. The height of the loop was adjusted for the amount of wind over deck (WOD). RADM Pierre Menet Trier recalled, "An important job was for a sailor to pull on a string to have the post folded by a spring a few seconds before the landing!"

French carrier aircraft had a mechanism where the hook was interconnected with the throttle. The hook was down when the

A suit with unusual circular lights. The signal is unrecognizable and probably a demonstration for the photographer. The assistant LSO has a radio handset. At night the second person on the platform did not worry about being seen.

throttle was reduced. The hook was raised when power was added. Thus, if a pilot did not like his approach he moved the throttle, the hook came up, and he rolled down the deck for another go. The *aviateurs* called this maneuver *Train Bleu* after the fast express train, which sped through stations between Calais and Nice.

To its credit the French navy was first to have transverse wires as arresting gear and first to land a multi-engine airplane on a carrier. In January 1936, the prototype Potez 56e landed aboard *Bearn* on a trial basis to see if it could be done.

First Night Landings

A few daring souls realized there would be a need for flying at night at sea as well as from land and bravely made the first shipboard landings in the dark. Credit for the first goes to LCDR John Dale Price of the U.S. Navy, who on 1 April 1925 landed a Vought VE-7 on USS *Langley*. Flt Lt Gerald Boyce made the first night landing for the Royal Navy on 1 July 1926 aboard HMS *Furious* flying a Blackburn Dart Mark II. By 1932, Japanese pilots were landing at night enough to justify the development of the *chakkan shidoto* light system.

Price remembered, "I made a total of 13 landings under various conditions of deck lighting and darkness, from full moon to no moon and from all lights to no lights (except the illuminated wands of the landing signal officer).

"The first landing was made in full moon with a row of flood lights 30 feet apart along the flight deck. The landing area was illuminated with 'dead' lights[5] 3 feet apart fore and aft, which outlined the arresting gear.

"As illumination of the moon diminished from night to night, so did the artificial illumination. First to go was every other flood light, then all flood lights. Then the dead lights were extinguished, leaving only the ship's running lights and the illuminated wands of the signalman. The object was to test the minimum illumination necessary.

"All landings were made without incident. It didn't seem particularly difficult at the time because the VE9 was a swell little airplane, practically foolproof.

"The operations were conducted off San Diego in perfect weather with a 24- to 26-knot wind over the deck (including the *Langley*'s speed)."[6]

A few years later, in 1929, every pilot had to do four night carrier landings per year. Four is hardly enough to be comfortable, so most of the landings were done when the sky was clear and the moon was near full or in the gloaming just after sunset. In the buildup leading to World War II the requirement for night CQ was eliminated, making the instances of later successful traps all the more remarkable. Effective night operations had to await the development of radar. The U.S. Navy had its first full-time night air group aboard light carrier *Independence* (CVL-22), which went operational in the fall of 1944.

A basic difficulty in night landings was making the LSO/DLCO visible to the pilot. A variety of gadgets and methods were tried before settling on lighting the LSO with electric lights. One of the oddest was an overall with fabric strips on arms, legs, and chest that glowed purple when an ultraviolet light shone on them. The LSO had difficulty seeing the airplane on approach and the ghostly stick figure was not well defined. "At the 90 we would be around 175 feet, 80 knots, and waiting for the 45 where, if we were lucky, the LSO would turn on the dustpan lights to give us an idea where the deck was. The LSO's fluorescent suit panels and paddles were illuminated by black light, which produced an eerie glow on the port side blunt end of the ship. His signals were discernible as long as he didn't get too excited and move the paddles too fast. If he did get a little spastic the black light–illuminated paddles and the panels became indecipherable and guesswork was required."[7]

The Brits came up with a set of three electric lamps, one on the Batsman's chest and one in each hand. Although only three dots of light lacked subtlety, the system worked and was also used in the daytime to assist in hazy or gloomy conditions. The tether of the wiring made a dash to avoid errant airplanes rather difficult.

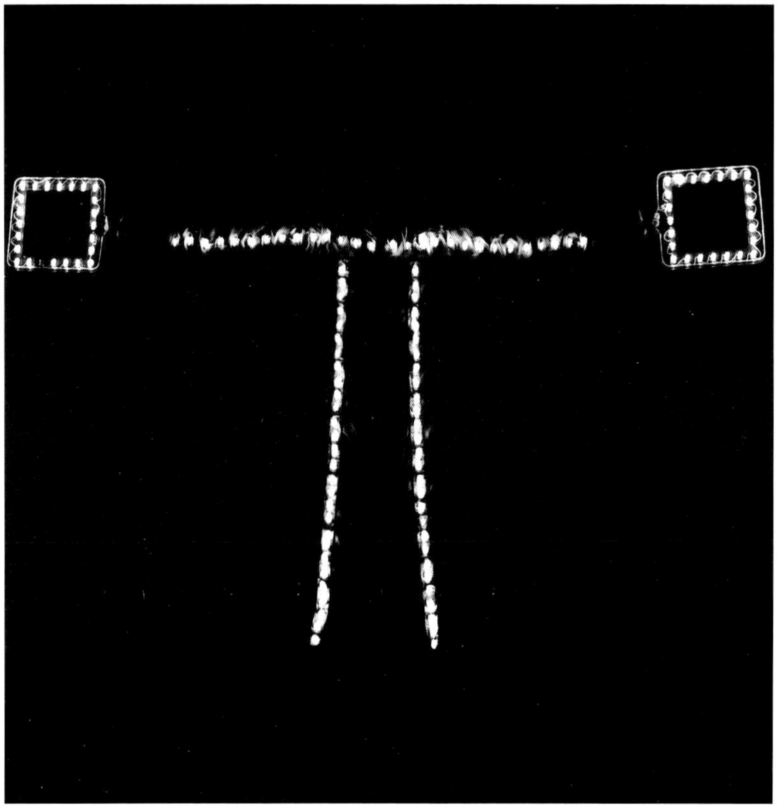

A drawback of the lighted suit was that the LSO became a stick figure with no dimension. The thin lines of lights were difficult to interpret. Although a variety of mechanical systems were tried, until the invention of the mirror, the lighted suit was the most practical system.

Chapter 3

PRACTICE, PREPARE AND COMBAT

1931–1941

USS Saratoga (CV-3) in New York City during a visitors' day in 1932. Her identifying black stripe is painted on both sides of the funnel. The nameplate on the bow was taken down when Saratoga went to sea.

By the end of the Roaring Twenties, aircraft carrier operations were routine, as much as carrier flying is ever routine. No longer was taking off and landing an experiment; it was now a sound procedure with equipment made for the purpose. The question became not, how do you fly at sea? but, what do you do with the capability of flying war planes off a ship? Where did aircraft carriers fit in the strategic picture? Each nation had different goals in mind and differing opinions within their respective services as well. In the United States, the controversy generated by Mitchell was dragging on, and even within the navy, the battleship versus aircraft argument continued. Great Britain was stuck with the problem of its air force trying to work in an environment it did not understand. In Japan, the conflict between army and navy was described as a "full-body contact brawl."

Preparing for the Real Thing

The United States Navy ran a series of Fleet Problem war games. The first with a carrier was Fleet Problem VIII in 1928 when airplanes from *Langley* dropped flour bombs on army and navy installations at Pearl Harbor. Fleet Problem IX the next year saw *Lexington* and *Saratoga* using their full capabilities defending and attacking the Panama Canal, including strikes against each other. (In one exercise, *Lexington* was attacked and theoretically sunk by her own aircraft despite a large "LEX" on the flight deck, "SARA" was painted on the sister ship. Soon after, *Lexington* had a wide black stripe painted horizontally on her exhaust stack and *Saratoga* a wide black vertical stripe on hers.) In the 1930 Fleet Problem in the Caribbean, the carriers were credited with sinking an entire battle fleet. The period also saw the introduction of United States Marine Corps (USMC) squadrons aboard ship. In the 1938 exercise, *Saratoga* pulled off a successful surprise attack on Pearl Harbor.

The emphasis in the Royal Navy was on torpedo attacks against an enemy fleet in harbor. This was the same concept that their first carriers had in 1918. Although the Royal Navy did not train for carrier versus carrier warfare, the emphasis on torpedo attacks did pay off at Taranto. All four active British carriers spent time in the Mediterranean with *Courageous* and *Glorious* basing in Alexandria and *Hermes* and *Eagle* going as far as the China Station, but except for the brief foray against the pirate fleet, their role was basically to show the flag.

Japan had better than war games. The aircraft carriers of the IJN went into combat in China for the first time during the Shanghai Incident of 1932. Compared to

USS** Lexington **in Panama Canal locks. The width of the locks affected the design of major warships. Radio masts were eventually moved to the edge of the flight deck where they could be swung to the side during flight operations; much simpler than rigging and derigging a mast as seen here.

The first Corsair was the SU type landing here aboard Saratoga *(CV-3). The SU has both a tailhook for the transverse arresting wires and arrow fittings on its axle for the longitudinal wires. Called "fiddle bridges," the rectangular pieces hold the wires off the deck.*

A Martin T4M torpedo bomber (the landing gears are separated so the long torpedo will fit under the fuselage) landing on Lexington *in 1930. The fore and aft wires have been removed with the installation of the Mk 3 AG. The circle was an aiming point for the pilots to judge where to touchdown.*

The Japanese A5M Claude was the finest carrier-based fighter of the 1930s, scoring many successes over China. The A5M was a completely Japanese product despite propaganda claims in the West. Compare it to the Boeing F4B and Fairey Flycatcher. (Phillip Jarrett Collection)

USS Constellation *(CVA-64), decommissioned 2003, was one of the last conventionally powered and conventionally named U.S. carriers.*

later combat in the Pacific, the missions over the month of February were skirmishes. However, they proved the effectiveness of bombing attacks and air-to-air combat (including the first aerial kill by a Japanese pilot) by carrier-launched airplanes.

Conventionally World War II began 1 September 1939, but Japanese carriers were in combat before then with their campaign in China. By 1937 *Kaga, Hosho,* and *Ryujo* were raiding Nanking and cities on the Chinese coast. These carriers worked as a unified task group[1] sending formations to attack inland targets from a fixed point in the China Sea (the U.S. Navy would be doing the same thing 35 years later over Vietnam from the same China Sea a hundred miles south). The IJN aircraft were at first inferior to Western– and Soviet Union–provided aircraft, but soon had the monoplane Nakajima A5M Claude[2] at a time when the U.S. Navy was flying F4Bs and F3Fs, and Britain, Fairey Flycatchers as primary fighters.

There was a lull in the Far East in 1939 as the European powers went to war. At the outset, German Stukas, although land planes, showed the effectiveness of dive bombers against land and sea targets. Japan and the United States had also been developing their own dive bombers and now worked on perfecting the machines and the tactics.

For the aircraft carriers the war began in the confusion of the Atlantic around Great Britain and then into the futile Norwegian campaign. The time had come to prove carrier development was worth all the expense and effort.

Taken in May 1940 from the flight deck of HMS Ark Royal, *this may be the last photograph of HMS* Glorious. *After recovering aircraft from Norway in June, the ship was sunk by the German battleships* Scharnhorst *and* Gneisenau *in the North Sea.*

Norway

The Royal Navy had a rough start. Eleven days after the war began in Europe, HMS *Ark Royal* barely avoided torpedoes from a U-boat. Two days later, three torpedoes struck HMS *Courageous* and she went down with all her aircraft and 518 of her crew. The carriers were being ill-used in anti-submarine patrols.

One of the most extraordinary and daring events in the history of carrier aviation took place in June 1940. Fourteen Hurricanes and nine Gladiators of the RAF landed aboard HMS *Glorious*. Not one of these airplanes had a tailhook. They were flown by pilots who had never landed on a ship at sea. Not one airplane was wrecked.

The British army had gone into Norway in a futile attempt to halt the German invasion. Air support was desperately needed but the flight across the North Sea was too far for fighter aircraft. In April, *Glorious* had taken 18 Gladiators that had flown onto a frozen lake. In two days 17 were destroyed. In late May, RAF 263 Squadron with Hawker Hurricanes and 46 Squadron with Gloster Gladiators craned their aircraft aboard *Glorious* and *Furious*. In range of Norwegian airfields, the RAF pilots took off and did what they could against the Luftwaffe.

Italy had jumped into the war on 10 June. France was about to surrender. (It did on 17 June.) British forces were needed elsewhere and a withdrawal was ordered. Rather than destroying the airplanes to avoid capture, a RAF squadron leader recommended flying them onto the carriers. *Ark Royal*'s deck was 200 feet longer than that on *Furious*, which meant the Hurricanes should be able to land. However, *Ark*'s elevators were too small to lower the non-folding-wing Hurricanes below. This meant the wings had to be sawed off to get them off the deck. The elevators on *Glorious* were large enough to handle intact Hurricanes.

Supermarine Walrus amphibious utility airplanes flew from the shore to *Glorious* for RAF officers to meet with the ship's DLCO. Fifteen-pound sandbags were put in the Hurricane tails to allow hard braking without nosing over. The air pressure in the tires was lowered to assist in braking, but otherwise they were stock RAF machines. On 7 June three Hurricanes successfully landed on *Glorious* aided by 40 knots of wind over the deck and were safely stored below. The next day, ten more Hurris, eight of the slower Gladiators, and four of the versatile Walruses flew aboard. *Glorious* and two destroyers were cleared to proceed home.

Tragically, all of these efforts were wasted. The three ships were attacked by the German battle-cruisers *Scharnhorst* and *Gneisenau*. Worried about fuel the captain of *Glorious* (a submariner with only 10 months aircraft carrier experience) did not have all the ship's engines on-line so could not outrun the Germans, who had gotten in range because no aircraft were airborne on patrol. He made other tactical mistakes as well.[3] Despite gallant efforts from the accompanying destroyers, gunfire sank all three Royal Navy ships. There were only 45 survivors. Besides all the RAF airplanes, five Swordfish of Naval Squadron 825 and a dozen Sea Gladiators of NAS 802[4] went down with the *Glorious*.

The standard U.S. Navy (and U.S. Army Air Corps as the P-12) fighter of the 1930s was the Boeing F4B. The formation here does not have the standard markings with colored and half-colored cowlings indicating flight lead and wingman, and one does not have the formation alignment lines on the top wing.

Bismarck

While the fighting in Norway raged, the German's most powerful warship made life hard for the Royal Navy. The successful pursuit of the *Bismarck* would not have been possible without aircraft carriers. No ship had the striking range of carrier-launched aircraft. On the same day *Bismarck* and *Prinz Eugen* sank HMS *Hood*, Swordfish from HMS *Victorious* nearly attacked HMS *Norfolk* before going on to *Bismarck*. Only one of the nine torpedoes fired struck, inflicting minor damage, but the Germans now had a threat from the air to worry about. Two days later, 26 May, *Ark Royal*, which had steamed quickly from Gibraltar, launched her squadron of Swordfish. Again, in grey and misty weather, the wrong ship was attacked. This time torpedoes were launched. The only reason HMS *Sheffield* did not become a fatality from friendly fire was that none of the torpedoes exploded due to faulty magnetic detonators.

The aircraft returned to *Ark Royal*, refueled, and rearmed with torpedoes with contact detonators; 15 Swordfish then set off for the German ships. *Bismarck* was hit twice. The first hit her heavy armor belt and caused little damage, but the second jammed *Bismarck's* rudder to the side. The damage was critical. Unable to steer properly or maintain full speed, the great battleship was doomed.

The Fleet Air Arm's Finest Night 11/11/1940

The attack on Taranto was spectacular. A fire on HMS *Illustrious* set the planned date back almost a month to take advantage of a full moon. By the new date the Italians serendipitously had all six of their battleships in the harbor as well as nine cruisers, eight destroyers, and many smaller vessels. The defenses of the port had been alerted and began firing as soon as the incoming Swordfish were within range. Tracer rounds in red, white, green, and blue from hundreds of 20mm cannon and machine guns ashore and on ships flamed across the sky. Bright explosions from more than 100 heavy anti-aircraft guns dotted the night. A pair of Swordfish in both waves dropped strings of flares landward. The bright, magnesium lights drifted down slowly under parachutes and provided a bright background to the dark ships assisting the pilots' aim. Overhead the full moon shone down, giving the entire scene a spectral unreality.

British torpedoes put three battleships out of action. In two hours the balance of naval power in the Mediterranean was radically changed.

In deep water, torpedoes drop easily. However, in shallow water, when dropped at airplane speeds and altitudes, a torpedo will plunge nose down and either porpoise uncontrollably or hit bottom. The FAA's solution was a thin wire from the nose of the torpedo to a spool on the belly of the aircraft. The wire held the nose up so the torpedo belly-flopped and was level to begin its run in. (Japanese and later, American, solutions were wood frames on the nose and tail to change the shape. The frames tore off on water impact.) Experts said that torpedo attacks in a harbor were impossible. The Royal Navy proved them wrong at Taranto.

The Japanese naval attaché in Berlin flew down a few days after and later a delegation of Japanese officers came and went over the attack with the Italians. An American navy officer was on board *Illustrious* as an observer and sent a comprehensive report to Washington. The Japanese learned from Taranto. The Americans apparently did not.

Carriers have an inherent complexity; the tanks for fuel, water, and gasoline can be interconnected to trim the balance of the ship. *Eagle* was not ready for Taranto because she had been bombed and her aviation fuel system contaminated. The five flyable Swordfish were transferred to *Illustrious*. Then, on successive days, three Swordfish crashed; the last on 11 November. The problem was traced to contaminated fuel and inspection showed that all the airplanes had bad fuel. In a frantic effort the maintenance crews managed to drain, purge, and refuel the airplanes hours before the launch that night.

The 21 Swordfish took off well after sunset. The attack was in the dark; the second wave dropping their torpedoes around midnight. The landings on *Illustrious* were two hours after that in the wee small hours. That the FAA kept pilots and Bats trained and current in night work (attacks had been previously made on Rhodes, Leros, Benghazi, and Tobruk) made the plan work. Only two aircraft were lost during the attack. None were lost at the ship.

Admiral Lyster[5] wanted to strike Taranto again the next night. Thinking of the harrowing event and that the Italians now knew the method of attack, one of the pilots was heard to say, "They only

Hangar Deck Landing

I was in VF-41 flying F4Fs from USS *Ranger* (CV-4) off the Bermuda coast, practicing for what later became the invasion of Africa. We had completed our strafing runs on the beaches of Bermuda and returned to the ship. I was the last in my four-plane division to land.

When the LSO gave the "cut," I complied and set the Wildcat down on the deck. Unfortunately, on contact with the arresting gear, my tailhook broke loose and rolled off into the sea. My fighter continued forward and was restrained by the barrier. The F4F went up on its nose, and still moving I found myself looking down at an airplane that had just been lowered to the hangar deck via the forward elevator. This violated the rule prohibiting elevator use during a recovery.

My plane was flipping inverted into the large hole on the flight deck where the elevator had been. I thought I would crash upside down on the hangar deck and be crushed on impact. I ran my arms down into the rudder pedals, forming my body into a ball, limiting my exposure outside the cockpit shell insofar as possible.

Instead of dropping onto the hangar deck, however, the wingspan of my Wildcat, now inverted, was just wide enough to have about a foot of each wing tip resting on the flight deck. I was now upside down in the F4F, hanging by my safety belt. The aircraft was gently rocking up and down over the open elevator hole.

Plane handlers removed the aircraft that had been on the elevator. The flight deck officer, several plane handlers, and the flight surgeon assembled to resolve the predicament. At first it was thought I'd fallen out of the cockpit because I was still trying to stay in a ball and was hard to see.

Finally, the elevator was raised slowly until it was close enough to my Wildcat that a couple of sailors could pat me on my back. I was told to release my seat belt, which I did. I was then lifted out of the cockpit. I stood up on the elevator, not a scratch on me.

In sick bay the flight surgeon checked me out and served me a slug of Old Forester in a paper cup. At dinner in the wardroom that evening, with all officers present, I was summoned to the captain's table. I was recognized by my CO and XO. I was described as the first pilot in the history of the navy to land on the hangar deck of an aircraft carrier. In honor of my accomplishment I was presented a large medal fabricated by the metalsmiths from a Prince Albert tobacco can.[7]

asked the Light Brigade to do it once!" Another wrote, "In the end we were told the idea had been cancelled as the weather report was completely unsuitable. I think that the Meteorological Officer was the most popular officer in the ship!"[6]

Naming American Carriers

United States Navy aircraft carriers were traditionally named after early ships of the navy or battles. (CV-1 *Langley* was named after a civilian, but there was no need for a rule with the first.) *Lexington, Saratoga, Ranger, Essex, Enterprise*; great names. (We always thought *Bon Homme Richard* was a strange name for an American warship, but "Poor Richard" would have been worse.) The rule (Confederate navy ships or battles won by the South during the Civil War were apparently not allowed) was followed through the great fleet buildup of World War II. With so many choices, what was the first exception to the rule?

When President Franklin Roosevelt was asked in 1942 where the Doolittle Raiders launched from, he whimsically replied, from *Shangri-La;* an imaginary land in a then-popular novel. In a stroke, the president's joke gave a major combatant a name from pop-culture. Franklin D. Roosevelt himself became an eponymous aircraft carrier within days of his demise (CVB-43).

The CVLs *Langley* (27), *Cabot* (28), and *Wright* (49) were people names. And what about CVAs *Randolph* (CV-15) and *Hancock* (CV-19)? Seems they were post-revolutionary ships, some named after founding fathers:

- USS *Langley* (CV-1), 1922
- USS *Cabot* 14-gun brig and first American armed vessel to engage an enemy, 1777
- USS *Wright* 16 December 1921, as AZ-1 USS *Orville Wright*
- USS *Randolph* 32-gun frigate in the Continental navy, 1776 (Peyton Randolph was president of the Continental Congress)
- USS *Hancock* schooner 1775 and frigate 1776 (John Hancock was president of the Continental Congress after Randolph. He was also a merchant-smuggler and very wealthy.)

U.S. Navy CVEs were supposed to be named after American bodies of water or islands, but with so many coming from the shipyards, battles or locations of fighting (When does a fight become a battle?) were put into use; for example, *Salerno, Sicily, Rabaul, St. Lo, Casablanca.*

HMS* Eagle *deck crew grabbing the wings of an angular Fairey Flycatcher, the Royal Navy's 1930s standard fighter. Because the carrier does not have arrestor gear nor does the Flycatcher have a hook, like all British airplanes of the era, it relied on a slow landing speed, the drag of the tailskid, and especially wind over the deck to stop after landing. The deck-edge netting prevents airplanes from going over the side. (Jennings)

A spectacular JATO takeoff of a P2V Neptune from the Franklin D. Roosevelt *(CVB-42). The smoke generated delayed operations on the flight deck as well as the launch of the next Neptune. One of the many reasons the concept was flawed.*

The major change of DH Sea Hornet from the Mosquito was to make the cockpit for only the pilot with a bubble canopy located farther forward for visibility. Visibility from the Mosquito was such that during trials of the "Mossie," the Batsman had to move out onto the deck to be seen and then scamper out of the way after giving the cut signal.

North American Aviation's AJ Savage was the first large multi-engine aircraft to operate regularly from CVs. However, difficulties with wing folding and engines tearing off on landing, a not uncommon problem, as seen in this photo, did not endear the AJ to carrier crews.

In modern times, USS *Kitty Hawk* (CVA-63) is an odd choice, although USS *Kitty Hawk* (AKV-1) was a cargo ship and aircraft transport that served during World War II. Following the assassination of President Kennedy, as a gesture of mourning, the last numbered conventional carrier (CVA-67) was named USS *John F. Kennedy*. With the first of the new class of nuclear-powered ships, USS *Nimitz* (CVN-68), tradition was ignored and continues to be with a series of presidents and obscure politicians.

Many Motors

Multi-engine aircraft have the advantages of carrying more payload, be it crew, armament, fuel or cargo, and offering more safety (having a second engine to get one home is comforting, especially over long stretches of ocean). Putting airplanes with two engines aboard aircraft carriers was an early idea.

The French were first. In January 1936, the prototype Potez 56e (designed as a transport, the Potez resembled a small DC-3) landed aboard FN *Bearn* on a trial basis to see if it could be done. The idea was not pursued.

A Lockheed 12, designated XJO-3 for experimental, made landings on USS *Lexington* (CV-2) in August 1939 testing the suitability of a twin-engined aircraft with a nose wheel for carrier operations. The idea was not pursued.

In March 1944 an adapted de Haviland Mosquito Mk VI (fighter/bomber version) piloted by Winkle Brown (adding yet another first to his list) made five landings aboard HMS *Indefatigable*. The British formed 618 Squadron with twin-engine Mosquito strike aircraft for carrier operations from CVEs, but it did not see combat before the war ended and the squadron was disbanded.

A USN B-25/PBJ made a couple of landings on USS *Shangri-La* (CV-38) in November 1944 (see Chapter Six). A Grumman F7F Tigercat was tested at the same time. The Tigercat became operational (although in a limited fashion), whereas the B-25 did not.

A derivative of the Mosquito, the DH Sea Hornet became the first multi-engine airplane to operate regularly on aircraft carriers beginning in June 1947.

Because this book is about landings, I will only mention the nuke-carrying Lockheed P2V Neptunes, which launched from CVBs after being hoisted on board. A Neptune with a tailhook did make 182 successful traps on arresting gear ashore at NAS Norfolk.

There were early jet fighters with two engines, but being small in size, they were not much different from their single-engine brethren. Early jets (F2H, F3D, Sea Vixen) used two engines for backup and sufficient thrust. The much larger AJ Savage first came aboard ship in August 1950, beginning a 10-year U.S. Navy carrier-based career.

The Royal Navy proposed a fleet surveillance, four-engine airplane in 1940. The engines were small, but the aircraft had great endurance. The before-radar idea was to launch the Fleet Shadower before sunset, follow the enemy fleet through the night, and land back aboard next morning. Two prototypes of the General Aircraft G.A.L.38 Fleet Shadower and Airspeed A.S.39 Fleet Shadower each were built, but neither ever landed on a carrier before the idea was dropped.

Although successful four-engine aircraft landings were accomplished, of course, by the C-130 Hercules (see Chapter Eight), the idea was not pursued.

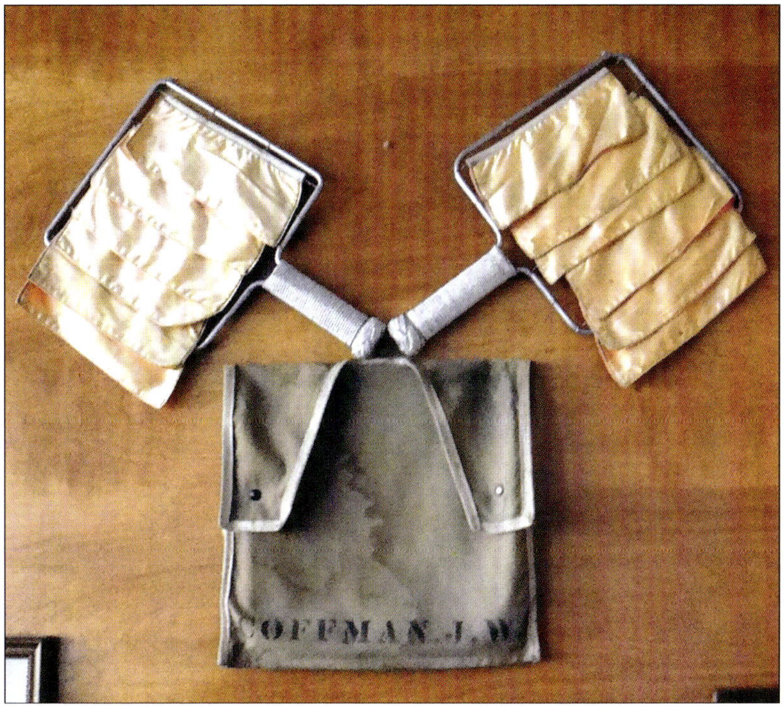

Examples of day paddles: (above) Fancy rope work on handles and canvas storage case. The fluorescent-type fabric is the same as the stripes on the coveralls. (LSO school collection) (top right) Another solution was grommets to let the wind through. The bright pink surface is stiffer than cloth. (Virginia Beach Military Aviation Museum collection) (bottom right) A good reproduction set for demonstrations. (LSO school collection)

Paddles Construction

The first paddles were semaphore flags (or sailors' white hats if one legend is correct) borrowed from the signal bridge. It did not take long to learn that in the wind the flag blew back flat and pilots had trouble seeing them. Possibly inspired by ping-pong, early LSOs made round paddles with handles of wood. Increasing the size of the disks made them easier to see. The problem this created was keeping such a large, flat surface area steady in the wind, not to mention the fatigue induced by holding the paddles at arms' length.

Who gets credit for the obvious solution (cut holes in the paddles) is unknown. The Royal Navy had the shipyard make the bats for DLCOs while in the U.S. Navy LSOs made their own with help from the ship's carpenter and, later, the metalsmiths. No two sets of paddles were the same and most were customized for the LSO who wanted them.

LSOs McCampbell and Konrad (also on the *Wasp*) are credited with creating paddles with strips of cloth on wires inside a metal

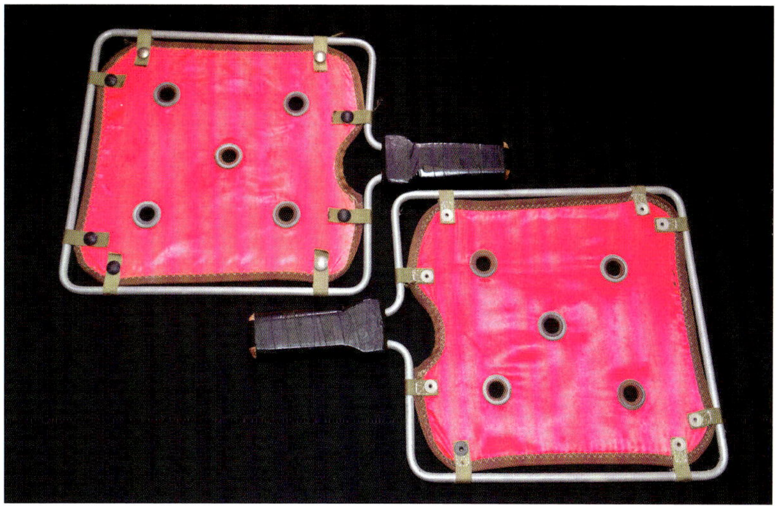

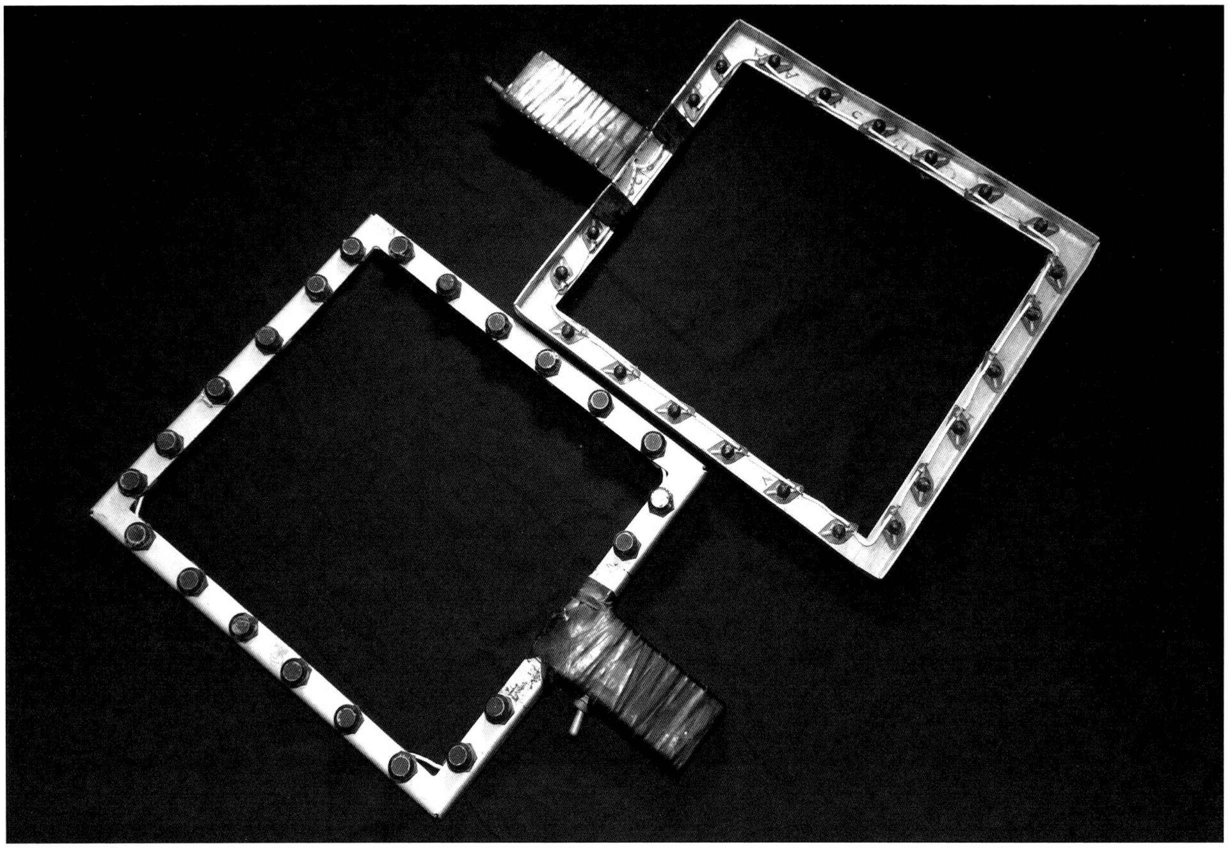

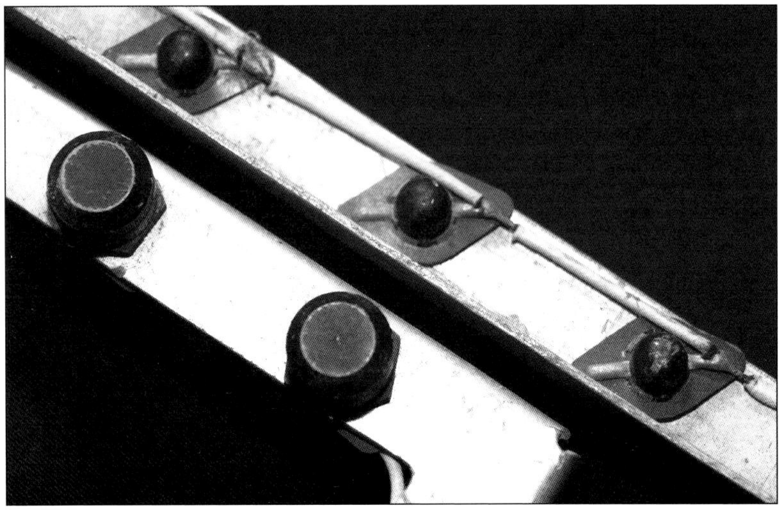

Examples of night paddles: (top) Lighted paddles, front (right) with the bulbs and back side, which has the switch to turn all the suit lights on. The tape on the handles probably means the paddles were made by the ship or squadron shop. With the open design, wind pressure was a minor factor, but the weight of the assembly was a bigger factor. (bottom left) Close-up with details of the light installation and wiring. (Virginia Beach Military Aviation Museum Collection) (bottom right) The handle was left at full length for stability. Set was broken up as souvenir gifts. (Courtesy LSO McClung)

A Loening OL-8A returning to USS* Lexington *after a relief mission to Managua, Nicaragua, after the devastating 1931 earthquake. The LSO is still using flags; soon after, paddles were discovered to be more visible than the wind-blown flags.

frame; aircraft tubing was a popular material. They are much lighter than solid wood. Even a few ounces make a difference after a long session on the platform.

A piece of cloth could be laced across the frame or wires run through strips of bright and strong material. When they fluttered they looked solid while still providing a minimum of wind resistance. Because a rectangle is easier to construct than a circle, square paddles became the norm.

For night work, the UV reflective cloth that outlined the LSO was also put in the paddles. When the electric suit was created the strings of small bulbs continued out to the paddles. DLCOs had two lamps with reflectors and a third on their chest. These lights helped in lowered visibility and could be seen from farther away, so were used in the daytime as well as at night. The problem with both lighted systems was that electric cords hindered an LSO's dash away from crashing airplanes and facilitated his getting zapped by short circuits in sea spray or rain.

LSO Platform

Like everything in aircraft carrier operations, where the LSO stood evolved as experience showed a better way. The first LSOs simply stood on the edge of the flight deck. When LSOs learned that pilots could see their signals better if they stood farther from the centerline, a platform was built that extended off the port side level with the flight deck. A solid platform became wet and slippery from rain or sea spray so the platform became an open-work grid. Made by the ship's carpenters of wood, the platform had open 1-inch squares. (They were lovely pieces of carpentry; I wonder if any survived?) An added benefit to standing on wood is its resilience; it is less fatiguing than metal.

Strong winds over the deck are good for landing airplanes but make it hard for LSOs to hold their arms out, so wind barriers were put on the forward side of the platform at the LSO's back. These screens evolved from wood boards slipped into slots for the Royal

The LSO platform on* Lexington *in 1937. Experience showed the need for more standing room; later platforms became larger with the addition of a wind break that folded down. There is no additional equipment, only the phone talker with his sound-powered headset.

Navy, to canvas in a steel frame and eventually to all metal. The screens had to be lowered for two reasons: The first was for clearance from airplanes moving on the deck. Second, when the sun was low after dawn or before sunset and the carrier was heading into the sun, the LSO was in shadow and his signals difficult to see.

With visual signals there could only be one person waving, so platforms did not have to be large. Trainees stood directly behind the controlling LSO and remembered to keep their arms at their sides. The phone talker stood in the catwalk near the platform and used flags; red for a fouled deck, green for clear deck. This sailor's sound-powered phones were on a circuit with the bridge, air operations (the tower), and arresting gear operators.

Getting to the platform was from a hatch onto the catwalk with a ladder up to the flight deck and on to the platform. For obvious reasons the platform and LSO were in an exposed position. This was also a hazardous position. It was not uncommon for a botched approach to put the airplane into the platform. Climbing down a ladder or making a leap onto a steel deck was not fast enough to avoid a crashing airplane. The solution was an escape net extending under and beyond the platform. Made of heavy, braided wire, the net was covered with padding and gave a fast way to jump, roll, and scurry down into the catwalk to run in either direction or into a hatchway.

When the mirror came into use, it became normal for a pair of LSOs to be on the platform, either for training or as a backup. The talker and spotter moved onto the platform as well. Equipment boxes were set at an angle on the edge for accessibility. Because the number of people no longer mattered, platforms could get crowded with trainees and spectators.

The modern LSO team (see Chapter Ten) needs a space for everyone and its equipment, so platforms have expanded accordingly.

A presumably practice platform evacuation. The netting is covered with a pad. The dark hole under the platform leads to the catwalk and nearby hatch into the ship. In the 1970s some East Coast carriers had platforms sunk below deck level as an unnecessary safety measure. With this arrangement the escape route was narrow. There were cases of over-eager leaps, which missed the net completely. If you were smart and first into the net you cleared off fast! More than one LSO had an arm or leg broken by his buddies landing on top of him.

In a scene from the early 1960s a Skyhawk is about to trap on USS Saratoga *(CVA-60). Three of the LSOs are wearing coveralls with fluorescent stripes, the talker is using flags to signal clear deck, the platform is varnished teak, and the wire rope of the safety net does not have a cover. The area the talker is standing in is the catwalk, which runs along both sides of the flight deck, except where there is an elevator. The back of the datum lights are visible to the left of the wind screen. Douglas A-3 Skywarriors are parked between the landing area and the island; possible on the* Forrestal *class.*

The new platform on Lexington with a workman's tools nearby. The platform bracing is sturdier and a safety rail has been added, but it does not yet have a full net for escape. Before catwalks were installed, safety netting ran full length on both sides of the flight deck. The drain scuppers have grid sections to keep level with the deck. Circa 1928.

In what is probably a posed picture (the paddle ribbons are limp so there is no wind, the equipment box is shut, and the cigar doubtful), LT W. F. Toby Tobin with paddles and LTJG J. E. Hyde are on the platform of USS Boxer *(CV-21) in 1952 during Tobin's third Korean deployment. The wood grid of the platform is covered with canvas and the safety net has extra webbing at the top.*

A posed photo taken while the carrier was in port (a 5-inch gun in vertical position is on the right, apparently there is no wind, and heavy industrial equipment is at left) shows the dress, equipment, and platform typical of the 1950s: a wood grid covered with canvas, a pair of equipment boxes with lids open, safety net thinly padded, and support stanchion wrapped with heavy padding. The deck edge scupper (drain) is covered next to the platform to keep the LSO from stumbling in it when moving onto the deck.

The escape route can be seen in this picture taken from the hatch into the ship; one jumped into the net, scrambled onto the catwalk, and ran aft, rarely forward, or into the hatch. The colors marking the LSO suits are bright in this 1950s picture. The LSO on the platform is using a paddle of each color while Toby Tobin clowning on the net has on his fluorescent pink sleeves.

Platforms in the 1970s could be crowded. While it took only two LSOs to properly work a recovery, there were trainees, LSOs from squadrons, and visitors. The white objects are sections of the curb, which went around the sides of the flight deck to keep airplanes and wheeled deck equipment from rolling over the side.

WAR IN THE MEDITERRANEAN AND ATLANTIC

1942–1945

Douglas SBD Dauntless in 1942. For Operation Torch, American airplanes had a yellow ring around the fuselage star to make them more obvious. **(*Flying* magazine 1943)**

Carrier aviation took on three distinctive roles in 1942, defined as much by geography as mission. The most significant difference between the Atlantic and Mediterranean and the Pacific was the enemy; Germany and Italy had no aircraft carriers. In the Pacific, the U.S. Navy and the Imperial Japanese Navy clashed in five major carrier-versus-carrier battles. Support of amphibious invasions became the other major task in the Pacific. Although there were seaborne invasions in the Mediterranean, only one, Operation Torch in North Africa, did not have Allied air support available from land bases.

Carriers in the Mediterranean During World War II

The carriers' main mission in the Mediterranean was to keep the sea lanes open to the Mid-East while running the gauntlet of the *Mare Nostrum*, "Our Sea," as Mussolini had declared it. The task was a difficult one as Italian and, later, Luftwaffe aircraft could easily control the Sicily-Malta-North Africa gap. The carriers and other ships of the Royal Navy had to fight off hordes of Axis bombers to get the supply ships though. The carriers themselves became supply ships of a sort, loading their flight decks with land-type fighters to fly off one-way to Malta. Operating within easy range of the enemy must have been frustrating, even frightening, to sailors whose own deck was locked by their cargo of airplanes.

Outside Gibraltar, after the German *Kriegsmarine* big gun ships were sunk or locked in port, the role of the carriers was to fight U-boats and protect the trans-Atlantic convoys. The Battle of the Atlantic was Anti-Submarine Warfare (ASW) at its height. Here the fast carriers with large numbers of airplanes could be replaced by many small carriers with smaller numbers of airplanes. The escort carrier's speed was sufficient to keep up with and maneuver around the slow-sailing merchant ships. More carriers were dedicated to ASW than any other mission.

At the time of Pearl Harbor, the United States had five carriers based on the East Coast. *Yorktown* (CV-5) had moved almost immediately to the Pacific in mid-December 1941. The brand-new

USS Wasp *(CV-7) on display (the aircraft are arrayed for appearance and the signal halyards are filled with flags) in 1941 before the United States entered World War II.*

RAF Spitfire on its takeoff run on USS Wasp*. An unusual event, there are more than the usual number of men watching from Vultures Row and other available spots.*

Hornet (CV-8) followed in March 1942. *Ranger*, which remained in the Atlantic Fleet for the duration, began shuttle runs to West Africa, flying off USAAF P-40 fighters, which continued across the continent to Egypt or India. The first of the American Escort Carriers, *Long Island* (CVE-1), also ferried aircraft to places like Iceland, Bermuda, and Trinidad between stints as a training carrier operating in Chesapeake Bay away from prowling U-boats. The fifth was *Wasp* (CV-7), which had been completed in 1940.

Malta Runs

The island of Malta was at the crossroads for Axis convoys going north to south as well as Allied convoys going west to east. Malta was deservedly called an "unsinkable aircraft carrier." The problem was to have enough aircraft to defend the island as well as attack Axis shipping. The nearest Allied base was at Gibraltar and it was too far away for fighters to make the flight. Consequently, carriers were drafted as ferries. HMS *Argus* and HMS *Eagle* carried Spitfires on the first runs, but could not carry very many. USS *Wasp* (CV-18) was loaned to the Royal Navy Home Fleet to assist. USS *Wasp* made her first trip in April 1942. Her F4F Wildcats were kept on the flight deck and 47 Spitfires put on the hangar deck. Within range, the Wildcats launched as fighter defense and the Spitfires that had warmed up below rode the elevators to the flight deck and took off. The level of proficiency the U.S. Navy had reached in carrier ops showed: 11 Wildcats and all 47 Spitfires were airborne in 61 minutes.

In May, USS *Wasp* made another trip. This time in company with HMS *Eagle*. *Eagle* carried 17 Spitfires while *Wasp* again had 47 on board. During the fly-off, one of the Spits crashed and another lost its auxiliary belly tank, and the pilot was given the choice of ditching or trying to land. In what is still considered an amazing event, the pilot made it back on board.

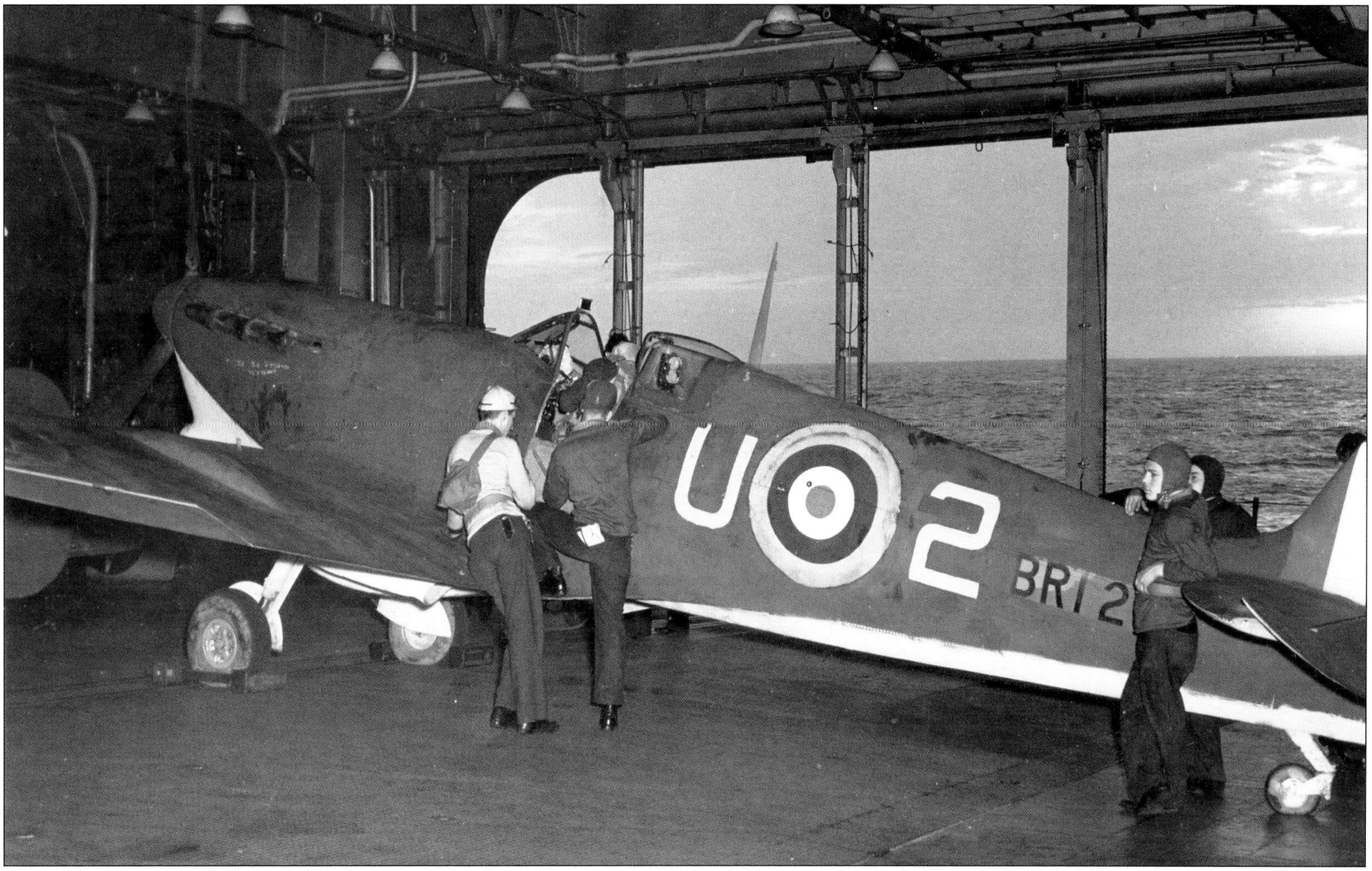

Because American hangar decks were open to the sides, airplane engines could be run without going to the flight deck. This was key to the fast launch of the Spitfires to Malta. Merlin engines tended to overheat when not flying so they were warmed up on the hangar deck, shut down, and started again on the flight deck immediately before takeoff.

Wasp turned west, made a stop at the Royal Navy base at Scapa Flow, and then went back to the States and on to the Pacific. Sadly, she was lost in fighting near Guadalcanal.

A poor quality but extremely rare color photo of LT David McCampbell working a recovery aboard USS* Wasp*. His paddles are bent aluminum tubing filled with an open-weave fabric for less wind resistance.

LSO David McCampbell

Dave McCampbell graduated from the United States Naval Academy in 1935 and by 1938 had earned his wings. He spent two years flying from *Ranger* with VF-4 before being drafted as LSO on the *Wasp*. He later said his most trying experiences were during operations in the North Atlantic, where he suffered frostbite despite an electrically heated suit. During the run to Malta, McCampbell had briefed the RAF pilots on takeoff technique and carrier ops in general. In passing, he mentioned that as LSO, if an airplane was making a dangerous approach he would probably jump into the safety net.

For almost all the Spitfires the launch went well, but a young pilot named Smith had his drop tank fall off. Without the gas in it he could not make it to Malta. He circled overhead while what to do was decided. The *Wasp*'s captain told McCampbell to bring the hookless, land-type aircraft with an inexperienced pilot back aboard. McCampbell later said he "dropped dead" at the idea.

Smith's first try was high and fast. McCampbell's arm signals, of course, meant nothing to the young British pilot. Remembering his briefing, McCampbell leaped into the net. Smith got the idea and went around for another try. The second approach was only slightly better, but possible. "He was still fast as hell so I tried to outguess him and gave him the cut far back from what I did for our own pilots."

LT McCampbell acting as the launching officer for Spitfire Mk VC fitted with a slipper fuel tank on its belly. It was the loss of this tank (possibly through pilot error) that resulted in a Spitfire landing without a hook back on the Wasp.

Smith chopped his throttle, but held off and did not touch down until halfway up the deck. The barrier had been removed and there was more than 35 knots of wind over the deck. Braking as hard as he could without going up on his nose, Smith came to a stop before falling over the bow.

McCampbell paced off 6 feet between the Spitfire's wheels and the edge of the deck! He congratulated Smith and asked, "How much time do you have in Spits?"

The astonishing answer, "About 128 hours overall, but this was my first time in a Spitfire." The crew awarded Smith honorary U.S. Navy wings.[1]

A grain ship MAC underway. The single lift (elevator) aft is partially lowered. The four arrestor wires are located almost amidships. MACShips were short by any standard with flight decks not that much wider than the wing span of the embarked Swordfish. (Canada Shearwater Museum)

"Dashing Dave" McCampbell stayed with *Wasp* during Pacific combat until she was torpedoed and he had to jump into the ocean. After 30 days' survivor's leave, McCampbell received promotion to lieutenant commander and assignment as senior instructor of landing signal officers in Melbourne, Florida. Although 32 years old, he next badgered his way into assignment to a fighter squadron, VF-15, on *Essex* (CV-9) in mid-1944. He was soon commander of Air Group 15 and finished with 34 kills as the U.S. Navy's top-scoring ace.

MACShips

Merchant Aircraft Carrier (MAC) ships were created in desperation for combating the German submarines that were devastating convoys across the Atlantic. There was no time to build aircraft carriers from the keel up, so oilers and grain carriers had flight decks added. These ships continued to carry their normal cargoes as well as operate aircraft for convoy defense. Nineteen MACShips went into service between April 1943 and April 1944 and served throughout the war. Thirteen were tankers of 8,000 tons with 460-foot-long flight decks, but no hangar stowage.

MV Alexia (Motor Vessel; MACShips kept their merchant designations and were crewed by merchant sailors. The fliers were a detachment from the FAA). A tanker MACShip that did not have a hangar deck could operate only three Fairey Swordfish. (J. Thomas)

Six were grain ships, which were even shorter, 420 ft, but had the advantage of an elevator and hangar spaces to put airplanes below. Both types of ships' beam-width caused problems. The Fairey Swordfish's wingspan of 45 feet was 8 feet from the deck edge (when on centerline) except beside the island where the clearance was only 27 inches.

According to Stanley Brand, "In conversion from original duty to MACShip, extra weight was added in the shape of accommodation, aviation fuel tanks, workshop equipment, and most of all, flight deck and its supports. In all, more than a thousand tons were added, much of it 30 feet above waterline. This had the effect of making her roll like a pig when sailing with waves coming in from abeam."[2]

When a MACShip rolled 15 degrees (not unusual in the North Atlantic) the bridge swung within 17 feet of the centerline, overlapping the wingtip by 7 feet. "Avoiding such a collision called for precision on the part of the DLCO (Deck Landing Control Officer) and split second reaction by the pilot whose controls were already almost on the point of stall.

Stanley Brand continued, "Bringing in an aerocraft to land on a deck with the stern rising and falling through 30 feet (forget the added complications of rolling 20 degrees each side of vertical if you can!) was no mean task for even an experienced Batsman (DLCO). Timing was the be-all and end-all. The aircraft had to be sinking steadily on its approach to the stern to arrive there as the stern was sinking, but about 3 feet above its lowest point of movement. There was always a steady moment at the lowest point before the stern started to rise again and it was during this steady interval that the cut signal was given and the hook engaged to arrest the aeroplane, and because the bow was at its highest the uphill slope on the deck helped to bring the aeroplane to a halt and reduce the load on the arrester wire.

"It was not the best situation to 'go round again' because the aeroplane was at its lowest and any obstruction forward was at its highest, so the timing of the approach to land was further complicated by the need to include consideration of the roll. The arrival of the plane at touchdown was best timed to coincide with the middle of a roll from starboard to port so that the port side was going down, not up, so an escape route free from obstruction [except for the Batsman] was available to the pilot who could swing violently left over the side of the ship. Poor old Bats! Into the net again!"[3]

Fairey Swordfish being positioned on one of the grainer MACships, probably during training, as three Swordfish was the normal complement. Aircraft are in the Atlantic color scheme of off-white with camouflaged upper surfaces. At Taranto the aircraft wore overall two-tone camouflage with light under surfaces. (Canada Shearwater Museum)

Batsmen were assigned to the aviation staff of a ship as primary duty and were not permitted to fly, although they were pilots. A frequent source of batsmen is interesting given modern attitudes toward combat fatigue.

Brand continued, "Often the best DLCOs were pilots of long flying experience who developed a nervous disposition because of stress caused by over-exposure to dangerous activity without relief. Unlike the RAF, which gave 7 days leave every 8 weeks to operational aircrew with a second-line posting after 30 operational flights, the Fleet Air Arm had insufficient manpower, or willpower, to adopt a similar policy.

"Men of great experience, living on their nerves but with the courage to carry on in spite of their misgivings were ideal subjects to become DLCOs and an inappropriate comment sometimes made by the insensitive was 'He may be a new DLCO but it is obvious that he has been Bats for ages.' There is no doubt that heightened reaction to danger with abnormally rapid response time was an essential qualification to control an incoming aircraft."[4]

Despite short decks (without wind, a laden Swordfish needed rocket assist to get airborne) and small hulls, which resulted in sterns pitching more than 30 ft and rolls of 20 degrees, despite having only one engine (maintained while exposed to wave and weather) and sea conditions that would quickly kill a crew that ditched, despite no radio aids to navigation and a horrendously slow cruise speed (75 knots due to a fixed-pitch propeller) the Swordfish crews persevered. (With 50 knots of wind—not uncommon in the Atlantic—and the convoy making 5 knots, if a Swordfish was 40 miles downwind of the carrier, it took two hours to return to "Mother.") Despite freezing cold and open cockpits (crewmembers were literally hoisted out after winter missions and frostbite was a frequent problem), despite no relief from almost continuous operations, the Swordfish crews persevered.

In the nine months before MACShips and escort carriers were introduced, 362 merchant ships were sunk in the Atlantic. In convoys escorted by MACShips, from their first voyage to the end of the European War in May 1945, only two merchant ships were sunk, and those by acoustic homing torpedoes (the U-boat did not have to extend its periscope). The Battle of the Atlantic was not won by MACShips, but if they had been introduced earlier many ships would have been saved.

Operation Torch

Operation Torch, in November 1942, was the first combined Allied amphibious operation. There had been major carrier battles in the Pacific that year, but the Island Hopping campaign had not begun. Torch was also unique because the objectives of the invasion were not only 500 miles apart, but had a neutral nation in between

Seafire in a not uncommon position after a deck crash; the main landing gear has either been torn away or crumpled into the wing, the wooden propeller blades have shattered down to nubs, and the long tailhook is hanging down mid-fuselage. In this 1945 photograph the Seafire is wearing the Pacific insignia with no red center and white bars to make its nationality more obvious.

Seafires being pushed on the deck of an RN CV in port. The cross-deck cables have been unhooked; the fiddle bridges are still in place. A camouflaged CVE is moored nearby.

them. The British targets of Oran and Algiers were in Algeria on the Mediterranean while the American objective of Casablanca lay on the Atlantic coast of Morocco. Between them was Spanish Morocco, a protectorate of neutral Spain, which dominated the southern shore of the Straits of Gibraltar. (Franco managing to remain neutral after accepting Hitler's aid in putting him in power is one of the 20th Century's greatest feats of statesmanship.)

The opposition to the Allies was also unique. France had signed an armistice in June 1940 and the northern part of the country was occupied by German troops. A French government headquartered in the small city of Vichy and headed by World War I General Petain had the southern section. Vichy French army, navy and air force units were based in both Algeria and Morocco. The loyalty of these troops was to *La Belle France* and how strongly they would oppose invasion by England and the United States was in question until the time the Allied soldiers came ashore. Hatred of the British was strong because of the perceived perfidy of the Royal Navy's shelling French ships at Mers-el-Kébir and Oran. In Morocco, what to do against the Americans was more in doubt. As it turned out, the opposition in the north was negligible while American forces on the Atlantic had a real battle.

Although the complete story of Operation Torch involves cases of uncertain, divided, jingoistic, and variable loyalties, complex political maneuvering, and clandestine activities worthy of a Hollywood thriller, such a saga is outside the scope of this book. (Just one example: A high-ranking American general was dropped in North Africa by a British submarine masquerading as an American submarine.)

The Royal Navy had been fighting in the Mediterranean since the start of the war, and except for the two runs to Malta by USS *Wasp*, had relied on their own ships. For Torch they added escort carriers, CVE, for the first time. The task forces assembled in the UK and staged in Gibraltar before heading for the invasion beaches. HMS *Formidable* and HMS *Victorious* constituted Force H and were given the role of general air defense. HMS *Furious* with escort carriers, HMS *Biter*, and HMS *Dasher* composed the Center Task Force against Oran, and the old HMS *Argus* with an escort carriers and HMS *Avenger* struck Algiers to the east. Thus, the composition of the RN's seven-carrier force was two fleet carriers, *Formidable* and *Victorious*, the elderly and smaller *Furious* and *Argus*, and three of the recently introduced CVEs.

For the preceding month, the pilots of the Fleet Air Arm (FAA) had been flying convoy protection missions with occasional victories by Martlet, Sea Hurricane, and Fulmar fighters shooting down aircraft of the *Reggia Aeronautica* (Italian Air Force). Indicative of the political sensitivities, the British carrier aircraft were painted with American insignia. Once Torch itself began on 8 November, they shot down four Dewoitine D520s in a dogfight, and elsewhere another D520, a Martin 167, and a German Ju 88 while flying cover for the landings at Oran. Both Oran and Algiers surrendered by the second day. Once the airfields ashore were captured, land-based fighters assumed the protective role and the Royal Navy carriers left the area. Two days after that, escort carrier HMS *Avenger* was torpedoed by a U-boat with a massive loss of life. For 802 squadron (Sea Hurricanes), HMS *Avenger* was the third ship they were on when it was sunk! (HMS *Glorious* with Sea Gladiators when sunk by German battleships after the Narvik evacuation in June 1940, HMS *Audacity* with Martlets when torpedoed in December 1941)

Torch also marked the combat introduction of the Seafire, the naval version of the Spitfire. *Formidable*, *Furious*, and *Argus* had Seafire squadrons embarked. The Seafire had the highest crash-to-landing ratio of any carrier-based aircraft.

Adapted Airplanes

LSOs and Batsmen adjust to the characteristics of the aircraft they wave, and every airplane type had unique traits; some only quirky, others hazardous. Sometimes the solution was to move the wave-off window farther out. Other times it was to recognize early signs of trouble and not let the problem get worse. With aircraft like the Seafire, however, LSOs became frustrated because the faults were nothing they could prevent. What seemed a normal approach could turn into an accident because of weak landing gear. Once the cut signal has been given, the LSO no longer had control or even influence. A wag once declared, "Don't watch after the cut, you'll only have to write a witness statement for the investigation." (Not true, of course, as a major part of the LSO's job is training, and critiquing all of a pilot's actions is important to that training.)

The Seafire (officially the Sea Spitfire, as the navalized Hurricane became the Sea Hurricane) was a forced attempt to adapt a landplane to navy carrier operations. Adding a tailhook and reinforcing the aft fuselage resulted in the highest landing accident rate of any aircraft in history. "Approaches were difficult, visibility was limited at best, landing gear collapses were commonplace, and the arrester hooks had a tendency to miss and bounce back

The Fairey Barracuda is seconds from touching down on HMS* Furious*. Dunstan Hadley wrote, "The mighty Barracuda was like no other aeroplane ever built. Designed to take over from the Swordfish and Albacore it was the latest, most up-to-date, most powerful strike aircraft in the Royal Navy. The wings were thick and bristling with radar aerials, boundary layer fences, grab handles, flaps, the pitot head, and bomb racks. The undercarriage looked massive as indeed it needed to be for the crunching deck landings it sustained. It had the most powerful Rolls-Royce Merlin engine ever built, boosted to about twice its intended power by a giant supercharger. However, owing to some misguided influence on the part of the 'Lords who rule the water' it had been designed not so much as a torpedo bomber but as an observer's aeroplane. The wings had been set high on the fuselage and large bay windows made of perspex built into the sides of the observer to 'spot the fall of shot,' which at the Battle of Jutland years earlier would have made the day for Beatty and Jellicoe." (Royal Navy Photo) [7]

into the fuselage frames, which buckled the airframe. More were lost to breaking their landing gear in hard landings than to all enemy causes." The invasion of Sicily was two months after Operation Torch and the Seafire continued its abominable record; in the first two days less than 50 of the 106 initially deployed survived because of landing accidents. By the time the invasion was over only 23 were serviceable!

Previous adaptations had worked. The Royal Navy had taken the graceful Hawker biplanes and successfully used them on carriers. The two-place Hind became the Osprey while the fighter Fury was the Nimrod in naval service. Both remained in frontline service until 1938. The pugnacious Gloster Gladiator added a "Sea" prefix and flew for the Royal Navy until 1945.

The U.S. Navy adapted the Boeing P-12 of the USAAC and made it the F4B series for carrier use. The biplane was active until the late 1930s. Probably the most blatant attempt at adapting for carrier work was the curious XFL-1, Airabonita. Bell Aircraft took their P-39 Airacobra and rearranged the landing gear so it had a tailwheel (at the time, a nose wheel was thought unsuitable for carrier ops), put a tailhook on and, *voila*, a Navy fighter to compete for a contract. The Airabonita didn't make it. The F2A Buffalo and F4F Wildcat did. Ironically, the first traps for a tricycle (nose wheel) aircraft on a carrier were in a P-39 by the famous "Winkle" Brown of the Royal Navy in a navalized RAF Airacobra Mk I in April 1945.

However, the increased weight and speeds required for fighters to be competitive in combat meant problems landing on a ship. It may have been expedient to take aircraft designed to fly off runways to sea but after 1940 there were no successful examples. The Hurricane to Sea Hurricane is arguably the last adaptation that worked.

There have been examples of hookless airplanes making landings on carriers, the most significant being the RAF flying on board HMS *Glorious* and the Spitfire on USS *Wasp* mentioned earlier. The experiments with the huge C-130 Hercules and the overloaded Vietnamese L-19 will come up later. All these were deliberate. Martin "Red" Carmody (later a veteran of three wars and rear admiral) made his first carrier landing on USS *Saratoga* off California in a SBD Dauntless. In the tedium of holding overhead, he had tuned the Automatic Direction Finder (ADF) to Bob Hope's radio show. (ADF worked on the same frequencies as commercial radio stations.) A woman was singing "Sleepy Lagoon" when his flight was given the "Cast" signal to land. While flying formation and then the landing pattern, he was not able to turn the volume off. In the groove, the song was "Tangerine" and the LSO gave him signals for small corrections to speed, line-up, and glide path. Crossing the ramp, Red mistook the LSO's arm waving for a cut, so he flared the Dauntless onto the deck and because he did not feel a tug on his straps, braked to a stop. The next thing he knew, the LSO was on the wing with his face in Red's screaming at him for not only ignoring the wave-off but forgetting to lower his tailhook.

There has always been a dichotomy in the U.S. Navy between East Coast, Atlantic Fleet, and West Coast, Pacific Fleet. In late 1942, the aviators of AirLant knew of the Pacific carrier battles, especially the victory at Midway in June. From admiral to airman they were eager to get into action. The reality was that the invasion of Casablanca was a rush job. An aircraft carrier and air wing take months to train to combat proficiency. USS *Ranger* had been operational since 1934, but all three American escort carriers were new and had not had time to work-up. During the four-day assault, fully one-quarter of U.S. Navy aircraft were lost, most operationally, i.e., not combat related.

The four escort carriers were designated ACV, Auxiliary Aircraft Carrier, at the time. The CVE designation did not come into use until July 1943. They were commercial tankers that the U.S. Navy had taken over in 1940 and used as fleet oilers. In 1942 they were converted into small aircraft carriers (553 feet long with 55-foot-wide flight decks, 11,400 tons displacement) while keeping their fuel carrying capability. Indeed, they were used to replenish the other ships in the convoy on the Atlantic crossing. Immediately after Torch they were transferred to the Pacific, where their dual capabilities made them the most useful escort carriers in the fleet. However, once they were commissioned as carriers time was short before they were needed for the invasion of Africa.

A lack of airplanes, pilots, and crews is why USS *Chenango*, ACV-28, was assigned duty as an aircraft ferry. She took 78 P-40F Warhawks across the Atlantic, which flew ashore on the third day. Many were damaged landing at rough airfields and their effective use hindered by a lack of parts and fuel.

USS *Santee*, ACV-29, was commissioned ten weeks before Torch and only left the shipyard days before sailing. Her embarked squadrons, VGF-29 and VGS-29, had only five experienced aviators between them. During the invasion they lost 21 of 31 aircraft.

The problems the *Santee*'s airwing had the first day were particularly bad, but typical of operational losses due to hurried training and inexperience. After takeoff on the first flight of the first day Thomas Blackburn, of VGF-29, could not fully raise the landing gear of his F4F Wildcat, but in his eagerness for action and self-perceived sense of duty as CO of the squadron, continued on into combat. As a result of the increased drag he ran out of gas while trying to find *Santee* and had to ditch in the ocean. Because his location was unknown Blackburn spent three days in a life raft before a destroyer, luckily, found him; an inauspicious debut for the man who later commanded the famous "Jolly Roger" Corsair squadron, VF-17, and became an ace with 11 victories over Japanese airplanes.

Escort carrier USS* Santee *(ACV-29), probably in October 1942 before Operation Torch.* Santee *was the only one in her class ever camouflaged in Measure 17. After a distinguished combat career as CVE-29, she became an escort helicopter aircraft carrier (CVHE-29) until struck from the Naval Vessel Register in March 1959.

During the few days of training USS *Santee* did get off Bermuda, a depth charge came off a launching airplane and detonated next to the hull. The tough oiler hull was unhurt but the entire ship was shaken badly enough that the YE homing device was damaged. The damage was not discovered because the accident happened on the last day of flying. Not only was the ship not where she was supposed to be, but Blackburn and his flight could not use the homing beacon. They had also radioed the ship, asking for a steer for home, but were not picked up by the ship's radar. A LTjg in the flight had lost oil pressure earlier and headed back to the *Santee* but was never seen again. The four nuggets in the flight gave up trying to find the ship and headed for a rough airfield ashore. Three of the four were wrecked on landing with the pilots becoming POWs for the remaining three days.

Two TBF Avengers crashed during takeoff later in the day and an F4F returning from CAP made a landing so "hot" that the tail ripped off and it went on its nose. Three operational losses: the result of too little training? Nine airplanes gone of thirty-one meant *Santee* lost 30 percent of her assigned aircraft on the very first day.

Casablanca-class escort aircraft carriers are the most numerous class of aircraft carriers ever built. Fifty were laid down, launched, and commissioned between November 1942 and July 1944. These were nearly one-third of the 151 carriers built in the United States during the war. The first class to be designed from keel up as an escort carrier, the Casablanca class had a larger and more useful hangar deck than previous conversions. The arrestor wires cover more than half the flight deck with the final barrier not far behind the island.

Overall, U.S. Navy fliers did well, claiming 26 Vichy aircraft destroyed and 5 probables, besides providing the only air cover the troops ashore had. The dive and torpedo bombers, in concert with surface warships, sank 6 submarines, 6 destroyers, and the cruiser *Primaguet*. The battleship *Jean Bart* had escaped from France days before the armistice with Germany and was only 75 percent complete and thus immobile at a pier in Casablanca. However, her anti-aircraft armament and one turret of powerful 15-inch guns were usable. The turret was put out of action late the first day by shelling from an American battleship, but repaired by day three. Bombs from *Ranger*'s Dauntlesses not only wrecked the turret, but put *Jean Bart* into the mud of the harbor.

On the third day, 10 November, French submarines escaped from the harbor and a pair of German U-boats came in from the Atlantic. All of the torpedo attacks were thwarted, including one involving an LSO.

Lieutenant Ernie Wood of VF-41 was on his way back to *Ranger* in his F4F Wildcat when he saw a submarine surface 100 yards behind the carrier. He said, "It was like the appearance of the Great White Whale in Moby Dick. I was very excited, and as I reported again to call someone who had something that might be effective, I saw the torpedo heading through the wake of the carrier dead astern. The sub captain must have been desperate to get us, so he came in quite close, and fired. Quite honestly I was hypnotized seeing that torpedo following the ship, which did not seem to have a chance."

Ranger turned and the torpedo passed close alongside. The LSO was just getting ready to recover aircraft and reported, "It missed us not by yards, it seemed just inches," He later claimed to be the only LSO who ever waved off a torpedo.[5]

As it did for the U.S. Navy, Torch provided a training ground for Fleet Air Arm pilots who fought in the Pacific including future aces.

Dummy Decks and ADDL

"Aerodrome Dummy Deck Landings" is the FAA term for practice at an airfield. Dunstan Hadley was a Fleet Air Arm pilot who received most of his initial training from RAF instructors; not that unusual for the time. After joining the Royal Navy and basic recruit training, Hadley went to an RAF Flight Training Squadron, FTS, in England where he soloed a Tiger Moth. He next went by liner and railroad to Kingston, Ontario, in Canada to a flying base where RAF instructors taught Royal Navy students in Harvards. Hadley received his wings in 1943 and went back across the Atlantic, where his final training was an all-navy operation. Advanced training in Miles Masters followed with one flight "to build one's confidence" in a Hurricane. Although most of his classmates were to fly the elderly Swordfish, Hadley and a few others became Fairey Barracuda pilots. During the three-month course he learned dive bombing, gunfire spotting, and the Barracuda's specialty, torpedo dropping. "We had notched up about 50 hours in the Barracuda and made 80 or 90 practice torpedo attacks. There was just one small detail of our training to complete: deck landing."[6]

The first step in preparing for landing on a ship was Aerodrome Dummy Deck Landings, usually just called ADDLs. A carrier deck was outlined on the runway with paint and the Batsman stood at the edge of the runway in the same relative position as he would be at sea. The Batsman's briefing to the new pilots, "The carrier circuit is at 300 feet. Get your wheels, flaps, and hook down and the hood open and bung the prop into fine pitch, then come round in a steady curve with plenty of power, hanging on the prop. Watch the Batsman and do exactly what he tells you. You will get fairly gentle corrections to your attitude to begin with to get you on the right line but as you get closer to the ship you must act more quickly as there is less time for the aircraft to respond. The Batsman will bring you gently down to finish your turn just before you reach the round-down; that's the end of the flight deck. When you get the cut, chop the throttle shut and the aircraft will sink on to the deck. If you get a wave-off open the throttle wide, only pull the wheels up as soon as it's safe to do so and fly off. Don't pull the flaps up until you get a bit of height and speed. For practice on the aerodrome you don't put the hook down, of course; just touch down and go round again."[8]

Although this is a good look at the flight deck of a CVE (USS Palau*) it is not what the pilot of a landing airplane saw; too high,the LSO is standing on the centerline with other people on the deck. The photo was taken from a blimp (two of the handling lines are seen from top to bottom in the photo). U.S. Navy blimps landed on carriers to refuel, resupply, and rearm.*

"Six tons and it lands like a suet pudding being dropped," Hadley said of the Barracuda, and added, "(We did) hundreds of ADDLs until we got it right.

"Sometimes the great 'Wings' (Commander Flying) himself came out to bat us. CDR R. N. Everett, RN, radiated fierceness and batted with fanatical zeal. I am sure he could have batted a Lancaster bomber in to a landing on a matchbox. He could hypnotize us from half a mile away. He had his own special groove in the sky, and you were in it, or else! He became so enthusiastic as the aircraft roared toward him that he danced out on to the runway, willing the aircraft to the very spot he had chosen, and he had to duck under the wing as the aircraft hit the ground. He surely got us down all right, but it was more shattering than the usual ADDL as he always disappeared under the nose much sooner than the other Batsmen, which meant that our period of guesswork was longer. He was the Navy's top Batsman and he knew it. I think even the birds obeyed him."[9]

For practice at night, dimlights marked the edge of the landing area and the Batsman held two lamps in his hands and had another strapped to his chest, all connected to a car battery on the ground, which prevented him from getting out of the way of an errant airplane.

Hadley and his classmates went onboard HMS *Ravager* in the Firth of Clyde on a wintery December day in 1943. *Ravager* was an American-built escort carrier 98 feet wide and 490 ft long, although only half of that was available for landing. Using the two *Barracudas* already onboard, two pilots at a time made four landings until each had eight deck landings and was considered as qualified. As on all carriers during landings, spectators crowded available viewing spots; the Royal Navy term for them was "Goofers." Flight decks are one of the most hazardous places imaginable. Talking about a late wave-off signal, Hadley wrote, "If it was too late the aeroplane came down anyway. The flight-party, crouched down in the walkways, behind gun emplacements or anything else handy, waiting for the crunch, then rushed out to gather up the wreckage and console the pilot."[10]

A DLCO giving a late-model Swordfish (radome on belly) the signal to fly lower. The wind barrier is down, possibly because a low sun angle placed the Batsman in shade where he'd be difficult to see. (J. Thomas)

Escort Carriers

They came with many names: Baby Flattops, Kaiser carriers, Jeep carriers, Woolworth carriers, Escort carriers, AVG, ACV, CVE. The Royal Navy named individual ships first with aggressive nouns (e.g., *Avenger*, *Battler*, *Attacker*), later with titles of rank (e.g., *Nabob*, *Emperor*, *Shah*). The United States Navy christened them with the names of bodies of water (e.g., *Long Island*, *Breton* (both sounds), *Gambier Bay*) or recent battles (e.g., *Casablanca*, *Tulagi*, *Guadalcanal*). During World War II, 122 were built and 8 were sunk. They defeated German U-boats, protected the vital supply convoys, and won the Battle of the Atlantic. In the Pacific, they escorted convoys, hunted submarines, and provided air support for island invasions and, in one remarkable combat, fought off Japanese battleships. More pilots and planes of the U.S. Navy flew off escort carriers than all the better known fleet carriers.

HMS *Avenger* (BAVG-2) was the first escort carrier to be sunk. Soon after Operation Torch, she was sailing alone toward Gibraltar when the U-155 torpedoed her. Avenger sank fast and only 12 of her 516 crewmembers were rescued. HMS *Dasher* (BAVG-5) exploded violently in the Firth of Forth after turning back from the start of a convoy in March 1943. Although a buildup of gasoline fumes was suspected, the exact cause was not determined and the British government attempted to cover up the disaster for morale purposes. On the other side of the world, USS *Liscome Bay* (CVE-56) was operating in support of the Tarawa invasion in October 1943 when a torpedo from a Japanese submarine hit the aft engine room and bomb storage area, resulting in major explosion. "She just went whooom; an orange ball of flame," reported an officer on a nearby destroyer. Less than one-third of *Liscome Bay*'s crew survived. Sailors began saying that CVE did not mean "Carrier Escort," but "Combustible Vulnerable Expendable."

USS *Gambier Bay* (CVE-73) of the Casablanca class was called the "Bonus Ship" because the Kaiser Shipyard in Vancouver, Washington, had a contract for 16 escort carriers in one month to which the Navy added two more. Not only were those 18 escort carriers completed, but *Gambier Bay* was added as the 19th! Designed for and manufactured in large-scale assembly lines, Jeep carriers were

Showing wear from service on North Atlantic convoys, this MACShip has her Swordfish parked aft with removable palisades to reduce the effects of wind. (Canada Shearwater Museum)

produced in numbers that gave the Allies a significant advantage in war at sea. Between the United Kingdom and United States there were 130 CVEs used in World War II. Having the ships was remarkable by itself; having them combat capable was even more of an achievement: 130 escort carriers meant 130 air groups of 20 to 30 airplanes, hundreds of pilots and aircrew to fly those airplanes, and 130 plus LSOs/Batsmen to bring them aboard. Training systems in both countries expanded rapidly and effectively, but training is not experience, and in naval aviation no position requires experience more than that of Batsman. The high level of non-combat losses during Operation Torch was largely a result of the rush to qualify.

LSO Dunstan Hadley

Dunstan Hadley's training is typical of how it was done in the Royal Navy. (USN pilot and LSO training are covered in Chapter Five.) After his first carrier landings, Hadley reported to 822 Squadron. After a few months training in Scotland, 822 had a last minute change of orders and was sent to Ceylon. The three squadrons of Barracudas and other aircraft were ferried to India on a carrier. The officers and men had a long and hot trip on various steamers via Suez. After more months of training and anti-submarine patrols the plan was for the squadron to embark in the fleet carrier HMS *Victorious*. The escort carrier HMS *Thane* was made available so the pilots could get refresher landings. At this time, Hadley had only his eight traps and they were half a year before. He expressed concern that *Thane*'s Batsman might not be in the same class as the one who had waved him on *Ravager*. He also wondered if he had forgotten how to deck land. His observer's reply was apt, "I don't think you did. It's like riding a bike. Until you can do it, it's impossible, but once you've done it you cannot ever imagine that you couldn't."[11]

HMS *Victorious* launched a major strike against Sumatra in October 1944. On return to Ceylon, 822 flew their Barras ashore and to an unhappy fate. Despite the efforts expended the Barracuda proved unsuitable for operation in the tropics and the personnel of 822 squadron returned to England. At home, Hadley received orders to DLCO training. His reply to the Admiralty could have been written by many others in a similar situation. "It is well known that

DLCOs are very carefully chosen from very experienced pilots who volunteered for the job when Admiralty Fleet Orders announce that volunteers may apply. I am a very junior pilot and I have not volunteered and I am not a lieutenant. Someone has blundered."[12]

After being chastised for his objection to his assignment by having leave and wine mess privileges denied for the duration of the three-week course, Hadley joined five other volunteers in a classroom. They were issued a fiberboard case containing "the latest gent's natty batting outfit" and a pair of bats, wooden handles with a circular metal frame with bright colored cloth stretched across. Their instructor explained, "This is day-glo cloth. It is fluorescent and you can see it for miles. The bats come supplied with handles 16 inches long for some obscure dockyard reason so we cut them down to about 6 inches as soon as we got them." He then went on to explain and demonstrate the signals while keeping up a patter, "Put your wheels down, you prune, hook; you clot; you've forgotten your flaps, idiot; you've made a complete balls-up of it, go around again."

For practical work the air station had pilots assigned known as "clockwork mice." Their job was to fly pass after pass to train Batsmen. Clockwork mice also had to certify new aircraft carriers by trapping each type of aircraft on each wire on each ship. This is the reason many pilots of the FAA (including Eric Brown with the highest number ever) had more than 1,000 carrier landings.

Hadley and his classmates stood on the end of the runway for ADDLs. Three airplanes at a time flew the pattern with one coming in every minute to give the trainees plenty of practice. They batted Swordfish, Barracudas, Martlets (Wildcats), and Avengers. At times, Cdr Everett came to watch, and when he could stand it no longer took the bats himself. "You must take charge," said Wings, "Make them do what you want them to do. Look, I'll show you." He whirled into action. His signals were firm and filled with fire. The pilots immediately noticed, even a half-mile away, that a human dynamo was now in command, and all their approaches became impeccable. As they neared the runway threshold the maestro went into a frenzy of activity, edging further and further onto the runway himself until, as he gave the cut signal, he had to duck low as the wing flashed over his head and the wheels hit the runway not 10 feet from him. "There, that's how to do it. That's better, you see, you're in control now. That's what you have to do."[13]

Besides batting practice, they were taught the other facets of a DLCO's job: launching aircraft, arranging them on deck, and moving them to the hangar deck. With teams of trainee handlers, they practiced moving airplanes about on the painted outline of a carrier. Fire-fighting training included a walk through flames wearing the full asbestos suit. Late in the course they got practical experience batting the pupil pilots also based at the air station. Finally it was time to go to sea for the real thing.

The ship was HMS *Trouncer*, one of the escort carriers built in the United States for Britain. After watching a classmate wave a dozen landings, Hadley went on deck and had his turn. The wind barrier was left down so that the instructor could stand behind him, but this also meant the full force of the 30-knot wind could be felt. "As soon as I held the bats there on the flight deck I knew what it was all about. Those bats were the size of dinner plates and as the wind caught them I was almost blown off the platform until I steadied myself and leaned back into the wind." The three Swordfish had their hooks up, and after hitting the deck powered up and went around again.

After about ten landings Hadley passed the bats to the next man. After each student DLCO had a go, tailhooks came down, the airplanes were trapped, the wires cleared, and the airplanes taxied forward with the barrier raised behind them. The pilots and batsmen then had a civilized lunch in the wardroom. The afternoon was a repeat of the morning. The pattern was repeated the next day using Wildcats. "They were much friskier than the Swordfish but good deck landers." The third day was Avengers and the fourth day the more challenging Barracudas. By the end of the week, Hadley had batted almost 100 landings plus launches and ranging aircraft. "That was that. We were now qualified DLCOs. A sticker was put in our flying logbooks to prove it to anyone who might doubt it."

Italy, Norway, France

After Operation Torch there were only five more operations involving carriers in the European Theater. Air cover from North Africa covered the Allied invasion of Sicily in July 1943. Two Royal Navy fleet carriers, HMS *Formidable* and HMS *Indomitable*, formed Force H and stayed in the area for the purpose of preventing the Italian surface fleet from interfering with the landings.

For the landings at Salerno on the Italian mainland that September, HMS *Formidable* and Royal Navy CVEs were brought from the Atlantic for direct support of the invasion. The early Mark Seafires again proved to be poor airplanes for carrier work; 10 were lost and 32 were damaged beyond repair. As soon as a suitable airfield ashore was captured they were flown off and the CVEs went back to Atlantic convoy duty.

The invasion of Anzio, January 1944, did not see carriers in action, nor did the massive amphibious operation that was the invasion of Normandy in June. Fascist Italy surrendered in September with its naval and air forces switching sides. Allied control of the Mediterranean was complete.

Far to the north USS *Ranger* was assigned to the British Home Fleet to cover a gap when the Royal Navy carriers were unavailable. The German battleship *Tirpitz* was anchored in Norway and constituted a "fleet in being" that threatened northern convoys. In August 1943, *Ranger* launched Air Group 4 on a sizable raid against coastal shipping and the Norwegian port of Bodö. All hands aboard were now Bluenoses, having sailed north of the Arctic Circle.[14] Although

Composite Squadron FM-2 Wildcats (F4Fs built by General Motors) on a CVE in the Atlantic. The one has been waved off, probably for having too close an interval. Wildcats and Avengers in the Atlantic were painted in light colors to make them harder to spot against the sky by U-boats, their main prey and opponents. Navy aircraft in the Pacific were camouflaged dark blue beause their main threat was from above and they wanted to blend in with the sea.

60 percent of the pilots were new, operational losses were few. Anti-Aircraft fire, or "Triple A," was responsible for shooting down or shooting up some aircraft. The two Luftwaffe snoopers who came near were shot down by F6F Hellcats. One pilot, Dean "Diz" Laird, who shared in both kills later became the only U.S. Navy ace with German as well as Japanese markings on his aircraft. Soon after the raid *Ranger* returned to the United States.

Attempts to sink the *Tirpitz* began in October 1942 with high-altitude bombing, which was ineffective. The first disabling damage was from miniature submarines half a year later. Forty Barracudas flying from HMS *Furious* and HMS *Victorious* damaged the battleship in April 1944. In August, the Royal Navy made repeated attempts using aircraft from five carriers (two of them escort carriers). The attacks failed due to inaccurate bombing, smoke, or fog obscuration and heavy AAA fire. Weather caused cancellations of planned attacks and hindered ones that did launch. The *Tirpitz* was a failure for the Fleet Air Arm and an example of a major surface ship surviving air attack. One has to wonder what would have come of the "Battleship Admiral's" argument against carriers if such an event had happened before Taranto or Pearl Harbor.

The fifth use of carriers was Operation Dragoon, the invasion of Southern France in August 1944. A major, well-executed amphibious operation, its significance is overshadowed by the Normandy landings two months before. Seven escort carriers participated, including two of the U.S. Navy, which were the first American carriers in the Mediterranean since USS *Wasp* 2½ years before. Embarked F6F Hellcats of the unique VOF-1 (Observation/Fighter Squadron) and VF-74 flew ground support missions as well as shooting down eight Luftwaffe aircraft, thus adding pilots to those from the Norwegian attack to the very small club of U.S. Navy pilots who could paint a miniature swastika on their fuselage. One F6F was credited with a double in the separate fights and sported four Nazi flags below the cockpit. The Seafires from the British carriers again had a disappointing number of non-combat losses.

Air, Surface and Undersea War

To the German U-boat crews, the first months of World War II were "The Happy Time" (*Die Glückliche Zeit*). The Kriegsmarine submarines cut a wide swath through merchant ships around the British Isles until the Royal Navy belatedly reinstituted the convoy system that had proven successful in the First World War. A second "Happy Time" came when they were turned loose on the United States soon after Pearl Harbor. The number of merchant sinkings was dramatic until Americans realized the threat, blacked out cities on the East and Gulf Coasts, and began convoys of their own. England would have lost the war without a steady supply of material from Canada and the United States. Winston Churchill wrote, "Battle of the Atlantic was the dominating factor all the war. Never for one moment could we forget that everything happening elsewhere on land, at sea, or in the air depended ultimately on its outcome." Called the longest continuous campaign of World War II, during the five years of the Battle of the Atlantic, the advantage shifted from one side to another. The final victory is aptly described as the convergence of technologies: radar, ASDIC/Sonar, forward firing depth charges, code breaking, operational analysis, long-range aircraft, and filling in the last gap, escort carriers.

There were too few escort ships to stay with the Atlantic convoys for long at the start. As more became available, especially from Canada, the range of coverage extended. Long-range patrol bombers extended coverage still farther, but a gap in the middle of the Atlantic remained a fertile hunting ground for U-boat wolf packs. As they became available, the first true escort carriers, the MACShips, stayed in company with the convoys. Losses to U-boats fell. At the Allied Atlantic Convoy Conference in early 1943, the Allies decided to shift from a defensive role to one of offense with the formation of specialized groups of ships centered on a CVE with the sole mission of finding and killing submarines. To the British these were "Support Groups." The American navy called them "Hunter-Killer (HUK) Teams." Freed from staying with a particular convoy, the HUK teams could chase a U-boat for days until the sub was forced to surface to its destruction. Between May 1943 and VE Day, the teams sank 53 subs and even captured one.

Flying from CVEs had a certain regularity. Unlike in the Pacific, where island invasions or raids came at irregular times with several hectic days followed by sometimes fairly lengthy periods with no flight operations, search patrols went out daily, all day. When a submarine was encountered either the action was quick or turned into a long "hold-down" chase. Most flights were hours of boredom with the landing at the end the most exciting event.

Escort carriers were about 500 feet long. Modern navy pilots marvel at landing on such a small ship, but the aviators of the day knew nothing else. Their first landings were on a CVE (or starting in 1943, one of the Great Lakes carriers), as were workups once in the Composite Squadrons, VC, which equipped the Atlantic escort carriers. The actual landing area for an escort carrier was the same as for the large carriers (the Essex class were 870 feet long), or CVLs. The extra deck area on the larger ships allowed for more aircraft and easier re-spotting but the arresting gear was the same. Lack of speed was a disadvantage of the smaller CVEs; if there was no surface wind, they could manage only 18 knots of WOD (wind over deck; higher is better) Another disadvantage was their sea-keeping qualities, or the lack thereof. The smaller the ship the more it is affected by wave action. The escort carrier LSO or Batsman, therefore, had all the challenges of waving malfunctioning or damaged airplanes flown by fatigued pilots plus much more frequent pitching and rolling flight decks. They had to be good. Yet, with the many CVEs being built, it was difficult to find enough experienced LSOs to man the platforms. Training LSOs became a high priority. The duty was not always desired, but it was important.

Chapter 5

CARRIERS SUPREME, THE PACIFIC

1942–1945

Rapid recovery in progress: The first Hellcat has wings folded and is following the director on the left. A chock man has his hand on the wing and walks along with the airplane, ready to throw the chocks in his right hand under the wheel in the event of a brake failure. The second F6F has cleared the barriers and the third is seconds from landing.

Japan operated 15 major aircraft carriers and 5 smaller ones between 1941 and 1945. Only the antique *Hosho* survived. Great Britain operated 13 fleet aircraft carriers and 53 escort carriers (most of which were built in the United States); 5 fleet carriers and 1 CVE were sunk. By the end of World War II the American navy had 108 aircraft carriers in operation: 30 fleet carriers, 5 of which were sunk, along with 5 smaller CVEs sunk during the war. Carriers fought carriers in five battles: Coral Sea, Midway, Eastern Solomons, Santa Cruz, and Philippine Sea.

Carriers in the Pacific

The devastating attack on Pearl Harbor was the culmination of aircraft carrier development: multiple carriers acting together to launch integrated formations of aircraft against an enemy fleet. The attack's planning and execution were superlative. The world will not see the like again. Naval tacticians and strategists will find errors and play what-if for years to come, but the attack worked. The United States Navy did not make carriers a principal weapon because of a change of thinking but because with the battleship force gutted in the bloody water of Pearl Harbor, it had to. That the American carriers were at sea was fortunate in that they avoided destruction, but sad in that they might have been an effective defense. Finally at war, the two nations used their aircraft carriers in ways unimagined by the creators of *Furious, Hosho*, and *Langley*.

Doolittle Raid 18 April 1942

The modern term is "power projection ashore." The Japanese demonstrated their mastery at Pearl Harbor. A small group of Army Air Force fliers off a U.S. Navy ship showed, albeit on a smaller scale, that the United States also understood the advantage of ships traveling undetected in the vast ocean, moving hundreds of miles a day, to launch points within the range of bombers and fighters hundreds of miles from their targets.

LSO Hank Miller

Although his work with the air force pilots had nothing to do with landing aboard a ship, his experience in flight operations made him perfect for teaching the bomber pilots how to get off the aircraft carrier. The initial plan came from a U.S. Navy Captain who had

March 1942, aircraft carrier* Akagi *with her distinctive portside island shortly after leaving Port Stirling, Celebes Island, for the Indian Ocean. The carriers and battleships are, from left to right:* Soryu, Hiryu, Hiei, Kirishima, Haruna, Kongō, Zuikaku, *and* Shōkaku. *Rolled futon mattresses have been lashed to the island to provide extra protection from bomb splinters.* (Naval Warship Photo Album: Aircraft Carrier and Seaplane Carriers*)

Crewmembers gather on the flight deck of Akagi *at Hitokappu Bay, Kuriles, Japan, in November 1941 prior to the attack on Pearl Harbor. The other carriers in the background are, from left to right:* Kaga, Shōkaku, Zuikaku, Hiryū, *and* Sōryū.

Flight crews briefing the attack on Pearl Harbor using a chalk diagram drawn on the carrier's flight deck.

LSO Miller with flag launching Doolittle's B-25 on 18 April 1942. Kneeling crewman to his right has the information board with the Hornet's *heading and course to target. The bomber's nose wheel is exactly on the stripe painted as a guide line. Unlike during normal flight operations, the catwalk is crowded with spectators.*

seen Army twin-engine bombers taking off from NAS Norfolk over the painted carrier deck used for FCLP. Two B-25 Mitchell bombers were secretly hoisted aboard USS *Hornet* in Norfolk, VA, in February 1942 and flew off the deck when far at sea.

Miller was an instructor at NAS Pensacola when he was drafted to train Dolittle's team. Miller went with the selected army air force crews to Eglin Auxiliary Field 1# in Florida. He had stripes painted on the runway the dimensions of a carrier deck with flags marking the distances. Miller coached the pilots in making carrier-type, minimum distance takeoffs. He accompanied them on *Hornet* all the way to their launch point. During the war he commanded the air groups on *Princeton* and *Hancock*, and during the Korean War was CO of *Leyte*. He retired as a RADM.

Battle of the Coral Sea 4–8 May 1942

Coral Sea was the first sea battle in which the opposing ships never saw each other. During two days of airstrikes, *Yorktown* was damaged and *Lexington* (CV-2) hit hard enough that she had to be scuttled. *Enterprise* (CV-6) and *Hornet* (CV-8) were in Pearl Harbor, having returned from Doolittle Raid. They sortied but could not reach the area in time. Japan lost the light carrier *Shoho*, but, significantly, sister ships *Zuikaku* and *Shōkaku* were damaged enough that they were not at Midway.

The day *Shoho* was sunk, *Zuikaku* and *Shōkaku* put together a 27-plane attack seeking revenge. The two American carriers detected the raid on radar and launched fighters. The running aerial battle dragged on for an hour.

LSO Norwood "Soupy" Campbell

"The weather was lousy," said *Yorktown*'s LSO. "A ceiling of about 300 feet variable, and black as the inside of a goat." Aircraft were coming in out of sequence. Campbell had a line of three coming straight in and he began waving the first. The airplane did not respond to his signals. No wonder, the airplane was a Japanese Val, and sensing something very wrong the pilot put the power on and climbed away. The on-deck speakers blared, "The planes on the starboard side are not friendly!" As Campbell recalled, "Every AA gun in the task force cut loose, shooting at anything or nothing. The sky was full of tracers." There was a Wildcat in the groove, and a 50-caliber gun near the stern opened fire on it. Campbell sprinted 30 feet to the offending gun, knocked the barrel off target, and yelled, "What in the hell are you doing? Can't you see that's one of our planes?" The sheepish reply was, "They all opened up, and so we did, too."[1]

After all of *Yorktown*'s fighters were safely on deck, Soupy Campbell realized he had incongruously almost brought aboard an enemy aircraft and had prevented a trigger-happy gunner from shooting down a friendly one.

Battle of Midway 4–6 June 1942

In one devastating morning, airplanes from *Hornet*, *Enterprise*, and *Yorktown* sank *Akagi*, *Kaga*, and *Soryu*. *Hiryu*'s aircraft struck *Yorktown* with three bombs. The crew had *Yorktown* repaired and back in action within the hour but a second group from *Hiryu* put two torpedoes in her. *Yorktown* lost power and began to list heavily. The emergency repairs had been so thorough that the Japanese pilots reported that they had destroyed another carrier. What was left of Japanese aircraft were now aboard *Hiryu*. Late in the day 24 SBD dive bombers from *Enterprise* made her into a blazing wreck. *Hiryu* survived the night but sank in the morning.

The peak of Japanese naval airpower was during the first attack on Midway Island, and the pilots of the Rising Sun were as good as they got until their ships were sunk from under them or were not there when they returned. However, the IJN remained a formidable force, as shown by a full deck load of A6M Zekes ready to fly off to the Battle of Santa Cruz.

LSO Robin Lindsey had gotten into the paddle-waving business almost accidentally. When VF-6 transitioned to Wildcats in May of 1941, Lindsay volunteered to "work out the boys" in FCLP. He had watched the Big E LSOs often enough to know the ropes. When the squadron was scheduled for CarQuals in F4Fs, *Lexington* was the available ship. But *Lex*'s LSO admitted he'd never seen a Wildcat and was reluctant to bring them aboard. So Lindsay was asked to fill in. "I said that if the boys gave me a vote of confidence I'd try anything," Lindsay recalls. Everyone got aboard, with no wave-offs. Lindsay still does not know what happened, but when he returned to Pearl Harbor and *Enterprise*, he found orders transferring him to ship's company as assistant LSO. When the senior LSO, Bert Hardin, became air officer, Lindsay took over the job.[2]

Late on the second day, 5 June, a search and destroy mission, which did not locate what was left of the Japanese fleet, was launched from the two CVs. To aid the planes returning in the dark, *Enterprise* and *Hornet* turned their lights on. Almost none of the returning pilots had made a night carrier landing. Significantly, the recovery was also Lindsey's first time waving at night. At first, the pattern went well, but soon, in the darkness and confusion, airplane after airplane appeared and were waved aboard. Lindsey turned to his assistant and asked, "For God's sake. How many more?"

"Dunno. Already have five more than were launched."

An excited Lindsey said, "Call the bridge; have 'em inspect all planes for meatballs."

A check of hangar and flight deck showed no Japanese airplanes and Lindsey completed the recovery without losing a plane. Later he laughed at his notion that the extra airplanes from *Hornet* may have been enemy. His debut at night earned him a commendation letter.[3]

The Battle of the Coral Sea the month before has been called a narrow victory for the Japanese navy. However, what happened

IJN Akagi was originally built with three flight decks but, like* Kaga*, was converted to a more conventional single, long, flight deck. Her sloped bow to assist with takeoffs is apparent. Because of her port side island, photographs of* Akagi *are sometimes reversed. In this case, a look at the wake and direction the airplanes are pointed gets it correct.

there had direct effect on the action at Midway. *Lexington* was sunk but much of her air group made it aboard *Yorktown*. *Yorktown* was damaged and went to Pearl Harbor, where after hurried and incomplete repairs (navy workers were still on board) she went to sea with an air group put together like a sandlot baseball team. Dauntless squadrons from *Saratoga*, on the West Coast having torpedo damage repaired, and a fighter squadron from *Lexington* brought her air group up to full strength. American squadrons could be easily reassigned as needed.

Shōkaku had been severely damaged and was in Japan for repairs. *Zuikaku* had less damage but had lost many airmen at Coral Sea. Because IJN policy was that aircrew must train with a ship, she was not considered battle worthy until replacements had arrived and been trained. Consequently, Japan's two best carriers were not at Midway.

At Midway, the United States Navy lost 1 aircraft carrier, 1 destroyer, and roughly 150 aircraft. Japan lost 4 aircraft carriers, 2 cruisers, and 250 aircraft.

In the aftermath, the Japanese revised procedures, especially in damage control, and modified their carriers. Significantly, recognizing the need for more aircrew, their training program was changed, but at the cost of shortening and rushing that training. The quality of the Japanese airmen steadily declined while the Americans steadily improved. Nor did the Japanese take their pilots out of combat either to become instructors or go on leave. The airmen's quip about rotation was, "*shinanakute wa kaeshite moraenai.*" (They won't let you go home unless you die.)[4]

Battle of Eastern Solomons 24–25 August 1942

The USMC landed on Guadalcanal in the Solomon Islands in August. Three American carriers—*Saratoga*, *Enterprise*, and *Wasp*—covered the landings and brought airplanes to Henderson airfield there. In response to the invasion, *Shōkaku*, *Zuikaku*, and *Ryujo* sortied from the major Japanese base on Truk. As the fleets converged and searched for each other, *Wasp* was detached to refuel and *Ryujo* sent to attack Guadalcanal. *Saratoga* sent 38 aircraft against *Ryujo*. At the same time, the American fleet was detected and *Zuikaku* and *Shōkaku* launched a strike of Vals and Zeroes against *Saratoga* and *Enterprise*. One hour later a second wave took off from the two carriers. The incoming formations were detected on radar and, in addition to airborne fighters, the American carriers cleared their decks by launching all flyable aircraft with instructions to go to Henderson or stay clear of the battle area until it was safe to return. *Saratoga*'s air group hit *Ryujo* with bombs and torpedoes, leaving her to be abandoned and sinking.

Enterprise was the first ship sighted and withstood most of the attacking force. By skillful maneuvering and heavy defensive anti-aircraft fire, she avoided many of the bombs but did take three bomb hits within a couple of minutes. Damage control teams rapidly readied *Enterprise* to land aircraft. American aircraft landed where they could, at Henderson or on the ships in the gathering dusk. *Enterprise* went to Pearl Harbor for repairs and on to the Battle of Santa Cruz. The United States lost 7 pilots, the Japanese more than 60 veteran aviators. The battle was considered to be a tactical and strategic victory for the U.S. because the Japanese troop reinforcements for Guadalcanal were turned back and because of that country's loss of ships, aircraft, and aircrew.

One week after the battle, *Saratoga* was torpedoed by a submarine, had to retreat for repairs, and so was not available at Santa Cruz. Two weeks after that, *Wasp* was also torpedoed, and sank, leaving *Hornet* and *Enterprise* the only American aircraft carriers in the Southwest Pacific.

Battle of Santa Cruz 25–27 October 1942

In the waters off the Santa Cruz Islands it was the heavyweights IJN *Shōkaku* and IJN *Zuikaku*, backed up by IJN *Zuiho* and IJN *Junyo* versus USS *Hornet* and USS *Enterprise*. It was not so much a match as a barroom brawl. The action was confused with both sides hitting the other hard. The battle was a tie in one sense, but it marked the end of Japanese domination in the South Pacific and, more importantly, the Japanese lost more aircrewmen than in the three preceding battles combined. More than one-half the elite aviators from Pearl Harbor were dead.

LSO Robin Lindsey

Enterprise's LSO Robin Lindsey, who had waved the night recovery after Midway, was on the platform on 26 October. *Enterprise* had been launching strikes and patrols all day. Some of the fighter pilots flew three missions. She had taken five bomb hits during three major

The peak of Japanese naval airpower was during the first attack on Midway Island, and the pilots of the Rising Sun gave as good as they got until their ships were sunk from under them or were not there when they returned. However, the IJN remained a formidable force, as shown by a full deck load of A6M Zekes ready to fly off to the Battle of Santa Cruz.

Eugene "Robin" Lindsey, LSO on Enterprise, giving a fast signal. After waving airplanes onboard Enterprise to a full flight deck, Robin Lindsey went from being a good LSO to a legendary one. He was always working to improve techniques and equipment for landing airplanes. The handle on the left-hand paddle is longer for better control in the wind while the right handle is shorter to give a rapid cut signal.

cuts to trap on the early wires. The hangar became crammed to capacity and airplanes were being parked on the arresting wires. Lindsey coached some onto the 3# wire. Then 2#. With 10 still to go, only the 1# wire was available. The phone talker relayed the order from the bridge to cease landings. Lindsey told him to pull the plug. "I don't want to hear anything from anybody." The *Enterprise* stayed into the wind.

The last Wildcat was flown by "Swede" Vejtasa, a former enlisted pilot who had shot down seven planes that day. He had let his less experienced wingmen land before him and was about to run out of gas. He and Lindsey had confidence in each other's abilities. The confidence was justified. Lindsey gave the slashing cut signal. Vejtasa flew perfectly and the Wildcat caught the first wire and stopped 20 feet from the parked airplanes. The crew burst into applause and shouts as Swede stepped from his cockpit and shook Robin's hand.[5]

Japanese attacks. The forward elevator was jammed in the up position. The flight deck was dented and had holes. As the second wave of Japanese torpedo and dive bombers came in he waved off the airplanes in the pattern and climbed into the back seat of a Dauntless parked on deck and started shooting with the twin 30-caliber guns. His assistant LSO, Jim Daniels, did the same. A Kate torpedo plane came in low across the stern. Both LSOs had a clear shot. The Japanese aircraft flamed, rolled over, and hit the sea. Back on the platform they argued over who should get credit.

Recovering their own airplanes was difficult enough, but several hours later, *Hornet* was bombed, began to list, and was put in tow behind a cruiser. Now Lindsey had to bring in airplanes from the *Hornet* as well as *Enterprise*. The forward flight deck with its inoperative elevator was soon covered and the handlers were lowering aircraft to the hangar deck using the 2# elevator amidships. The gaping hole past the only barrier may have rattled the returning pilots, but under Lindsey's firm guidance they were bringing them in and getting

U.S. Navy Pilot Training

With so many aircraft carriers coming off the ways the demand for pilots rose dramatically. During the build-up to war the luxury of having student pilots fly all types of naval aircraft went away. No longer was there time to fly not only fighters but floatplanes, flying boats, and multi-engine transports. The concept that a naval aviator could fly anything with wings lasted for many more years, but wartime training began to specialize. After primary training, students who became carrier pilots flew appropriate airplanes for the torpedo, bombing, or fighter role. Previous first-line types became advanced trainers. Torpedo droppers used Vought SB2Us. Early biplane dive bomber SBCs were used in training until the stalwart SBD Dauntlesses became available as fleet squadrons got SB2C Helldivers. Fighter training also started in biplanes, F3Fs, and F4Bs, and as F6F Hellcats took over, the now famous F4F Wildcat went to the Advanced Training Command. The entire U.S. Navy training command grew rapidly with new bases springing up all over the country.

Qualifying on the carrier, CQ, was sketchy at first. Some pilots did not get their first trap until in their assigned fleet squadron.

Green-shirted mechanics on the deck of a carrier working on a well-worn SBD Dauntless painted with large numbers and letters on the wings and fuselage sides. Oversize identification markings were placed on training aircraft to help identify overly exuberant student pilots indulging in flat-hatting or low-level aerobatics.

Escort carriers, *Long Island* (CVE-l) and *Charger* (CVE-30) on the East Coast ran CQ sessions in the Chesapeake Bay to avoid German U-boats in the Atlantic. The geographic configuration of the bay and heavy shipping traffic made efficient flight operations difficult.

A Carrier Qualification Training Unit (CQTU) was formed in 1942 based at NAS Glenview near Chicago, Illinois, with the service-type aircraft then in use: SBDs, TBMs, F4Fs, and later F6Fs and F4Us as well as SNJs. FCLP was performed at nearby outlying fields: Libertyville and Orchard Place Airport.[6] The CQTU was placed near Lake Michigan because of two special ships that were used to train carrier pilots. A large passenger vessel, the *Seeandbee*, which had been taking passengers and cars between Cleveland and Buffalo, was converted to an aircraft carrier in less than four months and as USS *Wolverine* began operations from the Navy Pier in Chicago in August 1942. In June 1943 a similar conversion, USS *Sable*, was added. Operations (if the wind was good) were very efficient. Five LSOs were assigned to the CQTU and alternated waving FCLPs and on the ships. (Three of the first LSOs assigned had become available when their former ships, *Lexington*, *Yorktown*, and *Hornet* had been sunk.)

Flights of six aircraft flew out beginning at dawn, and each pilot got eight landings before returning to shore. The next flight was waiting overhead. "When considered ready to go to the ship for the

The Grumman TBM Avenger, F4F Wildcat, and North American SNJ were all used for training in shipboard landings.

real thing, they were organized in flights of five to six planes with one of the qualifiers as the flight leader. However, it was quickly learned that unnecessary delays developed in locating the ship and once they arrived more delays occurred because of the poor flight patterns established. Early on, then, all flights to the ship were led by a CQTU staff pilot. This not only got the flights off to a good start but also seemed to be a psychological factor to the trainees involved in seeing the lead plane actually land aboard a carrier."[7]

One day, coincidently, D-day in Europe, *Wolverine* recorded 633 landings by all types of aircraft. (LSO Troy Guillory was reported as rather tired by the end of this day.) By the end of the war, *Wolverine* had logged more than 66,000 landings and *Sable* more than 58,000. More than 15,000 pilots had become carrier qualified on these two ships.

John Preston had been assistant LSO aboard *Yorktown* and reported to the CQTU at Glenview March 1943. He became the unit's commander that summer. Even after leaving that duty in late 1944, he found that the LSO label clung to him. Near war's end, as CAG-7, he landed aboard *Hancock* and parked his Hellcat during flight ops off San Diego. Reporting to the captain, Preston saw a TBM take a late wave-off and blow down the LSO screen. The metal frame hit the ship's only LSO, knocking him into the catwalk, unconscious. Preston offered to take over temporarily. With no other choice, John Preston became probably the only CAG to wave his own pilots aboard.[8]

U.S. Navy LSO Training

As the demand for carrier-qualified pilots rose, so did the need for LSOs to wave them, and those LSOs needed training of their own. The method used was classic apprenticeship. Pilots were ordered to ships where they worked with the experienced Paddles.[12] After a few months of assisting with FCLP and waving landings at sea they were considered qualified and assigned to a carrier of their own. Once the CQTU was established, prospective LSOs would be trained there before going to sea for more supervised experience before assuming duties as a ship's LSO. As devoted aviators, most regarded the job with ambivalence. They recognized the importance of the job, but would rather be flying. Most were drafted into the job.

LSO Robert Galer

LSO Robert Galer[13] in January 1941 was a Marine Corps 1LT and on his way to Hawaii. He joined his old friend Soupy Campbell on the LSO platform to watch him bring in the navy planes. Galer said, "I was curious about navy operations and bored with inaction since the marines were not flying."

At MCAS Ewa that summer, he was the Officer of the Day when the colonel commanding the Marine Air Group learned that the MAG was going aboard ship. The colonel looked at Galer and said, "Lieutenant, did I see you on the LSO platform coming out here?" Galer nodded.

"Did you know what the LSO was doing?"

Growing suspicious, Galer replied, "I thought so, sir."

The colonel looked at his watch. It was about noon. Glancing up, he intoned, "You are now the group LSO. You are relieved as Officer of the Day. You will start bounce drill for the group at 1400 today. Pick an assistant."

In desperation, Galer called his navy friend Soupy Campbell, who flew over with a spare set of paddles. For the remainder of that day and most of the next, the navy LSO gave his marine protégé an intensive course in waving. "Ergo, I was an LSO," said Galer.[14] (When VMF-211 went to its destruction at Wake Island Galer was kept in Hawaii because he was the only USMC LSO available.)

Hangar Deck Cats

Twin hydraulic catapults were installed in *Yorktown*, *Enterprise*, and *Hornet* during construction and by 1939 added to *Saratoga* (CV-3), *Lexington* (CV-2), and *Wasp* (CV-7). *Wasp*, *Lexington*, and *Yorktown* were sunk in battle and, later, in 1942, the hangar deck catapults were removed from *Saratoga*, *Enterprise*, and *Hornet* during rework in shipyards. Thus, of the navy's first eight carriers only *Langley* and *Ranger* never received hangar deck catapults.

Single H4A catapults were installed on the hangar decks of seven Essex-class carriers during construction. These ships were also commissioned with only one flight-deck catapult on the starboard side. Although capable of launching all of the aircraft types of the period, they were rarely used and proved a hindrance to movement on the hangar deck. The extra weight of the catapults was unwelcomed when it could have gone toward more anti-aircraft guns and radars; the catapults were removed by 1944.[15]

A Grumman F6F Hellcat catapulted from the side of a carrier underway. The height above the sea was a liability with no altitude to gain airspeed in a dive. Compare the height to the flight deck. Much like gunnery in the old days of sail, carriers had to wait for the "up roll" to ensure that the plane was launched into the sky and not the sea.

Island-Hopping Campaign

"Hopping" implies that invading one Japanese-held island after another and neutralizing enemy island bases was a simple playground game, but the sweep of the U.S. Navy and Marines across the Pacific was anything but easy. Vast numbers of ships, especially carriers, and airplanes were required. Although the large fleet carriers participated, it was the plethora of slow CVEs that became invasion specialists, softening defenses before the landing and providing close air support after the troops were ashore. Noteworthy were Marine Air Wings aboard navy escort carriers.

This side view of the hangar deck catapult shows why they were unpopular. The cat ran from one side of the ship to the other, not only taking up space on the hangar deck, but preventing movement fore and aft while the cat was being prepared or during launch.

Great Lakes Carriers

USS *Wolverine* (IX-64) and USS *Sable* (IX-81)[9] were the only aircraft carriers to sail the Great Lakes and the only aircraft carriers propelled by coal-burning steam engines driving side paddle wheels. (When there was no wind it took 150 tons of coal a day to make 16 knots, their maximum speed.) *Sable* was the first American carrier equipped with a steel flight deck (as a test for the armored flight decks planned for the Midway class CVs). They were war time expedients but did the job; each carrier logged more than 600 landings in a day, perhaps still an all-time record. By the end of the war, *Wolverine* had logged more than 66,000 landings and *Sable* more than 58,000. More than 15,000 pilots had CarQualed and hundreds of LSOs became qualified.

SS *Seeandbee* (a euphonious name based on the owner's company name, the Cleveland and Buffalo Transit Co.) was a luxury passenger liner and automobile ferry plying the Cleveland-Buffalo route. Built in 1913, she was one of the largest passenger liners ever to sail the Great Lakes, and her appointments would rival those of modern-day cruise ships. Stripped down to the former automobile deck, which was about 5 feet above the waterline, precious furniture, wood-work, mirrors, and other expensive furnishings all went over the side. Reconstruction from this level up incorporated living, mess, shop, and office spaces as well as strength members to support the flight deck, which was 26 feet above the waterline. A 5,000-gallon aviation gasoline tank was installed on the port side of the main deck to counterbalance the weight of the island structure on the starboard side.[10]

The flight deck was 550 feet long by 85 feet wide with a wider section amidships over the paddle wheels. There were nine arresting wires and three barriers. Forward of the island were two outriggers for parking aircraft. The crew was 18 officers and some 275 enlisted men.

The two "fresh water" carriers got underway at dawn with a flight of six aircraft over each ship ready for landings as soon as

Formerly the Great Lakes steamer* SeeandBee*, USS* Wolverine *(IX-64) at anchor in Lake Michigan in April 1943. The hull bulges out where the paddle wheel is located.

USS Wolverine *with the Chicago skyline. Flight operations could take place soon after leaving the Navy Pier if the wind was right.* Wolverine*'s flight deck was only 26 feet above the waterline.*

Unlike other carriers where the amount of smoke depended on the skill of the engineers, Wolverine *and* Sable *(IX-81) always had smoke because they burned coal. This soot made the deck dirty and one time all the LSOs on the platform had cinders in their eyes and landings stopped.*

USS Sable *with her customary trail of coal smoke and a Wildcat on deck. Neither* Wolverine *nor* Sable *left a wake behind because of paddle wheels on their sides.* Sable *had a steel flight deck with nine arresting wires and three barriers. The barriers were at the island, which meant little room for parking aircraft forward. The two outriggers by the island were used to get the LSOs and dud aircraft out of the way.*

One of the crash boats that accompanied the carriers going to the rescue of the pilot of a downed TBM Avenger. Lake Michigan was not always placid.

the ships were into the wind. Frequently, the down-wind leg of the landing approach was over the city of Chicago. Morning traffic jams were caused by commuters who slowed to watch.

The severity of the first winter moved carrier training briefly to San Diego, where it did not go well. So by March 1943, *Wolverine* was cutting through the lake ice with her two-plane guard boats following in her wake while commercial shipping had not yet dared to go out onto Lake Michigan.[11]

Typical of the naval aviation "you can hack it" attitude of the day was a late switch of airplane types when the weather was not cooperative. With no surface wind the 16-knots *Wolverine* and *Sable* could make was not sufficient for qualifying in service-type aircraft. Because all pilots had flown the SNJ in training (although sometimes months before) they were given a couple of quick FCLP periods and sent out in the trainers for their first traps.

Training Paddles

Training Landing Signal Officers was part of the program at the CQTU. There was no formal LSO school or even a set length of instruction. Most candidates began training elsewhere then were sent to NAS Glenview to spend several weeks doing FCLP before being assigned to one of the ships for three or four months. With two to three trainees at a time, the platforms were a bit crowded.

The Next Training Carriers

In October 1945, CQTU Glenview was transferred to NAS Saufley Field, Pensacola, Florida. The unique "Great Lakes Carriers" were retired (and soon scrapped). Carrier training remained in the Pensacola area until the U.S. Navy went to single base training in 1972. CQTU underwent changes of name and organization, but not of purpose.

The pilot is part way out of the cockpit of this ditched Wildcat. Because Lake Michigan is fresh and cold water, sunken aircraft have only minimum corrosion and the lake bottom has become a source for warbirds to be restored, some to flying condition.

To facilitate training, a carrier was based at Pensacola (when tied up at the pier in the old section of the air station, the ships provided inspiration for generations of flight students).

- The veteran USS *Ranger* (CV-4), there for a short period in late 1945
- USS *Saipan* (CVL 48), 1946–1947, the first of a series of light carriers
- USS *Wright* (CVL 49), March 1947–January 1949
- USS *Cabot* (CVL 28), *1949–1950 (*1967–1989 she served in Spain as *Dédalo*)
- USS *Monterey* (CVL 26), January 1951–June 1955
- USS *Saipan* (CVL 48), 1955–1957, the only carrier based in Pensacola twice
- USS *Antietam* (CVS 36), 1957–1962, first to CQ student naval aviators in jets
- USS *Lexington (CVA/AVT-16),* 1962–decommissioned 1991, had more traps than any carrier in history with 493,028
- USS *Forrestal* (CVA/AVT-59), *1991,* after less than a year as CQ was shifted to fleet carriers

A deck crash like the one that befell this Avenger could stop operations for the day if the wreck could not be cleared. A return to port was an option if time and distance were right. Sailors are attempting to secure this wreck for the trip back to port.

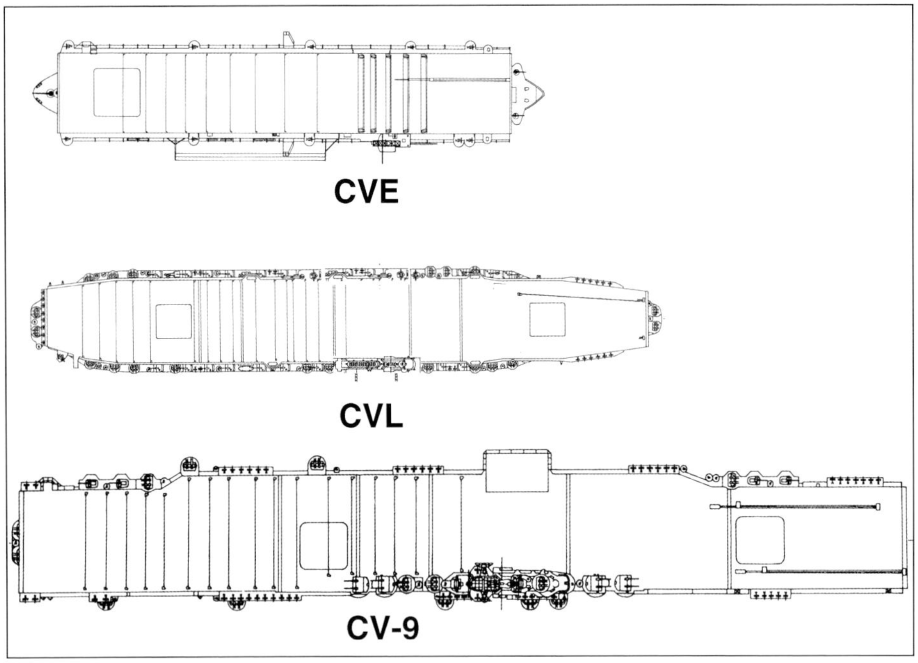

A size comparison of the three types of carriers used by the U.S. Navy in World War II. Pilots whose only experience had been on CVEs or CVLs referred to the Essex class ships as "Big Decks."

Battle of Philippine Sea 19–20 June 1945

The largest carrier battle in history was seven fleet and eight light carriers of the United States Navy versus five fleet and four light carriers of the Imperial Japanese Navy.

By June 1944, the Japanese had nearly rebuilt their carrier forces in terms of numbers, but their planes, many of which were obsolescent, were largely flown by inexperienced and poorly trained pilots. *Taihō* (at the time, the largest aircraft carrier built), which had been commissioned early in the year, was the equal of *Shōkaku* and *Zuikaku*. Although classified as fleet carriers the ocean liner conversions *Junyo* and *Hiyō* had limited capability. The light carriers were *Ryūjō*, *Chitose*, *Chiyoda*, and *Zuihō*.

The Japanese were hoping for the *Kantai Kessen*, the Final Battle. The location of the American fleet was known because the carriers had been flying in support of the invasion of Saipan. Their plan was to commit all the fleet to battle with the hope that their numerical inferiority would be overcome by the ability to use aircraft from both the carriers and shore bases in the Marianas.

On the first day, Japanese airplanes from Guam were detected inbound and 35 shot down. The American fighters were recalled and other aircraft launched to clear the decks when a strike from the west was picked up on radar. The attackers were intercepted 70 miles out and 25 downed; 16 more were shot down closer in but none came near the American carriers. The second attack wave was engaged at 60 miles with 97 of the 107 airplanes shot

An SBD Dauntless on a bad landing with the LSO well out onto the deck. Why no wave-off?

Hellcats were the fighters that racked up the score during the "Marianas Turkey Shoot." This one has been given the cut, although lined up left, or LUL. A sled is being towed behind to provide a target for practice bombing and strafing.

A very casually dressed Dick Tripp has just given a Cut to a Hellcat and is watching the landing before catching a few more rays. Compare the dress and equipment with those of today's LSOs.

down. After launching her airplanes, *Taihō* was hit by a single torpedo from an American submarine, which did not put her out of action but began a chain of events that culminated in her death. The third strike lost only 7 aircraft with 40 returning to their carriers. Midday, another U.S. Navy submarine torpedoed Pearl Harbor veteran *Shōkaku*, ripping open gasoline lines and tanks that exploded violently within minutes. A fourth attack lost 9 while diverting to Guam and encountering a U.S. carrier group. The remnants had 30 of their number shot down by Wildcats over Orote Point airfield on Guam.

By the end of Day 1 the Japanese had lost more than 350 planes, the U.S. Navy, 30. The carrier pilots, and soon all of America, called the day the "Marianas Turkey Shoot."

"At dusk [a pilot on USS Essex] was present on the flight deck for one of the most interesting moments of an event-filled day. I was watching in awe as the LSO worked his magic and brought a plane aboard every twenty seconds. Plane after plane landed. Finally, there was one more guy left to trap. He made a beautiful turn to final, with his plane silhouetted against the sunset. As he approached, the LSO began jumping up and down and waving his paddles, giving him the wave-off. But this guy was committed and kept coming in. The LSO dropped his paddles and jumped into the net. At the last minute, the pilot sucked up his gear and took the wave-off. It was a Zeke! The meatballs under his wing were unmistakable. No one on deck fired a shot as he staggered back into the air. We were barely able to close our wide-open mouths, let alone fire a gun!"[16]

On the second day, the American carriers moved west seeking the Japanese fleet. They had no luck for most of the day. Finally, in late afternoon, they found it 310 miles away, and going farther west 23 more miles every hour. A strike of 240 planes from all the aircraft carriers was launched and was enroute when it was discovered the Japanese task force was another 60 nautical miles farther away. A planned second strike was canceled. The first was not recalled. Those fliers knew they would be operating at the limit of their range.

The attack took place just before the sun set. Twenty American aircraft were lost due to enemy fighters and extremely heavy anti-aircraft fire, but they damaged *Zuikaku*, *Junyo*, and *Chiyoda*, and an Avenger sank *Hiyo* with a torpedo. The problem became how to fly the distance back with dwindling fuel, find the carriers, and land in the dark.

Despite Admiral Mitscher (who had become Naval Aviator 33 in 1916) ordering all ships to turn on lights and escorts to fire star shells, valuing the lives of pilots more than the threat of enemy submarines, 80 airplanes were lost, most by ditching in the sea, many in crashes on deck.

By the end of the Battle of Philippine Sea, the IJN lost 3 carriers, 433 carrier-based aircraft, and 200 land-based planes, 90 percent of its naval air assets.

Leyte Gulf Battles 23–26 October 1944

Although the Battle of Philippine Sea is the largest carrier-versus-carrier battle, the Battle of Leyte Gulf is the largest naval battle of all time. Sibuyan Sea, Surigo Strait (the last battleship battle), Cape Engano, and Samar may be considered battles in their own right by virtue of the forces involved. Except for the battleship-versus-battleship engagement in the Surigo Strait, aircraft

LSO Dick Tripp wearing more conventional coveralls while waving on Yorktown. However, he does not have shoes on; just another eccentricity typical of LSOs. Tripp is a member of the Ten Grand Club (LSOs who waved more than 10,000 passes).

Well out on the deck and braced against the wind, a Batsman brings in a Martlet (unlike the Avenger that began FAA service as the "Tarpon," the American name "Wildcat" was not adopted). Bats is dressed for the tropics and using the three lamps for visibility even in the daytime.

The hangar deck of USS Essex *(CV-9) with an F6F Hellcat and TBM Avenger being worked on. Buried farther back is an F4U. Starting in late 1944, Corsairs carrying radar were sent out in detachments as night fighters.*

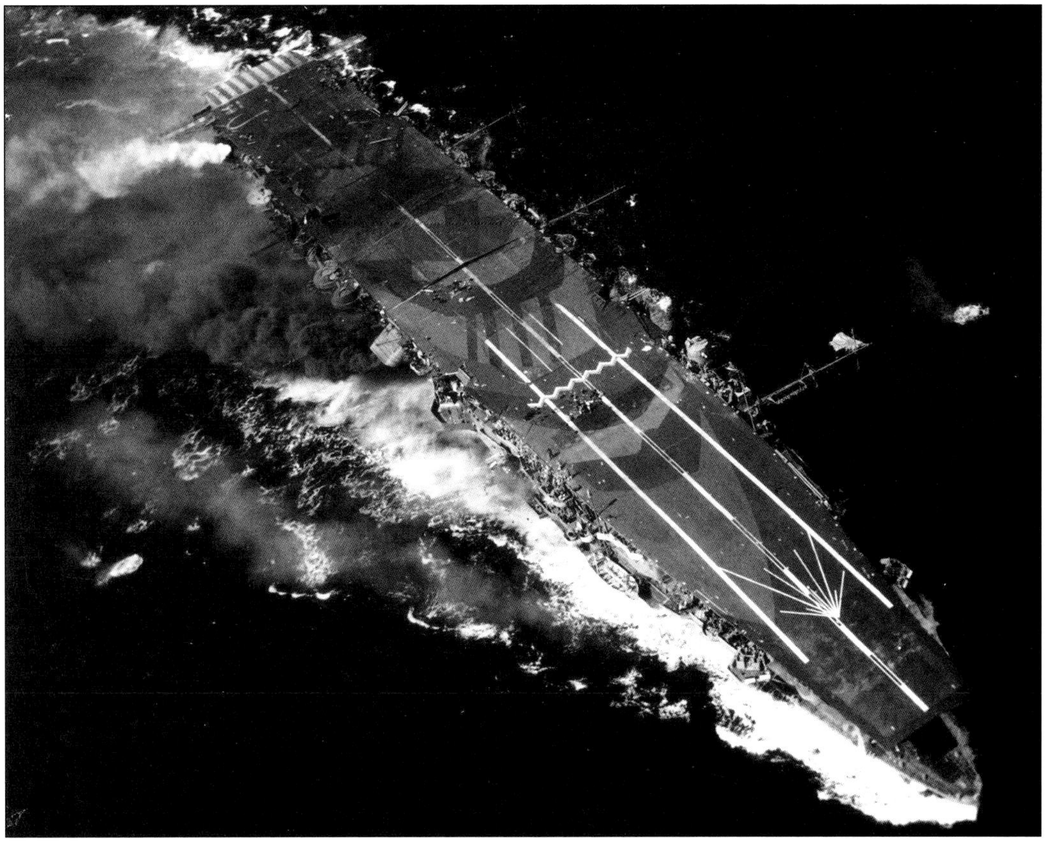

IJN* Zuihō *during the Battle of Leyte Gulf acted as a decoy; she had no airplanes on board, and met her end under the bombs of U.S. Navy aircraft. Like other Japanese carriers still afloat late in the war,* Zuihō*'s flight deck was elaborately disguised with painted gun turrets and false decks. A vent of steam came out the apex of the angled lines near the bow to assist the helmsman in getting the WOD correct.

carriers were in each. The Japanese placed their remaining carriers together in the Northern Force, tasked with baiting the American carrier task forces away from the landing beaches of Leyte. The Center and Southern Forces were then to wreak havoc on the invasion troops and ships. American forces located the Center and Southern Forces, but not the Northern Group of carriers. The force that wanted to be found was not, while the two that wanted to be undetected, were.

The Center formation included the giant battleships IJN *Mushashi* and IJN *Yamato*. Airplanes from six U.S. Navy carriers in three separate attacks put 17 bombs and 19 torpedoes into *Musashi*, which left the force in an attempt to run aground but sank first. USS *Princeton* (CVL-37) was hit by bombers flying from Luzon, exploded, and sank.

Former LSO Dave McCampbell shot down 9 enemy planes and his wingman 6 in one mission. With his score up to 30, McCampbell became the U.S. Navy's top ace.

In a move that remains controversial, when the Japanese carrier force was located ADM Halsey ordered all the big American carriers north to engage. In the confusion of who ordered what and garbled communications between commanders, the Leyte beachhead was left with only three escort carrier groups, Taffy-1, -2, and -3, and their escorting destroyers and destroyer escorts. Even after the earlier air attacks, the Center Force remained formidable. Eleven destroyers, eight heavy cruisers, the *Yamato* and three more battleships came through the San Bernandino Strait. The Taffy groups did not hesitate and rushed their Dauntlesses, Avengers, and Wildcats in the air loaded with whatever ordnance was at hand. The CVEs had a single 5-inch gun and all in Taffy-3 claimed hits on the Japanese ships. Three of the destroyers drove straight at the battleships, firing guns and launching torpedoes. All three were sunk.

Heavy shells fell around the unarmored CVs. USS *Gambier Bay* was hit and sank (the only U.S. Navy aircraft carrier sunk by gunfire). The airplanes attacked with bombs (non-armor piercing), rockets, machine guns, and even depth charges. Some pilots continued making mock attacks after they were out of ammunition. Damage to the Japanese ships was limited, but the ferocity of the assault convinced ADM Kurita that he had run into the main American carrier group and he turned his fleet around and headed back through the San Bernandino Strait. Of the five battleships he had started with only IJN *Yamato* remained battle worthy.

The depleted Japanese carriers managed to have 75 aircraft attack the 3rd Fleet. Most were shot down and did no damage. At dawn 30 Japanese fighters were shot down and 180 American planes began a series of attacks that lasted all day. By the end of the day, 527 sorties had been flown. *Zuikaku, Zuiho, Chitose,* and *Chiyoda* were no more.

Late to the Party

The British aircraft carriers came to the Pacific War late; understandable considering the demands of war in Europe that kept the Royal Navy occupied in the Med and northern waters. As the fleet expanded with new ships and the domain of the Third Reich shrank, the Admiralty committed to the formation of the British Pacific Fleet (BPF) for the start of 1945.

British carriers had operated east of Suez in the Indian Ocean and had based ships at the naval base at Trincomalee, Ceylon, in the earlier years of the war. The raids they undertook were small with limited results. In April 1944 HMS *Illustrious* worked with USS *Saratoga* attacking Sumatra in the first U.S./UK carrier operation.

The debut of the BPF was with three "I"s and a "V" (*Indefatigable,*

Indomitable, Illustrious, and *Victorious*) for aircraft carriers in a successful attack on the Palembang oil refineries on Sumatra in January 1945.

The BPF continued working-up in Australia, learning to work with American forces and developing an effective supply train of oilers, ammunition, and stores ships. In addition to the four fleet aircraft carriers there were six Royal Navy Escort Carriers. All operated a mix of British and American aircraft: Fireflies, Seafires, Corsairs, Hellcats, and Avengers. This variety presented problems in obtaining spare parts; even the American-built airplanes had enough differences to be unique.

One adaptation to the Pacific Theater was elimination of the classic British roundel with the red ball in the center. It was too easily confused with the Japanese *Hinomaru*'s red disk. To make the insignia even more obvious white rectangles were added to the sides to look similar to American markings.

The BPF went into action as part of a combined Allied task force during the Okinawa Campaign in March. *Formidable* replaced the battle weary *Illustrious* in time for the onslaught of kamikaze attacks.

Thirty-two days of operations was the longest a British battle force had been at sea since the days of Nelsonian fighting sail. In July and August the British aircraft carriers joined U.S. Navy task forces striking the Japanese home islands.

The Royal Navy took more than a proportionate share of damage from suicide attacks. Kamikazes scored direct hits on *Indefatigable, Victorious,* and twice on *Formidable.* Thanks to their armored flight decks, a benefit that would be incorporated in future carrier design, all were soon back in action with only limited damage.

In an indication of what naval air power had become, there were no aircraft carriers in Tokyo Bay for the surrender ceremony. They were all off the coast in case something went wrong; yet, they still put up more than 100 aircraft for the flyover of the Japanese surrender on USS *Missouri* (BB-63) in Tokyo Bay.[17]

The flight deck of a Royal Navy CV in the Pacific is filled with American-built Corsairs and Avengers. The British roundel first had its red center eliminated so that it was not mistaken for a Japanese hinomaru *in the confusion of battle; then, following the American's lead, white rectangles to change the overall shape from a circle.*

This photograph could be titled "How the United States Won the War." Popularly labeled "Murderers' Row," it is a display of the production, training, and organization capability of the United States. The view is over the flight deck of USS Ticonderoga *(CV-14) crowded with F6F Hellcats. Riding at anchor in the fleet anchorage at Ulithi Atoll in December of 1944 are the second USS* Wasp *(CV-18), the second USS* Yorktown*, the second USS* Hornet *(CV-12), and USS* Hancock *(CV-19).*

NEW ROLES
1946–1955

The new USS* Coral Sea *(CVB-43) has 63 airplanes visible on the flight deck with room for more. The CVBs were built with low profiles to minimize shock from a radical new weapon, the atomic bomb.

At the end of World War II the United States Navy had 98 carriers in commission. The following 10 years saw three events that shaped the future of carrier aviation: the drastic downsizing of the American and British navies, the arrival of jet aircraft, and the war in Korea.

Peace Strikes

Bring the boys home was the cry. And it was not only the troops who were done, huge numbers of ships and planes were cut. In a year and a half, 68 U.S. Navy carrier air groups were disestablished. USS *Tarawa* (CV-40), which had only been commissioned in 1946, along with *Princeton* (CV-37), made a six-month deployment with Air Group 1 onboard. The air group pilots averaged 16 traps for the half year and one of them said, "The navy had 22 aircraft carriers when we left and only 6 when we returned!"[1] The three CVB, heavy carriers, which were begun during the war, became operational and brought a much-improved capability. *Midway* (CVB-41), *Coral Sea*, and *Franklin D. Roosevelt* (CVA-42) had armored flight decks, improved elevators, and catapults capable of launching the heaviest airplanes coming into use. These carriers were more than 100 feet longer and 20,000 tons heavier than the Essex class and planned for loads of 137 aircraft.

USS Franklin D. Roosevelt *at her commissioning on Navy Day, 27 October 1945, at the New York Naval Shipyard. Reflecting lessons learned in the final months of the war, she has no less than 18 5-inch guns in turrets along her sides for anti-aircraft defense.*

The ability to launch heavy aircraft was important because the United States Navy needed to have the capability of delivering atomic bombs. The newly created USAF was insisting it be the only service allowed to do so. The early bombs weighed 5 tons and there was at first no carrier able to accommodate airplanes that could carry such a load. After a period during which P2V Neptune[2] patrol bombers launched from the ship in a rather impractical plan (it did lead to some spectacular rocket launches to prove the possibility), the North American Aviation (NAA) AJ Savage arrived. The largest airplane to regularly operate from aircraft carriers, it could haul an A-bomb, drop it on a target 800 miles away, and land back aboard the carrier. For LSOs the Savage was a challenge.

Another new and even larger aircraft carrier had the keel laid in 1949 and was canceled the same year. USS *United States* was designed to carry large sea-going bombers and reverted to a flush deck to ensure clearances. To speed operations CVA-58 had five elevators

Carriers Around the World

France	
HMS *Colossus*	1951 to France/*Arromanches*
USS *Langley*	1951 to France/*La Fayette*
USS *Belleau Wood*	1953 to France/*Bois Belleau*
Canada	
HMS *Warrior*	1946–1948 loan to Canada/*Warrior*
HMS *Magnificent*	built for Canada/*Magnificent*
HMS *Powerful*	built for Canada/*Bonaventure*
Australia	
HMS *Vengeance*	1954 loan to Australia/*Vengeance*
HMS *Majestic*	built for Australia/*Melbourne*
HMS *Terrible*	built for Australia/*Sydney*
Argentina	
Warrior (via Canada)	1958 to Argentina/*Independencia*
Venerable (via Holland)	1968 to Argentina/*25 de Mayo*
Holland	
HMS *Venerable*	1949 to Holland/*Karl Doorman*
Brazil	
Vengeance (via Australia)	1957 to Brazil/*Minais Gerais*
India	
HMS *Hercules*	built for India/*Vikrant*

The size of the AJ-1 Savage is apparent in this picture taken onboard USS Oriskany *(CV-34) in 1952. The number of red shirts (ordnance men) and open bomb bay doors indicate the occasion was probably a familiarization with the navy's new nuclear weapon delivery aircraft.*

This LSO, with the windscreen down, has just given the cut to an AJ-1 Savage on USS Midway *(CVB-41). Judging from the wire caught in the tailhook and the wheels that are not on deck, it is an in-flight engagement, which means a hard landing; not good in a Savage, which had notoriously weak engine mounts.*

A later-model AJ Savage in the post-1955 gray-and-white scheme landing on USS Bennington *(CV-20) after her modification to an angle deck. The four lights on the port side are the source lights for the mirror OLS. Instead of the standard four CDPs, there are six. The dashed line marks the center of the axial deck for takeoffs.*

National Carrier Transfers

Colossus Class (Light Fleet Carriers) built 1945/46	
Colossus	1951 to France/*Arromanches*
Venerable	1949 to Holland/*Karl Doorman* 1968 to Argentina/*25 de Mayo*
Vengeance	1954 loan to Australia/*Vengeance* 1957 to Brazil/*Minais Gerais*
Warrior	1946–48 loan to Canada/*Warrior* 1958 to Argentina/*Independencia*
Triumph	Korean War, decomm 1955
Glory	Korean War, decomm 1956
Ocean	Korean War, Suez Crisis, decomm 1957
Theseus	Korean War, decomm 1962
Perseus	aircraft maintenance carrier to 1954
Pioneer	aircraft maintenance carrier to 1946

Majestic Class (Light Fleet Carriers)	
Majestic	built for Australia/*Melbourne* 1955
Magnificent	built for Canada/*Magnificent* 1948
Hercules	built for India/*Vikrant* 1957
Powerful	built for Canada/*Bonaventure* 1952
Terrible	built for Australia/*Sydney* 1948
Leviathan	not completed/scrapped
U.S. Carrier Transfers	
Langley (CVL-27)	1951 to France/*La Fayette*
Belleau Wood (CVL-24)	1953 to France/*Bois Belleau*
Cabot (CVL-28)	reserve 1967 to Spain/*Dedalo*
U.S.-Built CVE	
HMS *Biter*	1945 to France/*Dixmude*

One of the popular Colossus class (Light Fleet Carriers), built 1945–1946, HMS* Warrior *was loaned to Canada for two years and kept her name. Half of the Colossus class carriers built went to other countries.

and four catapults. Policy decisions favoring USAF strategic bombing over naval warfare by the Truman administration led to the cancellation.[3]

Ten Colossus class light fleet carriers were built in the UK but none were completed before the end of World War II. Four of them became the initial carriers for Holland, Argentina, Australia, and Brazil and the fifth became France's first modern carrier. Two were aircraft maintenance carriers, which did not fly fixed-wing aircraft. The remaining four served the Royal Navy effort in Korea.

Six Majestic class ships were begun with one never finished and the others going to other countries. The Illustrious class carriers, which had fought so splendidly in the Pacific, operated in fits and starts for a decade, eventually suffering from obsolescence and budget cuts.

Jet Promises, Jet Problems

The first jet carrier landing was made by LCDR Eric "Winkle" Brown in a prototype DH Vampire aboard HMS *Ocean* 3 December 1945. Earlier, in November of that year, a Ryan FR-1 Fireball had landed on the escort carrier USS *Wake Island* (CVE-65), supposedly using only the jet engine; however, any "first" claims are spurious as it was an emergency procedure by that hybrid power airplane. The first American jet carrier landing was on USS *Franklin D. Roosevelt* by LCDR James Davidson in a McDonnell FH-1 Phantom 21 July 1946.

The Vampire never entered naval service. Brown's comment: "The jet's engine acceleration response was very sluggish"; an early observation of a problem affecting all jets but especially critical for landing aboard. In the event of a wave-off, because a jet took so long to come up to full power, LSOs and Batsmen had to move the decision point, the Window, further out.

Trials were made with twin-jet Gloster Meteors but they, too, were deemed unsuitable. The Supermarine Attacker (an oddity, a jet with a tailwheel) first flew in June 1947, but was not in squadron service until the very end of the decade. The Royal Navy relied on prop-driven aircraft until well into the 1950s.

Meanwhile, the three American naval jet fighters begun during World War II (Phantom, Fury, Pirate) were making their first flights. The sea trials of the FH-1 Phantom[4] were not experiments but acceptance trials. Fleet squadron VF-17A used 16 Phantoms and carrier qualified an CVL-48 *Saipan* in May 1948. The straight-wing FJ-1 Fury also went into squadron service, while the Pirate was such a poor performer that only 33 were built and it never went to sea.[5] By 1949 Grumman's F9F Panther and McDonnell's twin-engine F2H Banshee had begun their long service with the U.S. Navy.

A twin-engine FH-1 Phantom about to trap with its long hook. The bar in front of the windscreen flipped up when the tailhook was lowered. Its purpose was to keep the barrier cables from riding over the nose (there was no prop in the way) and slicing into the cockpit, which was kept open in case of a ditching.

Casual Training

According to navy aviator "Screws," "Transition to jets [note: probably 1950] meant flying an F4U Corsair [or riding in an SNB, for us Ensigns] from Miramar to North Island, where the old-time jet jocks of VF-721 [they'd had their F9Fs for four months] gave us a few system lectures in the morning, followed by our first fam flight in the afternoon. They were too busy with their own work to bother with a "chase pilot," but we'd never heard of such a thing anyhow. Air Pac required 20 hours in type before starting FCLP, and 30 hours before CarQual. The boats were all straight deck. We flew flat, paddles passes; when you got the cut it was either a landing or a crash. Eight landings for me to qualify, one more on the ORI (Operational Readiness Inspection) in Hawaiian waters. My tenth carrier landing in Panthers was with 33 hours in jets and at the end of my first combat mission, and with flak holes in my airplane."[6]

Korea

The Korean War began 25 June 1950, when North Korea invaded South Korea. The two carriers in the area, USS *Valley Forge* and HMS *Triumph*, made the first aircraft carrier strikes into North Korea on 3 July after a week of repositioning and resupply. Korea was out of range of USAF fighters based in Japan, a situation that existed until

One of the popular Colossus Class (Light Fleet Carriers), built in 1945–1946, HMS Warrior was loaned to Canada for two years and kept her name. Half of the Colossus-class carriers built went to other countries.

Flying the Seafire

Commander David "Shorty" Hamilton, Royal Navy, had a total of 550 day and 117 night, accident-free, deck landings in Supermarine Seafires, Hawker Sea Furies, Grumman Avengers, turboprop Fairey Gannets and jet DeHaviland Sea Vampires, Supermarine Attackers, Hawker Sea Hawks and DeHaviland Sea Venoms, and Sea Vixens. Of these, 106 were in Seafire XV and XVIIs. He became a qualified DLCO and trained other Batsmen.

The models I refer to are the later version of the Mk XV, which had a deep fuselage aft of the cockpit, and the Mk XVII with a cut-down fuselage and bubble canopy; both with Griffon engines of 2,000 hp. These were the first to be fitted with a "sting"-type arrestor hook at the extremity to the fuselage.

The main differences from a Spitfire: (a) folding wings, done manually, (b) arrestor hook, (c) longer stroke oleos to absorb the deck landing impact and, in the Mk XVII, fittings to allow for catapult launches, (d) a strut installed in front of the tail wheel to stop an arrestor wire tearing it off, (e) a green indicator light, in the cockpit, to show hook down. A feature that I have never seen mentioned is treadless tyres, introduced to prevent any sideways strain on the undercarriage during deck landing, which could be absorbed by skidding. Also, anyone who had flown the Merlin-engined version had to remember that the Griffon prop rotated in the opposite direction, and rudder trim was reversed.

First flight: The cockpit was small, but just right for me and one felt very much a part of the plane. There had been no thought of ergonomics; buttons, levers, and switches were placed wherever it was convenient for the designer/manufacturer. After start up, and with engine temperature and pressures correct, run the engine up to high revolutions to check for magneto drop, not before getting a member of the ground crew to stand in front of the tailplane, lean over, and put all his weight on it. If that is not done the slipstream could lift the tail off the ground and put the propeller into it. Having reached the runway and done the cockpit check, which included full left rudder trim, you open the throttle and, in spite of full trim, find one still has to add left rudder to keep straight. Having applied full throttle there is still

The Mk 47 Seafire is very different from its Spitfire progenitor with a high tail, bubble canopy, and contra-rotating propellers. The small extension is to prevent the cable from snagging on the tailwheel before being engaged by the tailhook in the fairing at the bottom of the rudder.

a likelihood that you will wander off to starboard, and while you are trying to counteract you realize the aircraft is airborne and skidding madly. Now you have to raise the undercarriage before the airspeed limit is reached and, at the same time, wind off the full left rudder trim.

The rudder trim wheel is on the left side near the floor but the undercarriage lever is on the right sidewall. This is where three hands would be useful. Undercart has to come first. So, take your left hand off the trim wheel and transfer it to the control column; grab the undercarriage lever with your right hand. Move it down, pull to the left, swing it up through about 90 degrees, push it to the right and then down, to lock it. Then change hands back to wind off the trim. While this is going on the plane is wandering about like a drunken sailor and your chums are standing on the tarmac having a good laugh. The remainder of the flight is magic and the landing a doddle because your heart rate is back to normal and the brain untoppled. The first question you were asked was "How high were you when you got the gear up?" It soon became the norm to take off with less than full throttle.

Carrier style: the major change was the reduction of circuit height from the standard 1,000 feet ashore to 300 feet, which was that used for carrier landings. From then on every landing you made was from that height and it used to annoy the RAF somewhat at their airfields, but who cared? From the standard, square Tiger Moth and Harvard circuit one changed to 180-degree banked turns at the end of each straight. At the end of the downwind leg, a steady descending curve to the runway, with some throttle applied, was the aim. The two reasons were, firstly, one could see the runway out of the left-hand side of the windscreen all the way until wings were leveled at the last minute and, secondly, a nose-up three-point attitude had to be carefully maintained at the lower end of the speed range. These two items were of major importance when deck landing.

We started intensive Aerodrome Dummy Deck Landings [ADDLS] at RNAS Milltown, a satellite airfield about 10 miles from Lossiemouth. We flew carrier-style circuits all day, doing touch-and-goes each time, under the orders of the Deck Landing Control Officer [DLCO], who stood on the left side of the runway, which was marked out with white paint, as a flight deck landing area. The Batsman was always an experienced deck landing pilot. The average session was 8 ADDLs in about 20 minutes and there were several sessions a day. One was usually considered ready to deck land after approximately 100 of these.

First Deck Landing: We had to rendezvous with the fleet aircraft carrier HMS *Implacable* in the English Channel and flew south in pairs, refueling at RAF Acklington and RAF Waddington on the way, finishing at RNAS Lee-on-Solent. There are two major handling matters with the Seafire to bear in mind, when taking it to the deck. Firstly, the aircraft is small with a large amount of horsepower up front. If the Batsman gives you a very late "wave-off" and you slam open the throttle at slow speed the aircraft tries to rotate round the propeller; a torque stall, usually fatal. Secondly, the plane has a very low drag airframe and if you are only a little fast on landing it is possible to float gracefully over all 10 wires into the crash barrier.

On 22 June 1948 I flew out to the ship, steaming in Lyme Bay. On arrival I was instructed over my [four channel VHF] radio to join the circuit and land. Flying up the starboard side of the ship, one could see the "Aeroplane" flag, red and white, displayed at the yard arm. This indicated to all ship traffic that the carrier was operating aircraft and to keep clear. Passing up the ship's starboard side, at 300 feet and 150 knots, I closed the throttle and did a 180-degree turn to port. By the time that was completed the undercarriage, flaps, and hook were lowered and I radioed, "four green." I locked the cockpit canopy open as I flew downwind, the plane settling comfortably at 75 knots, and when opposite the ship's island I started the final turn. This is where both concentration and pulse-rate are at maximum.

The plane is now in a nose-high three-point attitude and the speed is kept steady at 65 knots, about 5 percent above "engine on" stall. The only way to see is to crane the head as far left as the open cockpit will allow; you can just see the Batsman and the port side of the flight deck. Your eyes flicker between the Batsman and the airspeed indicator, to the total exclusion of all else. The flight deck is now getting closer; "Bats" signals minor corrections, which you comply with instantly. Concentration, concentration; still airspeed and bats, bats and airspeed; finally the round down flashes past under the port wing; the batsman gives you "cut"; you level the wings, close the throttle, and at the last moment ease the stick back a touch, to land in a three-point attitude. There is a thump and then a rapid stop as the arrestor wire grabs hold and your shoulder straps dig in at the 2-1/2-g deceleration. You have become a member of a very exclusive club.

The Seafire rolls back under the tension of the wire, let it for a few seconds; then apply the brakes. Two flight deck handlers run out, free the arrestor hook from the wire, and clip it back in the up position (thumbs up; a burst of throttle). You taxi forward over the wire barriers, which are immediately raised behind you, ready for the next landing. Following the ballet-like signals from an aircraft handler you are parked as close as possible to other aircraft in the deck park known as Fly One. By the time you vacate the cockpit the next plane has landed and is taxiing up the deck. The flying operations proceed like clockwork; with a worked-up ship and squadron, the landing interval is between 25 to 35 seconds. Eight good landings and I was qualified on the Seafire. (Published with author's permission)

An F4U Corsair with flaps full down going off the bow catapult. Cat operators are working the controls from the catwalk. During the Korean War Corsairs changed status from fighters to attack aircraft.

A Douglas AD "Able Dog" snarled in the wires. The Skyraider was the USN's heavy hitter with six ordnance stations on each outer wing and three racks capable of 1-ton loads on the inner wing and fuselage.

Along with the Hawker Sea Fury, the Fairey Firefly was a major FAA combatant in Korea. A game the British pilots played was to lower their tailhooks and go trolling for telegraph and telephone wires. Usually the snapped wire fell off, but sometimes the plane returned to the ship with a snarl of it still on the hook.

United Nations troops drove north late in the year. USS *Valley Forge* was soon joined by USS *Philippine Sea* and by the end of 1950, nine American carriers were rotating in and out of the Far East. Five carriers (four British and one Australian) worked back to back for additional air power from the start to end of the conflict. HMS *Triumph* was relieved by HMS *Theseus*, followed by HMS *Glory*, the Australian HMAS *Sydney*, HMS *Glory* for her second stint, HMS *Ocean*, then *Glory*'s third deployment, which lasted almost to the armistice while HMS *Ocean* and HMAS *Sydney* wrapped up the action and loitered for a few more months, just in case. The carriers' time on the line were sequential with only a few days overlap.

LSOs Ashore, Part 1

The first recorded use, other than for practice, of LSOs ashore was in October 1939. USS *Ranger* had been searching for a German supply ship that had left Mexico for a rendezvous with the *Graf Spee*, but because a hurricane was approaching the Gulf of Mexico she had to leave the area. Bombing Squadron 3 (VB-3) moved ashore to Carter Field on the U.S. Naval Base Guantanamo, Cuba. Carter Field was on the west side of the bay and had not been used since World War I. When the maintenance troops arrived the only residents were an old Cuban and a pig in a shack. The usable runway was so short and the approaches so restricted that the SB2U Vindicators landed on Paddles control. VB-3 spent two weeks at the primitive airfield. As it turned out, the ship SS *Emmy Friedrich* had been scuttled before the squadron even left Norfolk.

On Guadalcanal in 1942, navy Seabees built an additional landing strip by tamping down sod a mile from Henderson, the main field. Officially "Fighter 1#," the pilots called it "the cow pasture," which was a good description. When VMF-224 pilots flew their F4F Wildcats there, Major

The LSO has given the cut to a Skyraider and he and the other Paddles are looking up the deck to watch the trap. The spotter has binoculars trained on the next airplane in the pattern while the talker has placed a deck condition flag.

USS Valley Forge (CV-45) was known as the "Happy Valley," sometimes sarcastically as she set a record for time at sea. The light-colored planks make up a section of her wooden flight deck that was replaced. The outer dashed yellow lines are Foul Lines over which no personnel or equipment is allowed during landings. The landing F4U Corsair has its flaps full down. The four ordnance stations on each wing are apparent and the silver object is either a fuel tank or unexpended napalm.

A Vought SB2U Vindicator assigned to the Commander Air Group 4 on USS Ranger (CV-4). The oversize insignia are markings of the Neutrality Patrol. Vindicators were based in Guantanamo during the search for a German freighter.

Bob Galer, the CO, fell back on his LSO training and waved the airplanes to ensure safe approaches for the first landings on the rough runway.

The brutally cold weather and mountainous terrain made the fighting withdrawal from the Chosin Reservoir in Korea a test of men and machines. Without close air support flights from the carriers off shore the battle would have been lost. A Marine aviator put a carrier-type aircraft to another use. VM0-6 was based at Yonpo with light observation aircraft and helicopters. CAPT A. F. McCaleb, had flown TBM Avengers as artillery spotters and received permission to try taking out casualties in them. He landed the first "Turkey"[7] at Koto-ri even as bulldozers were finishing the crude strip, and took out several wounded men. Landing on "the unbelievably high, short airstrip" required considerable airmanship for a safe landing. McCaleb realized that having an LSO on the runway would help pilots get down safely.

He contacted CAPT Malcolm Moncrief, an F4U pilot and an LSO. McCaleb flew Moncrief into the strip, where the latter set to work. The TBMs flew incessantly; some pilots as often as 11 trips a day, relying upon Moncrieff's paddles to get them onto the small field gorged with other planes and equipment. The casualties were flown 35 miles to Yonpo; 160 during the first 10 days of December. A Marine LSO, standing exposed to harassing fire, bringing in carrier planes on a landing strip almost in enemy territory became part of the legend of the Chosin Reservoir.

The most famous LSO (probably the only one known to the general public) is the fictional "Beer Barrel" created in James Michener's novel *The Bridges at Toko-Ri* (made into a popular movie of the same name in 1954). In the book Michener wrote a vivid description of the role and mystique of the LSO. "There always came that exquisite moment of human judgment when one man standing alone on the remotest corner of the ship, lashed by foul wind and storm; had to decide whether that jet roaring down upon him could make it. This solitary man had to judge the speed and height and the pitching of the deck in the wallowing of the sea and the oddities of this particular pilot and those additional imponderables that no man can explain. Then, at the last screaming second he had to make his decision and flash it to the pilot. He had only two choices, he could land the plane and risk the life of the pilot and the plane and the ship if he had judged wrong. Or he could wave off and delay his decision until next

A TBM Avenger pressed into emergency service as a medical evacuation aircraft at the Yonpo airfield in Korea.

With a crushed wing tip tank and shattered canopy ENS Jackson lands his F9F Panther with a mild swerve. His wingman ENS Crow flies upwind after dropping Jackson off for a Paddles' talkdown.

time around. But he could defer his job to no one. It was his, and if he did judge wrong, carnage on the carrier deck could be fearful."

LSO LTJG Robert "Dog" Fannon is likely the inspiration for "Beer Barrel." Fannon was the LSO on one of the carriers Michener visited during his tour. Fannon may have been more colorful than some, but was representative of the era demanding the most of LSOs: early jets, on straight decks, in miserable Korean weather, and in combat.

In later years, Dog was a pilot flying the TF/C-1 COD, which made regular runs to aircraft carriers within range of the VRC squadron's shore base. In 1956 *Yorktown* (CVA-10) made her last cruise before having a mirror installed. The COD flew a nice pass and shut down while still in the arresting gear. Almost immediately, the door of the TF flew open. An obviously agitated Fannon emerged and strode rapidly back to the LSO platform. There, he grabbed the *Yorktown* LSO by the front of his flight suit, and delivered a legendary message, "Listen, Sonny, I saw what you were doing. *You* were giving *me* signals when I came aboard. Don't you *ever* do that again! Whenever I come out here, you just stand there with a roger signal and watch the cockpit. When I nod my head, you give me a cut. Understand?" For a long time thereafter, whenever the COD came onboard *Yorktown* its pass was an automatic OK-3.[8]

Korean combat differed from the Pacific campaigns, which had established the value of aircraft carriers. Carrier aircraft attacked supply lines; flew deep support missions; sought out targets of opportunity; bombed bridges, railroads, and highways; and escorted air force bombers on special missions; in all weather, day and night. There were never more than four carriers in action at the same time. U.S. Navy and Marine aircraft flew 276,000 sorties (only 7,000 less than the totals for World War II in all theaters). They dropped 177,000 tons of bombs; 74,000 more tons than during World War II. In terms of American effort, navy and marine aircraft flew more than 30 percent of action sorties in Korea, opposed to less than 10 percent in World War II. The importance of aircraft carriers was no longer in doubt. Construction of new super-carriers was begun. New developments, aircraft, and techniques were coming, which radically changed carrier aviation and made a safer and more effective fighting force.[9]

Blind Landing

On 17 September 1950, flying an F9F-2 Panther, Ensign Edward D. Jackson Jr. flew through steel cables strung across the Han River. The snapped cables whipped across the canopy and punched out the windscreen. Jackson was knocked unconscious with severe facial injuries. When Jackson came to he found himself blinded by shards of plastic and blood. His wingman, Ensign Dayl E. Crow, talked Jackson out to the Yellow Sea and USS *Philippine Sea* (CV-47). When the

Jackson being lifted from the cockpit. Medical personnel are in white jerseys. Jackson eventually recovered his sight. The stick in front of the Panther's windscreen is the guard for the Davis barrier.

time came to dirty-up, the flaps came down only on one side. LSO LTJG "Les" Bruestle took control over the radio and despite the battle damage and blindness talked Jackson into a cut for the 4# wire. Jackson survived with 36 stitches and an emergency blood transfusion. The Panther and Jackson both flew again.

LSO Leslie Hofto

LSO Leslie Hofto went through the NROTC program at University of Washington, graduated in 1947, and stayed an extra year as an engineering student and a varsity rower. His first assignment was flying AD Skyraiders with VA-75, which deployed to the Mediterranean where he picked up his waving qualification. As LSO, Hofto was assigned to CVG-7 staff and got his flight time with his VA-75. CVG-7 was in Korea in *Bon Homme Richard* (CVA-31), popularly called "Bonny Dick," from May 1952 to January 1953. Although everyone else went home, Hofto was extended for three months to work up a newly arrived air group that had World War II LSOs who were unfamiliar with jets. He also had a complaint common to LSOs of that era: not enough flying. Mostly he did engine run-ins and only limited combat ops. However, he showed himself to be in the ranks of the great Paddles a year after Korea when he was the senior LSO on USS *Bennington* (CVA-20) during the near disaster that was Operation Mariner.

The September 1953 Operation Mariner was an ambitious, multi-national, trans-Atlantic fleet exercise. USS *Wasp* (CVA-18), USS *Bennington*, and the Canadian carrier HMCS *Magnificent* ("Maggie" to those who knew her) and 22 other ships were in the Task Force. Despite being 460 miles from the nearest land, Cape Farewell, Greenland, 52 U.S. and Canadian aircraft were launched from the three carriers; AD Skyraiders and F4U Corsairs from the American carriers and TBM Avengers from Maggie. No jets were launched; fortunately, as it turned out. After an hour, the weather began to deteriorate and a recall was issued. Ten Corsairs managed to land, but by the time the eleventh tried visibility was down to a few yards. Several aircraft attempted approaches but none could see their ships in the murk.

The 42 aircraft had been airborne for three hours. The Corsairs and Avengers had only an hour until they ran out of gas. The fog blanket grew to 2,500 feet thick. Overhead the airplanes held while alternative plans were considered. The airfield on Greenland was too far for the Corsairs, had unknown weather, and it would be after dark for the planes even if they did make it. A mass ditching into the frigid ocean was proposed. A U.S. Navy submarine 110 miles west reported a relatively clear area. The aircraft were told to head for the sub and ditch alongside. And then a miracle.

As the gaggle of airplanes passed over enroute to the submarine, a break appeared in the clouds. Still not good; visibility about 2 miles under a 300-foot cloud base, with 12-foot ocean swells and a wind gusting up to 40 knots. The ships headed into the wind and all aircraft were told to return immediately for landing.

LSO Hofto was worried. Before Operation Mariner he'd had only a relatively brief three-month pre-deployment period to work his pilots through field carrier landing practice and carrier qualification landings. Some of the pilots had yet to qualify at night. On the platform aft on the flight deck, Hofto watched the results of the trauma the pilots were experiencing: marginal visibility, increasing darkness, and low fuel states, all mere moments away from ditching at sea. None of the pilots was inclined to stray very far from a carrier, once discovered. Aircraft materialized out of the low-hanging clouds and pilots quickly jockeyed themselves into the groove. Some aircraft descended below the ragged, 75-foot ceiling only to pop right back up and disappear. The congestion around *Bennington* was continuous and Hofto never lacked for a plane at the cut position. At one point he counted the lights of nine aircraft approaching *Bennington* simultaneously, five between the 180-degree position and the cut, with four more stretched out in a line astern of the ship. He took all comers as fast as the deck was cleared, but the wave-off–to–cut ratio was about five to one.

One AD pilot flew an exceedingly fast approach. In a judgment call, Hofto gave the pilot a cut signal at a distance three times farther out than normal. The pilot responded properly by chopping his throttle and Hofto continued to wave signals, "bending" the Skyraider up, then down, over the pitching ramp to a successful trap. Then, apparently trying to conserve fuel, an F4U Corsair came into Hofto's sight at the 180-degree position of the landing pattern. The Corsair was in a clean (gear and flaps up), fast glide and put on a mini–air show. The Corsair pilot continued his approach, reducing power and rapidly lowering gear, flaps, and hook. But he was

Panther as Movie Star

Besides his 13.5 kills in World War II, George Duncan is known for his F9F ramp strike on *Midway* (CVB-41) July 1951. You know the one; it's been used in a bunch of movies. So many that he was told that he should have joined the Screen Actors Guild. His first landing that day was fine; the spectacular crash occurred on the second. Because it was a test program the movie camera coverage is exceptional. After hitting the ramp, the forward section of the Panther rolled up the deck, tearing off the canopy and Duncan's helmet. Amazingly, his only injuries were minor burns. Duncan was later captain of *Ranger* (CVA-61) 1962–1963. The crash sequence was used in *Men of the Fighting Lady* (realistically as an F9F), *The Hunt for Red October* (standing in for an F-14 Tomcat), and, even sillier, in *Midway*, where the SBD Dauntless (flown by "Captain" Charlton Heston) morphs into an SB2C Helldiver in the groove and crashes as Duncan's Panther!

Duncan's F9F crash sequence: Settles below the ramp (top left), Impact and the Panther bursts into flame (top right), The cockpit section rolls up the deck ahead of the fireball (bottom). Amazingly, Duncan had only minor injuries.

slow in getting power back on. Hofto watched as the F4U's tailhook splashed through wave tops before the unidentified pilot took his own wave-off and disappeared upward into the clouds.

Heavy seas caused *Bennington*'s stern to pitch up and down through a considerable arc. Timing his cut signals to achieve a safe hook-to-ramp clearance was a "crap shoot" for Hofto. Aware that minimum fuel states were prevalent, he ignored marginal approaches and resorted to wave-offs only when the deck was fouled. He also attempted to cut every plane late, both to provide the most stable portion of the pitching deck for landing and to enable quick clearing of the landing area after the trap. It was not an easy task. In one case Hofto flashed a cut to an AD but the pilot held off. The Skyraider floated precariously over the wires, appearing to be headed for a messy collision with the aircraft parked forward. At the last moment the deck fortuitously heaved upward. The pitching deck caught the tailhook in a late wire and literally snatched the plane to a safe arrested landing.

In another instance, Hofto cringed as the deck moved rapidly upward after he gave a cut signal to a Skyraider pilot. The plane's hook barely cleared the ramp as the deck reached maximum up-pitch and the pilot had to "horse" his aircraft downward to chase the deck as it dropped away beneath him. The plane caught the 12# (last) wire and a "clear deck" was called almost as soon as the hook disengaged.

One of the last aircraft to trap on board *Bennington* was a nugget pilot in a Corsair. Separated from his section leader and "flying on fumes," the young pilot had twice descended into the miserable weather and, not finding a carrier, twice climbed back to on top. Descending for a third and perhaps final time, he flew his Corsair down to 40 feet above the water to stay beneath the fog. There he spotted a string of flares and followed them, but the pilot couldn't locate the carrier visually and, at a 40-foot altitude, was headed for a life-threatening rendezvous with the ship's fantail.

On the LSO platform, Hofto signaled a frantic wave-off. Hofto's assistant LSO fired red flares and screamed "Wave-off! Wave-off!" over the radio. Recognizing his perilous situation at the last moment the Corsair pilot jammed his throttle to full power for a frantic wave-off. Cocked-up in a near-stall attitude, the F4U climbed agonizingly to clear the end of the flight deck. Hofto resisted the urge to dive off the LSO platform into the safety net. Instead he rapidly switched signals from a "wave-off' to a "roger," then gave the cut signal. The F4U slammed down on the deck and the tailhook engaged an arresting gear cable for a successful trap. Seconds later, the Corsair's engine quit from fuel starvation.

Les Hofto didn't bother with the usual LSO debrief for pilots, but the omission had nothing to do with the celebrating. Hofto's assistants hadn't been able to keep up with the normal platform book-keeping. In fact, they couldn't even keep track of the wave-offs during the hectic period and were just thankful that no one went into the drink.[10]

Paddles' Versus Bat's Signals

As visual signals developed in the early years the Americans and British, as with which side of the road to drive on, diverged. When British carriers were integrated into the task forces in the Pacific in the last years of World War II, they shifted to the American system, but reverted on return to Royal Navy control. The shift happened again for Royal Navy ships participating in the Korean War. This disparity in signals led to some interesting events.

In the early 1950s, the Tophatters, VF-14, were flying F4U-5 Corsairs from the deck of USS *Kula Gulf* (CVE-108). The ship was involved in an Atlantic Fleet exercise in the Caribbean, and one of the other participants in the evolution was a British carrier.

Kula Gulf was steaming with a ready deck one afternoon while trying to avoid an approaching storm when an urgent request for landing was received from the leader of a flight of eight airborne British F4U-4 Corsairs. They couldn't trap on their own carrier because it was beneath the worst of the storm, the Brit flight leader reported, and their fuel states dictated a prompt recovery. *Kula Gulf* responded that the deck was ready and invited the Brits to come onboard.

When word was passed that Royal Navy Corsairs were to be recovered, the VF-14 LSO hastened to his station on the aft port platform, and the U.S. Navy F4U drivers scrambled topside to watch the show from Vulture's Row. The Royal Navy Corsairs broke formation smartly ahead of the ship, turned downwind, and made good approaches, up to a point. When close-in on final, the Brits seemed unresponsive to the LSO's visual paddle signals, in some cases placing themselves in precarious positions. Low fuel states or not, all eight Royal Navy Corsairs received wave-offs on their first passes. A few managed successful traps on their second passes, but the rest didn't get aboard safely until their third pass at the deck.

After completion of the ragged recovery, the judgments of the observing U.S. Navy Corsair drivers was that the Brits "must have had very little carrier landing practice." On the other hand, the deplaning British pilots complained vehemently about "that crazy Batsman" (British for LSO).

Post-flight briefing placed things in better perspective and revealed that the Brit Tailhookers weren't such bad aviators after all. The shortcoming was a need for closer attention to universally understood tactical signals when conducting international exercises. In both services, the "Roger" signal from the LSO or batman-paddles held horizontally in outstretched arms, meant "OK, continue the approach." When the American LSO dropped his arms to a below-the-horizontal position, it meant "You are low (below the safe flight path), bring it up." Arms above the horizontal meant "You are high, bring it down." In the Royal Navy, on the other hand, those signals meant the opposite. When the Batman's outstretched arm signal dropped to a below-the-horizontal position, it meant "You are high, bring it down," and so on.

The Brit aviators managed to get safely onboard *Kula Gulf* by seat-of-pants flying, ignoring the impulse to follow the LSO's signals.[11]

Double Trap

According to Bob Atherton, "I was around for the transition from paddles and straight decks to the mirror and the angle. They sure made a difference, but I have to say lots of wires saved me one day when I was flying, not waving. You gents ever heard of a double trap, two airplanes at once?

"The Corsair was called the hose-nose for a good reason. That R-2800 engine stuck way out. The F4U-5 was particularly bad with the extra length and the cooling intakes on the sides of the cowling. I was on my second cruise and had over a hundred landings in the F4U. Because I'd been sick at the beginning of the *Roosevelt*'s deployment and sent back to the states, it had been months since I'd landed on the ship. The CAG told me to be overhead when the *Franklin D. Roosevelt* pulled out of Barcelona and I could get a few passes then a trap or two. The ships had their own SNJ trainers in those days to keep the aviators in the ship's crew current and the SNJ would be there with me.

"It wasn't normal ops. The carrier was turning, trying to find the wind. The SNJ was in front of me, but at one point, flying perpendicular to the ship so I figured I was number one. The technique in the Corsair was to keep turning until the cut; even then, you could only see half the LSO. His right arm gave me all sorts of corrections; figured it was sort of refresher training. Wound up high and well to the right when he gave me the slashing motion that means cut. Two absolutely mandatory signals, right? Cut and wave-off. So I chopped the power and put in a side-slip to get down. As the wing dropped I could see the SNJ on the 1# wire. Something was very wrong so I pushed the throttle up. The R-2800 didn't like that, hiccupped, and blew black smoke. I pulled it back to idle, but the burst had given me enough of a boost to land on the 11# wire, the last one. The sailor working the barriers was alert enough to drop them so I didn't snag my prop, or worse.

"The crash klaxon was blaring and the flight deck was empty; everyone had cleared off. I just sat there thinking my career was over. Finally, the Air Boss called out to get those airplanes clear, there were others to land.

"I waited down in the ready room for the summons to the bridge. Went to chow and bed still waiting. By the next day, knew I was okay. Apparently the ship and SNJ pilots had screwed up so bad they just wanted to keep it quiet."[12]

USS* Coral Sea *preparing to launch in 1955; the destroyer is getting into position as plane guard. The air wing is a varied mix, some dark blue, others all metal, including "long-" and "short-" nose F2H Banshees, FJ Furies, AD Skyraiders, and AJ Savages.

Indochina 1947–1953

The end of the war saw Indochina with the communist Vietminh in control of much of the northern area, Tonkin. Eager to regain its former colony, France dispatched troops in the former aircraft carrier *Bearn*, which arrived in Haiphong in February 1946. By the end of the year a civil war had broken out. FN *Dixmude* was a CVE built in the United States for Britain, where she served a busy three years as HMS *Biter*, escorting convoys and hunting submarines before going to the French navy. In early 1947 she went to Indochina with a squadron of Douglas Dauntlesses and a load of Spitfires for the air force. The SBDs began strikes

Let's Add a Hook

Although several aircraft have made it from the flight deck to the air force, the A-7 Corsair II and F-4 Phantom II being the most obvious examples, airplanes designed for runways that gained sea legs are few and far between. In the primordial days of jets, the successful P-80 Shooting Star and its two-place trainer version, the T-33, both had tailhooks added, but it was not until the TO/TV was heavily modified to the T2V Sea Star that it flew regularly at sea. Although the FJ-2 and FJ-3 Fury were navalized F-86 Sabrejets, folks forget that the F-86 was a North American Aviation re-do (granted, a major one) of the navy's original FJ.

Hooks were hung on and trial deck landings made with two other North American Aviation Co. products. In November 1944 on USS *Shangri-La*, LCDR Bottomley made the first carrier landing in a B-25 bomber. After inspection he took off and made another trap before flying off to NAS Norfolk. The same day, LT Bob Elder logged 25 landings in a P-51 Mustang. For a variety of reasons, the Mustang did not make it into the navy inventory. The Marines did use Mitchells, designated PBJ, ashore in VMB squadrons during World War II. (The P-51, if accepted, probably would have become the Sea Horse.) The F7F Tigercat flew its CarQuals at the same time and was accepted, but had problems on the ship and saw combat only ashore during Korea.

After the Sea Gladiator, Sea Hurricane, and Sea Spitfire,[17] the British adapted several RAF aircraft for carrier flying. There was Sea Mosquito, Sea Hornet, Sea Fury, Sea Vampire, Sea Venom, and Sea Vixen. (Hardly the most original names.) There was a Sea Hawk as well, but it did not originate as an air force design.

The French made the Fouga Magister into a carrier-capable trainer as the CM.175 Zéphyr. The most recent example is the RAF Hawk jet trainer, which immigrated to America in the late 1980s and became the McDonnell Douglas T-45 Goshawk in which U.S. naval aviation students get their first traps. The U-2 also became carrier capable. (See sidebar, "The U-2 at Sea," in Chapter Nine.)

Hawker Seahawks doing a simultaneous start using explosive cartridges. Indian navy Seahawks saw combat during the Indo-Pakistani War.

On 15 November 1944, LT. Bob Elder performed the first "trap," or carrier landing, of an Army Air Forces aircraft with a North American P-51D Mustang. Appropriately re-named the Seahorse for Navy duty, the P-51 successfully landed aboard the USS Shangri-la *(CV-38) while being evaluated along with the Grumman F7F Tigercat and North American PBJ (B-25) for possible carrier operations, none of which came to pass. (Courtesy of Artist Craig Kodera)*

against the Vietminh, especially in the center area, Annam, which was out of range of the air bases at Saigon and Hanoi. After five weeks of operations, *Dixmude* returned to France to pick up more airplanes for the air force. Returning in October, in three weeks she launched 200 sorties before going to France and then the United States for F6F Hellcats and SB2C Helldivers to replace the obsolescent Dauntlesses.

Dixmude sailed across the Pacific and offloaded the airplanes in Saigon. In the meantime, FN *Arromanches,* which the Royal Navy had operated as HMS *Colossus* for a year, arrived in theatre with her air wing of Seafires and Dauntlesses. After only two months she went back to France for overhaul. There were no carrier operations for 1949 and most of 1950 until *Arromanches* returned with newer aircraft. She was joined by FN *La Fayette,* a carrier of similar size that had been USS *Langley* (CVL-27). Both stayed until the end of the civil war. Despite the infamous loss of Dien Bien Phu (naval aircraft flew one-third of the missions in support there), the French did not lose the war but were defeated at the conference table in Geneva, which divided Indochina into the countries of North and South Vietnam.

LSO W. F. "Toby" Tobin Jr.

After LSO W. F. "Toby" Tobin Jr. was awarded his wings in 1949 he went to the LSO school, which was then at NAAS Corry Field in Pensacola, Florida. Considering his later reputation, he wasn't keen on the idea, but the job had several perks, including becoming jet-qualified.

The first issue of* Naval Aviation News *appeared in September 1943. Filled with articles of historical interest, current news, and safety information,* NavNews *has been avidly read monthly ever since. The October 1952 issue featured LSOs and Toby Tobin in his tiger suit on the cover.

When the Korean War began, Air Group-2 (CVG-2) was needed in WestPac, immediately. Those members of air group who were not lucky enough to fly to NAS Alameda, California, rode in two troop trains for the cross-country trip. Tobin remembers it as "a wonderful time," with little to do but party and watch the scenery. After a few months of combat, USS *Boxer* (CV-21) lost one of her propeller reduction gears and was back in Alameda by November. "Very neat! Very nifty! Back alive in 1950!" Then the Chinese entered the war, and after only three weeks at home CVG-2 went back out on *Valley Forge* (CV-45). CVG-2 cross-decked to the *Philippine Sea* (CV-47) in March 1951 so that "Happy Valley" could go to the United States for an overdue overhaul. "Phil Sea's" deployment ended in June. After a decent turnaround Tobin was back onboard *Boxer* with 27 other pilots who had made all three of the group's cruises. At that point, Tobin said, three-quarters of the guys were so good "they would fly up to the blunt end and we would whack 'em."

The French navy had asked for a qualified LSO and Tobin lucked into the unique assignment. One problem, though, was that he didn't speak French. Of course, the airplanes didn't care. Neither, it turned out, did the French aviators. "They were so anxious to practice English on me that I didn't have to learn French." Another problem was that most of the *aviateurs* were British trained and had to learn reverse up and down signals.

After some NATO exercises on *La Fayette* Tobin went to *La base d'aéronautique navale de* Karouba, Bizerte, Tunisia, to conduct FCLP for the newly formed *Flotille* 14, flying F4U-7 Corsairs. "Those who have landed F4Us aboard CVLs will appreciate that the combination of the narrow deck of the light carriers and F4Us, especially the F4U-7, was not a happy marriage," but all of the aviators of 14-F were outstanding and qualified aboard *La Fayette* without incident.

Tobin at work on the French CV* La Fayette. *The wooden platform has an extension and his use of solid paddles is unusual.

A Grumman F6F-5 Hellcat from Escadrille 1F prepares to land on the French carrier* Arromanches *(R95) operating in the Gulf of Tonkin.

La Fayette went to Indochina in spring of 1953 with a squadron of Hellcats and another of Helldivers. Besides his waving duties, and although technically illegal, Tobin flew several missions, thus "Le Tobe" became the only two-war Hellcat pilot.

Night Landings Normal

As the Pacific War progressed the need for night operations at sea became apparent. The basic problems were to find the ship and see the deck and DLCO/LSO signals. Sufficient lighting had to be balanced against being sighted by the enemy. Variations abounded as trial and error determined what was worth keeping.

A variety of ideas were noted in the listing for the recovery of Swordfish after the Taranto attack in November 1941:[13]

- Each plane had a light on its undercarriage by the arrester hook and turned on its running lights just before landing.
- Neon batons were used by the officer controlling the landings.
- Red obstruction lights marked the superstructure.
- Flame floats with delayed action were dropped astern.
- Each side of the stern was lighted by a green and red shaded light.
- The carrier blinked the letters "P" and "S" from the port and starboard sides of the ship
- Green and red arrow-directing batons were used for directing and spotting the planes around the deck.

Fluorescence

Both the Royal Navy Batsman and U.S. Navy Paddles used lighted wands initially. Whether the legend of pilots being inspired by the glowing costumes of dancing girls at a night club is true or not, ultra-violet lights shining on the LSO wearing special-fabric stripes became the preferred method. The cloth strips were fastened by small metal snaps. The system was workable with two problems: the signals were hard to recognize if the LSO moved his arms too fast and the UV light made the approaching airplane look blurry. Robin Lindsey's solution: "My method was to cut the visor off a baseball cap and by using an elastic band around my head hold the visor inverted just under my nose, cutting off the ultra-violet light."[14]

Full Timers

In November 1943 a radar-equipped TBF Avenger with two F6F Hellcats on its wing intercepted a Japanese raid and shot down two Betty bombers. Only two of the planes landed back on USS *Enterprise* before dawn, completing the first American night combat mission to begin and end in the dark. (The missing F6F was flown by the CAG, ace Butch O'Hare.)

Project Affirm at NAS Quonset Point, RI, had been working on night tactics and equipment using the experience of the pioneer night squadrons in the Pacific and the RAF. A specialized night fighting squadron VF(N)-101 began flying from *Enterprise* New Year's Day 1944. The navy's first full-time night air group was Air Group 41 (CAG-41) aboard CVL *Independence,* in the fall of 1944. When the Japanese battleships and escorts were transiting the San Bernardino Strait before the Battle of Samar, Air Group 41 sent Avengers airborne that night, tracking the large enemy force. For reasons still unclear, Admiral Halsey ignored their valuable information.

By the end of CAG-41's first cruise, their record was 46 enemy planes shot down, 30 of them at night, 20 destroyed on the ground, and three ships sunk, one of them at night. By the time of the strikes on Tokyo, the *Enterprise* air group, CAG-90, had become the first big-deck night air group. Under CDR Bill Martin, Air Group 90 included veterans of his old VT-10, which had bombed Truk shipping in the dark twelve months before. Flying night Hellcats and specially modified Avengers, Martin's men "approached nocturnal carrier aviation with an enthusiasm approaching evangelism."[15] With the concept proven, night-carrier-landing training became a requirement for all carrier pilots by August 1945.

Electric Suit

Both LSOs and DLCOs were free to modify and adapt their dress and equipment. As Batsman Jack Thomas wrote, "For night landings the Batsman replaced his bats with a pair of hand-held lamps with another lamp strapped to his chest, so I made a modification for day landings (especially in conditions of poor visibility) by strapping on an extra fluorescent disc to my chest. Wearing a red rugby shirt with a blue and yellow baseball cap this made me more visible."[16]

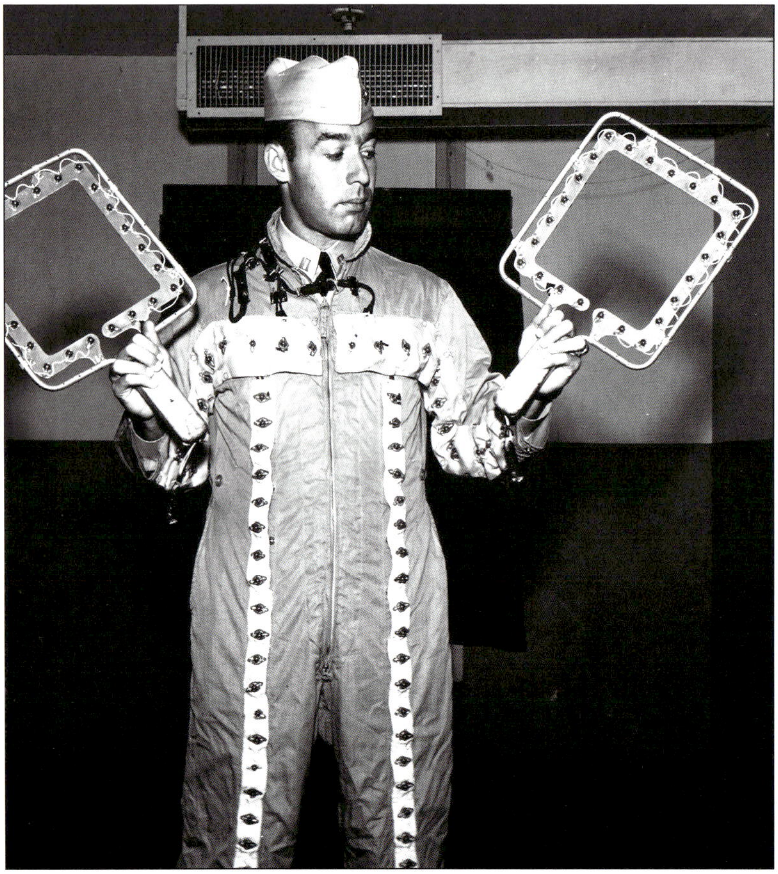

The small snaps are barely visible on the four cloth strips that hold the lights. The connecting plugs and the lights add to the overall weight. Ironically, refinements to the lighted suit came at the time when the mirror Optical Landing System (OLS) was coming into use. [USN via Thomason)

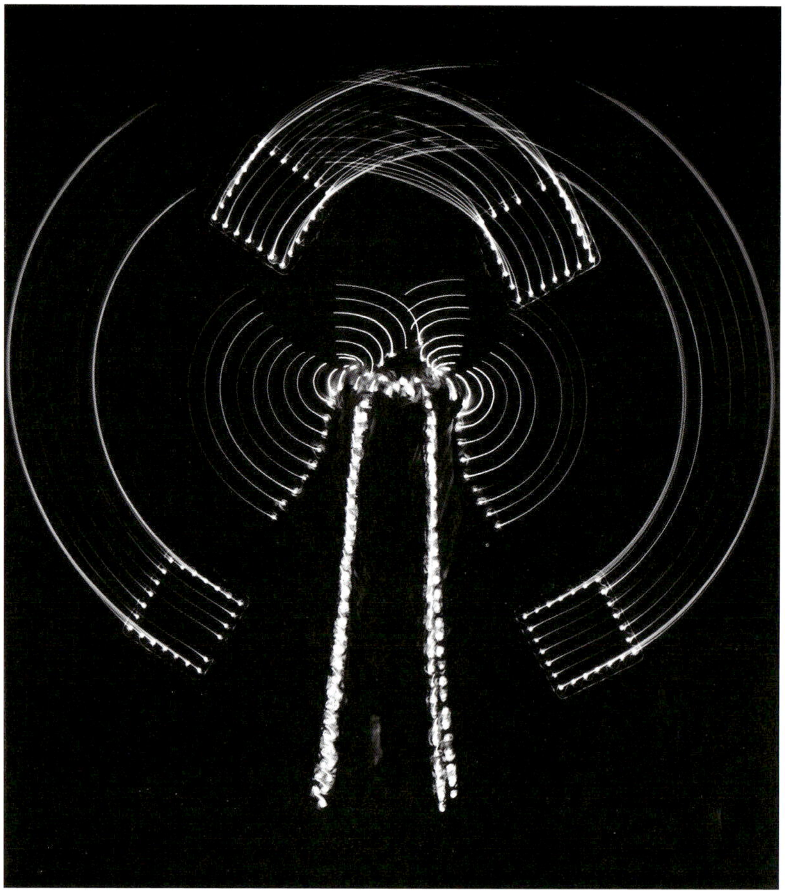

A demonstration of the wave-off signal by an electric-suited LSO. The camera exposure time makes the lights look streaked. (USN via Thomason)

An LSO wearing an electric suit at twilight. Pilots called landings at this time of day "Pinkies."

U.S. Paddles made an electric suit by rigging a series of small light bulbs onto the coverall arms and legs in the same pattern as the fluorescent fabric panels. A wired set of paddles went with the suit. A toggle switch on one of the paddles turned the lights on and off. There were electric plugs to connect the paddles to the sleeve, the right side to the left and to the battery. The lights were wired in parallel, requiring double wires. The paddles were significantly heavier. The suit was heavier and certainly awkward. With all the connections and wiring the risk of shock when salt spray or rain caused a short circuit was high; not a good thing in the middle of a recovery on a dark stormy night.

The electric suit remained in use until OLS revolutionized the LSOs job.

An A3D Skywarrior landing during the period when paddles and mirror, straight and angled deck were in use.

The VF-61 "Jolly Rogers" (with a skull and crossbones flag on the fuselage) F9F-8 Cougar trapping on USS Intrepid's *(CV-11) straight deck. Twelve wires are visible; #4 was caught. Open canopies for carrier takeoffs and landings were standard because early ejection seats needed altitude and speed to work. Until the A-4 and F-8, all USN tactical aircraft had canopies that slid back instead of flipping up. The yellow axial stripe that marked the deck run has numbers showing the distance remaining to the bow.*

Even a large ship is subject to wind and wave. USS Coral Sea *(CVA-43) has an F2H Banshee on the catapult. Like DLCOs launching Swordfish off CVEs, the cat officer will time the launch so that the bow comes up.*

Chapter 7

LANDING AT SEA REVOLUTION

A trapped F-8 Crusader. The nose strut is compressed, power is up, and the director is already running toward the cockpit.

The decade that included the Korean War saw two major innovations in aircraft carrier aviation: the angled deck and the mirror landing system. Another development was of an evolutionary nature: the remarkable steam catapult, which enabled the launching of much heavier aircraft.

Lessons learned during World War II and Korea resulted in programs for U.S. Navy aircraft carriers to improve their capabilities. The Royal Navy made similar changes to their carriers on a selective basis.

Same Carrier, Piston Era to Jet Age

Project 27A[1] was completed on nine USN carriers beginning with *Oriskany* (CV-34) in October 1947. More were planned, but by late 1953 Project 27C was in effect. Project 27A modified Essex class carriers with strengthened flight decks; H-8 improved hydraulic catapults, jet blast deflectors (JBD), and special weapons (nuclear bomb) facilities, along with increasing aircraft fuel storage. The 5-inch guns and turrets were removed, increasing deck space, and squadron ready rooms were moved below the hangar deck for added protection and comfort with an escalator rigged on the side of the hull to transport equipment-laden aircrew from the second deck to the flight deck. The program to update the three CVBs had a different designation but accomplished the same items.

Project 27C included all of the items of 27A and changed the appearance much more than removal of the gun turrets had: streamlined islands, "Hurricane" (no openings or breaks from bow to flight deck) bows, new C-11 steam catapults with prominent bridal catchers (called horns), Mk5 constant runout arresting gear, and the biggest change, angled decks. All of the angled-deck, Essex class conversions were commonly referred to as "27 Charlies."

The Angled Deck

Shifting the landing area diagonally had many advantages over the straight deck, wires, and barriers system. There was more deck available forward for an aircraft park and space for catapults. The

Essentially a Navy carrier-based version of the Air Force's fabled North American F-86 Sabre, the FJ Fury brought swept-wing operations to aircraft carriers in the mid-1950s. Shown here with North American test pilot R. A. "Bob" Hoover, the FJ was capable of transonic speeds, yet could land aboard Essex-class carriers. (Mike Machat Collection)

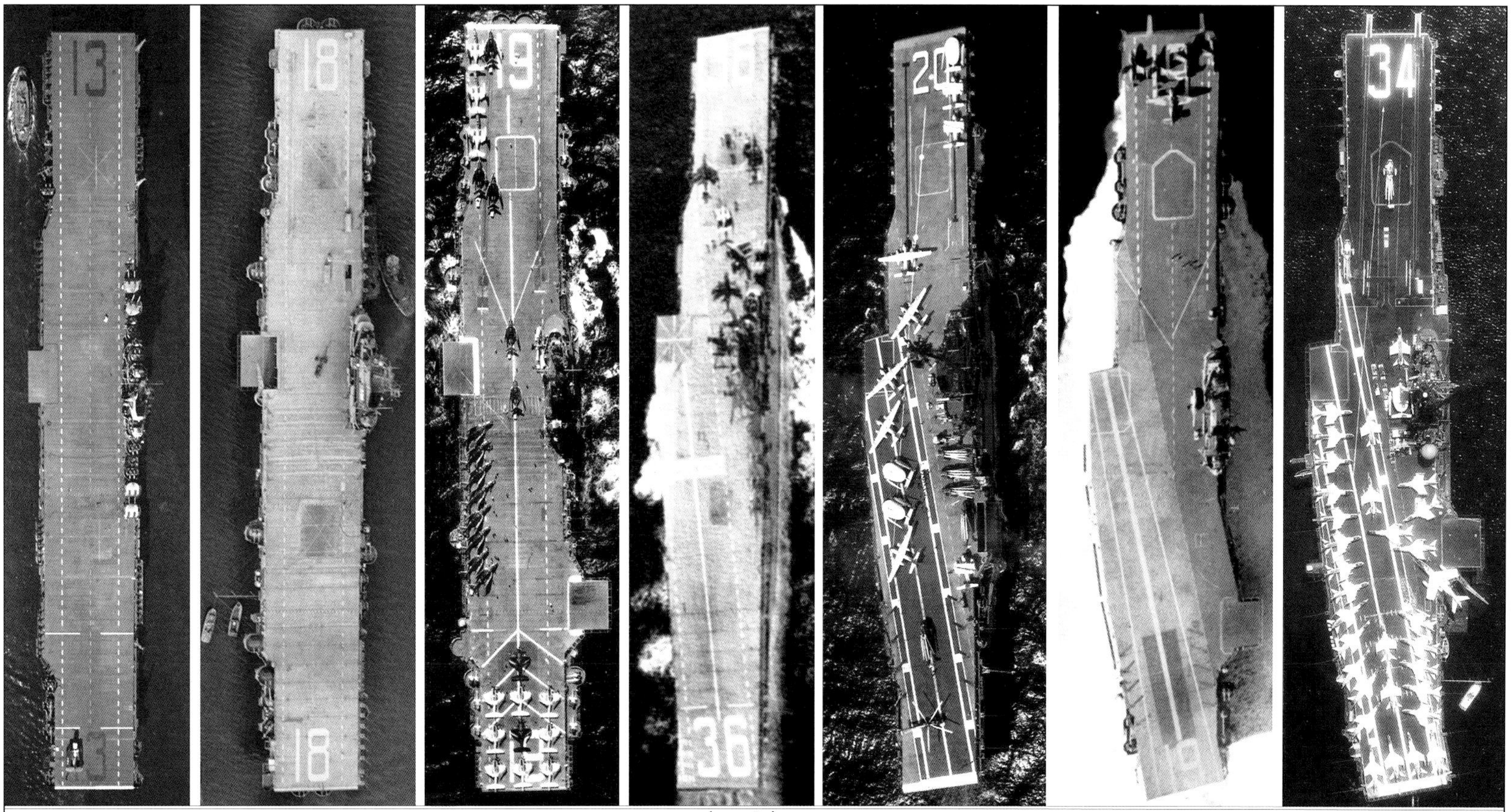

Modernizations of the U.S. Navy Essex class aircraft carriers (left to right):

- ***USS** **Franklin** **(CV-13), a "short hull" type as delivered 1944***
- ***USS** **Wasp** **(CV-18), after her SCB-27A conversion in late 1951: new hydraulic catapults, new island, removal of the deck guns, new bow***
- ***USS** **Hancock** **after her SCB-27C modernization, circa 1955: like SCB-27A but new steam catapults and relocation of the aft elevator to the deck edge***
- ***USS** **Antietam** **(CV-36) after the installation of an experimental angled deck, circa 1954***
- ***USS** **Bennington** **after SCB-125: enclosed hurricane bow, angled deck, and starboard deck-edge elevator***
- ***USS** **Hancock** **after SCB-125 in April 1957. Starboard deck-edge elevator is now located farther aft, forward elevator was enlarged***
- ***USS** **Oriskany** **(CV-34) received SCB-125A, 1974 starboard deck-edge elevator was located farther forward***

(United States Naval Institute Proceedings, *September 1975*)

overhang allowed the island to balance farther out on the other side, widening useful deck area. With nothing but open deck in front, landings became much safer; in case of the hook not catching a wire the airplane could take off again instead of being damaged by the barrier or, worse, going forward into the pack of planes parked forward. Offsetting the landing area was such an obvious improvement that it is a wonder the idea was not thought of much earlier. Before coming up with the three huge inventions (steam catapult, mirror, and angled deck) the Royal Navy expended much time, energy, and money on the dead-end Flexdeck.[2]

At a meeting deciding Flexdeck was not going to continue, the angle deck was proposed. By 1952, HMS *Triumph* had a 5-degree angled landing area painted on her deck and a series of test landings were flown. The idea crossed the Atlantic, and a few months later the experiment with a painted angle deck was done on USS *Midway* (CVB-41). The arresting gear remained in its axial position, so all the trial landings were touch and goes. USS *Antietam* (CV-36) came out of the shipyard with her landing area and arresting gear angled 10-1/2 degrees, and by April 1953 had proven its effectiveness with 15 types of aircraft, both prop and jet, making landings.

After working with the new deck configuration a pilot commented, "To an experienced tailhooker, landing a jet airplane on an angled deck was sheer bliss."

HMS *Ark Royal* was launched May 1950, and by February 1955 had an angle deck of 3½ degrees and a mirror. USS *Forrestal* was commissioned October 1955 and had been built from keel up with an angle deck at Newport News Shipbuilding. From then on all aircraft carriers had angled decks, either as conversions or original construction. USS *Lake Champlain* (CVS-39), the exception, remained active until 1966.

The angle deck introduced another factor. To get the best wind for landings the carrier simply headed into the wind. Now the ship handlers had to combine the ship's movement with the natural wind to have the component straight down the angle. This also had

USS* Antietam *as the Training Command CV (T-28 clearing the landing area). The mirror is on the right side, a location used before experience showed the port side was preferred.

HMS* Ark Royal *was completed in 1955 with a shallow angle. Three squadrons of Seahawks are lined up; Sea Venoms are on the bow and turboprop ASW Gannets are aft. (Ministry of Defence)

Well-known and compelling photo sequence shows one of the primary advantages of the angled deck. A Vought F8U-1 Crusader from VF-11, the Red Rippers, snapped a main gear strut while landing aboard the USS Franklin D. Roosevelt *(CVB-42) in 1962. The magnesium strut ignited and the jet rolled off the end of the angle deck, but the pilot ejected at the last second using his Martin Baker F5A ejection seat and survived the mishap uninjured. Martin Baker then used this photo sequence in a very successful ad campaign. (US Navy)*

the advantage of blowing the exhaust gasses from the ship's boilers off to the side. When there was no wind the carrier had to make its own. This meant that a right-hand crosswind made line-up more difficult. It also meant that stack gas would be in the groove.

Steam Catapult

Over the years several different methods of powering a catapult were tried. The first used a simple dropped weight and pulley system. A spinning flywheel was tried. Gunpowder and compressed air systems were common on ships to launch floatplanes throughout World War II. Hydraulic power proved the most efficient for multiple, successive launches, and was used on aircraft carriers. Because of the physics of operation, hydraulic catapults had an upper limit on the weight of the airplanes they could get to flying speed. All of the force is applied in the first instant, with little moderation. This causes severe strain on the airframe, and pilot. (From personal experience, a shot on a hydraulic cat at even moderate weights is like getting whacked in the back of your skull by a 2 x 4 oak board.)

Recognizing that jet aircraft needed more powerful accelerators (as they called catapults) the Royal Navy developed steam-powered catapults. The key was a self-sealing strip that allowed a piston to move the entire length of the cylinder without losing the pressure driving it. The German V-1 Buzz-bomb had used such a device for ground launches with steam from a *Dampferzeuger*, which generated steam chemically and not from heated boilers.

An experimental catapult was built on top of the deck of HMS *Perseus* in 1950. Tests began with wheeled dead-loads and then unmanned aircraft with clipped wings were fired into the sea. In final tests, all types flown by the FAA were launched with pilots. In all, more than 1,500 launches were performed. In January 1952 HMS *Perseus* went to the Naval Air Engineering Center in Philadelphia on the Delaware River to demonstrate the steam catapult to the United States Navy. Both British and American pilots flew the tests. An example of the power of the new catapult was the launch of an F3D Skyknight with 10 knots of tailwind; the H8 hydraulic catapult would have needed 28 knots headwind. The catapult was adapted as the USN C11 catapult by April.

USS *Hancock* had the first installed in June 1954 and the C-11 became standard for the Essex class 27C conversions and on the three CVBs. Capable of launching a 70,000-pound airplane, the steam cat gave the U.S. Navy what they needed for the atomic bombers.

The Mirror

The second revolutionary change to shipboard landings was invented by LCDR H. C. Goodhart of the Royal Navy. Goodhart realized that a narrow beam of light could be projected at a set angle to give pilots a visual reference. The story is, he conducted a simple experiment in his office using his secretary's pocket mirror and a flashlight.

The mirror on HMS* Albion*. A natty-looking DLCO in white coveralls and a beret is using a crank to adjust the mirror's height to get the hook-to-ramp clearance for the next airplane type to land. The Royal Navy practice was to place the DLCO with the optical landing system instead of on a separate platform. He is provided a safety net.

A Seahawk landing on a RN CV. The source lights are on the left edge of the flight deck. The plane guard helicopter, unlike USN practice, stays to the left of ship, inside the landing pattern.

He used her lipstick to draw two horizontal reference lines on the mirror and blocked the light to a single beam. Goodhart had her stand back until the dot of light was between the lines and walk forward, stooping to keep the light centered until her chin was on the desk.

In order to make the light bright enough to be seen at a distance, several automobile head lamps were put in a row shining toward the mirror. They were on a rheostat to vary the light's intensity for differing weather and visibility conditions. The mirror had a gentle concave shape so that the light could be seen in a plane about 30 degrees on both sides of the centerline and to focus the row of lights into a single bright disk. It did not take long before the pilots began calling the light the "Meatball."

A Lady Named Clara

Clara: radio call for "I do not see the ball." Short for "Clarify," as in, "Clarify why I am not seeing the meatball" or a possible TINS: an LSO in the early days of the optical landing system became frustrated with a certain pilot's apparent lack of attention to the ball. He called the pilot in and the pilot vigorously denied the charge that he was spotting the deck. The next day, to prove his point, the LSO covered the OLS ball with a pair of feminine under garments (exact type unknown) that he had borrowed from his ladylove whose name was . . . Clara.

Seems at any gathering of LSOs, Clara-related tales pop up. In mirror days, the first two aircraft trapped, but the third called "Clara." It turned out that the source lights were burned out. During a recovery with the MOVLAS (movable lights) on the starboard side, the first three F-14s in a flight trapped, but the fourth called "Clara." In this case, a helicopter had been parked in front of the lights all along. But the ultimate deck-spotter had to be the pilot who, after trapping at night, called the tower and told the air boss which deck edge lights were missing.

Putting It on the Deck

Another factor in determining the correct landing spot is hook-to-eye distance for airplane type. Because of fuselage length and attitude, at approach speed the vertical distance from the pilot's eyes to the point of the tailhook has to be corrected so that the hook hits the deck short of the target wire when the pilot is looking at a centered meatball. On mirror installations this was done by raising or lowering the entire assembly. The mirror was stabilized in pitch only by the ships gyros.

Before landings started the LSO performed a pole check using a mirror on the end of a 12-foot-long pole placed on a marked spot on the deck to check the angle. By looking straight up at the mirror he saw the same ball and reference lights the pilot did.

Red lights to signal a wave-off and green lights to replace the cut signal were operated by the LSO with buttons on a handle called the "pickle." The complete unit was officially an Optical Landing System, OLS.

Radios for the LSO had been a headset with a lip microphone and the transmit switch built into the handle of one of the paddles. Now that his hands were free, the LSO could use a radio handset instead of wearing a headset. Thus the classic pose of the modern LSO: handset held to an ear and the pickle in the other hand ready to signal wave-off or cut. When the deck was foul, not ready for a landing, the controlling LSO held the pickle up to show he was aware of deck status. In a well-trained air wing, on an experienced ship, clear decks frequently came only seconds before the aircraft would have been waved off.

Experience revealed problems with the mirror. Keeping the large glass surface clean was important and difficult. Flight deck debris, salt spray, and rain blew on it, blurring the image. A solution for the mirror getting dirty or foggy was to blow hot air across it. In rare circumstances, early or late in the day, the sun shone on the mirror, completely obscuring the ball.

Did the mirror mean no more LSOs? At first that was the thought. However, the landing accident rate shot up without LSOs and they were soon back on the platform. The job had changed; it was not as physical and pilots made their own corrections. The training function of Paddles did not change. They continued to grade each pass and critiqued them. Ashore, they waved innumerable FCLP passes before allowing pilots to go to sea. They kept records, looking for error trends. Their voice over the radio settled shaky pilots, giving guidance in emergencies or assistance in bad weather. Above all, LSOs remained responsible for that last second critical decision to allow a landing or give wave-off.

HMS *Illustrious* began sea trials with the new OLS in October 1952. A year later HMS *Indomitable* performed more extensive tests, which included both British and American pilots. Some of the U.S. Navy pilots had never before landed on a carrier at night. No airplanes were

The source light rack is in the foreground for this mirror installation at a naval air station. Except for FCLP, all flights returning from any mission will make carrier approaches.

LSOs' concentration is such that they tend to move toward approaching airplanes without thinking about it. Unlike paddles days, movement onto the deck is restrained by the length of pickle and handset cables.

damaged in more than 100 landings. The U.S. Navy took until August 1955 before the development squadron VX-3 did the first American mirror landings on USS *Bennington*. LCDR Bob Dosé[3] flew an FJ-3 Fury for two days of landings. On the second day LCDR H. C. MacKnight in an F9F-8 Cougar logged the first U.S. Navy night traps using the mirror OLS. OLS were put on all American carriers and at shore bases in 1956 and 1957. The accident rate in 1954 was 35 accidents for every 10,000 landings; by 1957 the rate had dropped to 9 per 10,000.

The introduction of OLS made both carrier navies adapt to something the other had been doing all along. The Americans began flying a descending approach from higher starts as the Royal Navy did, while the Brits had to react to seeing whether they were high or low U.S. Navy Paddles–style and make their own correction rather than being directed to fly up or fly down.

Typical Recovery

Landing on an aircraft carrier at sea is a complicated and difficult evolution. To explain how it is done, we'll go straight through an ideal day approach and landing with numbers at places requiring further comments, which are in the following paragraphs.

The formation of airplanes flies up the starboard side of the carrier at 600 feet with tailhooks down. Passing the bow the flight leader breaks left in a steep turn. The #2 pilot continues as he counts seconds to establish the interval. At 6 to 12 seconds he makes his break turn. #3 and #4 have also been counting. At the same interval as #2, #3 breaks and #4 resumes his count to turn downwind with the same interval between the airplanes. (1)

In the break the pilots use G, idle thrust, and speed brakes to slow down and lower wheels and flaps. When abeam the LSO platform they will be at approach speed with landing checks complete. From the abeam position each begins a turn of slightly more than 180 degrees across the wake and lined up on the centerline of the angle deck. (2) When the pilot sees the meatball he calls his identification, type of aircraft, that he is flying the OLS, and the fuel remaining in hundreds of pounds. "304, Skyhawk, ball, 1.8." (3)

On the platform the spotter checks the airplane wheels, flaps, and hook and calls, "All down. Foul deck! Gear set for A-4." The LSO repeats, "All down. Foul deck," and raises his arm with the pickle. At the pilot's call, the LSO replies, "Roger ball." When the preceding plane clears the landing area a large indicator light goes from red to green. The phone talker hollers, "Clear deck!" Paddles drops his arm and repeats, "Clear deck."

The pilot uses changes of pitch and power to keep the ball centered and stay on speed (4) and small banks to stay lined up on the centerline. At touchdown, the pilot goes to full power and puts the speed brakes in preparation for a bolter. (5) A good engagement throws him against his shoulder harness. As the airplane stops he pulls the throttles back to idle. The tension on the CDP pulls the airplane backward. The wire goes slack and the airplane rolls past it, freeing the hook. The director signals "apply brakes" to stop the roll and then signals "come ahead" to taxi clear of the landing area. In the cockpit the pilot puts on a burst of power while raising the hook and flaps, and starts the wings folding. (6)

The LSO has been watching the landing all the way. When the aircraft has trapped, or boltered, he tells the writer that the wire caught, a grade for the pass, and any comments. He must do this quickly; the next aircraft is about to call the ball. Some wit observed that LSOs have an attention span of only 20 seconds; 10 seconds to watch the pass and 10 seconds for comments. A good recovery will land 20 aircraft in less than 10 minutes. (7)

Even on a clear day with a steady deck this LSO has gone as far on deck as the handset cord let him. Complete concentration from both pilot and Paddles is vital. Grumman A-6 Intruder has wingtip speed brakes extended.

(1) Away from the restrictions over land the break at the carrier is a chance to show off. Speeds may be more than 500 knots, the turn made at 80 degrees bank, and 6 or more Gs needed to slow down. A favorite expression is "Ya gotta look good at the boat." Looking good applies to not just the break but also to the interval downwind (the same for all aircraft) and the landing itself.

(2) Good pilots watch the signs of wind: wave appearance, size, and direction plus the carrier's wake size, to judge when to start their turn.

(3) Zip Lip means radios will not be used except for emergencies. The reason is for tactical security in case the enemy is monitoring the frequency. To remain proficient, the U.S. Navy makes Zip Lip a normal procedure. Pilots do not call the ball unless something is wrong with the aircraft or fuel is low. The LSO signals he has control by flashing the green cut lights for a couple of seconds. An entire launch and recovery cycle can be done without a word said on the radio.

(4) Naval pilots are inculcated from the start with the idea that pitch equals speed and power equals altitude. To fly the ball, the pilot uses the stick to stay on speed while moving the throttles to correct for high or low. The two are, of course, interrelated in that adjusting one requires adjusting the other.

This is the camera's view in close. The pilot does not see the ramp and only notices the LSO in his peripheral vision. His scan is on the centerline and meatball (which is slightly low).

In the early 1960s angle-of-attack indicators began appearing in carrier aircraft. These eliminated the need to guess a correct airspeed based on weight, underwing stores, or odd configurations. By sensing the angle air is flowing over the wing an optimum speed can be held. The first indicators were dials with a needle in the instrument panel. These required a split scan with the pilot's eyes moving from inside to outside and back. An angle-of-attack indexer with three symbols for fast, on-speed, and slow was mounted on top of the glareshield or on a canopy bow to keep it in the same visual area of the ball and reduce the pilot's scan.

(5) Jets and turboprops have slow acceleration times; by going to full power at touchdown the airplane is ready to fly off the angle in the event of a bolter, whether caused by the hook not catching a wire, a "hook skip," or the airplane flying past the last wire. LSOs will call "Bolter, bolter!" when they see this happen.

For the years between the introduction of the mirror and the last piston-powered airplanes at the ship the technique was to fly the same pattern as the jets and fly the ball until the LSO signaled cut with the green lights and/or by radio. The pilot then chopped the power to idle, looked at the deck, and timed his flare to touch down on all three wheels.

(6) The minutes after landing are the busiest of a flight. Here is what you would be doing in a typical airplane, in this case an RA-5C Vigilante:

An RA-5C Vigilante at the moment of touchdown on USS Kittyhawk (note the smoke coming off the tires as they spin up). A C-1 COD is in the foreground. Another Vigilante, two F-4 Phantoms, and yellow tugs are parked on Elevator #4 forward of the LSO platform. The white and yellow deck markings are faded and covered with grime late in the carrier's deployment to the Tonkin Gulf.

AOA, Indexers, Approach Lights

An attempt at a fairly simple external indicator of aircraft attitude was attempted as far back as the 1940s. The system was nothing more than a light with three colors of glass plate in front. Mounted in the wing leading edge, the box showed a different color, green/amber/red, depending on the angle one was looking at the light. The setting of the light was adjustable on the ground and was calibrated by sighting against angled stripes painted on the vertical fin. The drawback was that the color of the light was the actual attitude of the aircraft only when on the glide slope. The system was an improvement over no external speed indication at all for night approaches.

Gerry O'Rouke's description of night FCLP for F3D Skyknights: "As the low, moving lights came around, settling even lower toward the trees, the dim silhouette of the airplane had almost to be imagined. It was there, outlined by the wing and fuselage lights, almost shrouded by the multicolored approach light that told the LSO what the plane's flight attitude was. Too slow was red, on speed was amber, too fast was green. The sound of the engines mounted, and small changes in throttle settings were detectable through ever-so-slight changes of pitch in their whine."[4]

The invention of a true Angle of Attack (AOA) sensor, not simply an attitude indicator, gave pilots a way to read the wing's performance. [5] A small vane or probe on the nose gave a reading on a gage. The system was refined by placing a three-symbol (fast/on speed/slow) indicator in the pilot's outside scan. [6] The same indications were shown to the LSO as three colored lights variously mounted in the port wing leading edge or on the nose landing gear. Unexplained is the change in meaning of the colors; red became fast, amber/yellow remained on speed, and green now meant slow (perhaps a traffic light analogy? Green means go faster, red means slow down). Many Paddle's TINS begins, "He was low and going green." On some aircraft two lights could remain lit while changing, e.g., green and amber looked white, a little slow.

A Crusader pilot described the transition to the new gadget like this: "We had a whole squadron full of F8U-2Ns (freshly painted) awaiting us, with AoAs. For initial CarQuals (day and night) in *Independence*, 138 to 140 knots was pretty much the (airspeed) gauge. Only during many bounce periods preceding our 1960 Med deployment did we shake hands for a tentative look-see arrangement with the AoA. And never was such a piece of gear so rigorously double-checked against our airspeed indicators. Seems funny now, but change away from what's kept one alive so far isn't a casual affair. Ah, the memories. I can almost smell the cockpits and feel that drop of perspiration running down my neck."[7]

As soon as you feel a solid tug on your shoulders (even with the harness locked your torso lurches forward a couple of inches), pull the twin throttles back to idle and thumb the speed brakes in. Push and hold the nosewheel steering button on the control stick so that the nosewheel stays straight during pull back. Quickly reach beside the throttles and move the handle to start the flaps up. Look to the right for the director in a yellow shirt. When he clinches his fists, step on the brakes to stop moving backward. Switch hands so that your left thumb is holding the NWS (Nose Wheel Steering) button down and reach over to the right forward console for the tailhook handle. The director swings a thumb up into the palm of his other hand. Raise your hook by twisting the handle and pushing it in. Switch hands without letting go of the NWS button so that you can push the throttles up to start taxiing forward.

Once moving forward, push the throttles back to idle, steer with your feet on the brake pedals as needed. The director crosses his arms across his chest. Switch hands again and reach all the way back on the right and put your hand on the wing-shaped handle. Don't take your eyes off the taxi director! Twist it to unlock and then pull up hard to fold your wings. (There's a switch on that panel, which allows the tail to fold as well.) Switch hands for what should be the final time to hold the NWS and move the throttles as needed to get to a parking spot. Frequently, you are the next to last to land, so after your J-79 engines are shut down you remain in the cockpit while a tow bar and tug are hooked up to push you into the Vigi's usual spot aft of the island while you act as brake rider.

(7) The writer is usually another LSO, especially a trainee. The sailors who were spotters and phone talkers picked up the shorthand and could write if necessary.

Paperwork

Naval aviation tends toward understatement. A night recovery of 28 airplanes in bad weather that went smoothly got a simple, "Good work, guys," call from the air boss over the 5MC flight deck speakers. A perfect landing is merely "OK." Despite movie images, braggarts are uncommon and harassed by their peers when they do pop up; yet recognition for a job well done is important. For landing at sea there is the Greenie Board and Golden Hook.

Landing Grades

A normal, well-flown pass to a trap is "OK." A pass with errors but acceptable performance is "Fair," (OK). A poor pass, but not bad enough to warrant a wave-off is a "No-grade." A wave-off, WO, is considered bad for grading purposes. However, because there are reasons for a wave-off besides pilot technique, there are foul-deck wave-offs (FDWO), which are usually "freebies," and own-wave-offs (OWO), which may be good or bad depending on the reason. Bolters (the symbol is a "B" with an arrow through it) are bad unless caused by a hook skip (the symbol is an arc over the wire number). Another negative is a cut pass, a dangerous maneuver past the wave-off window. Outstanding passes, especially under poor weather conditions, at night, with aircraft malfunctions or battle-damage or combinations thereof, are "OK underlined," (OK). To quantify the grades a numerical value is assigned to make recordkeeping and computing averages, individual and squadron, possible.

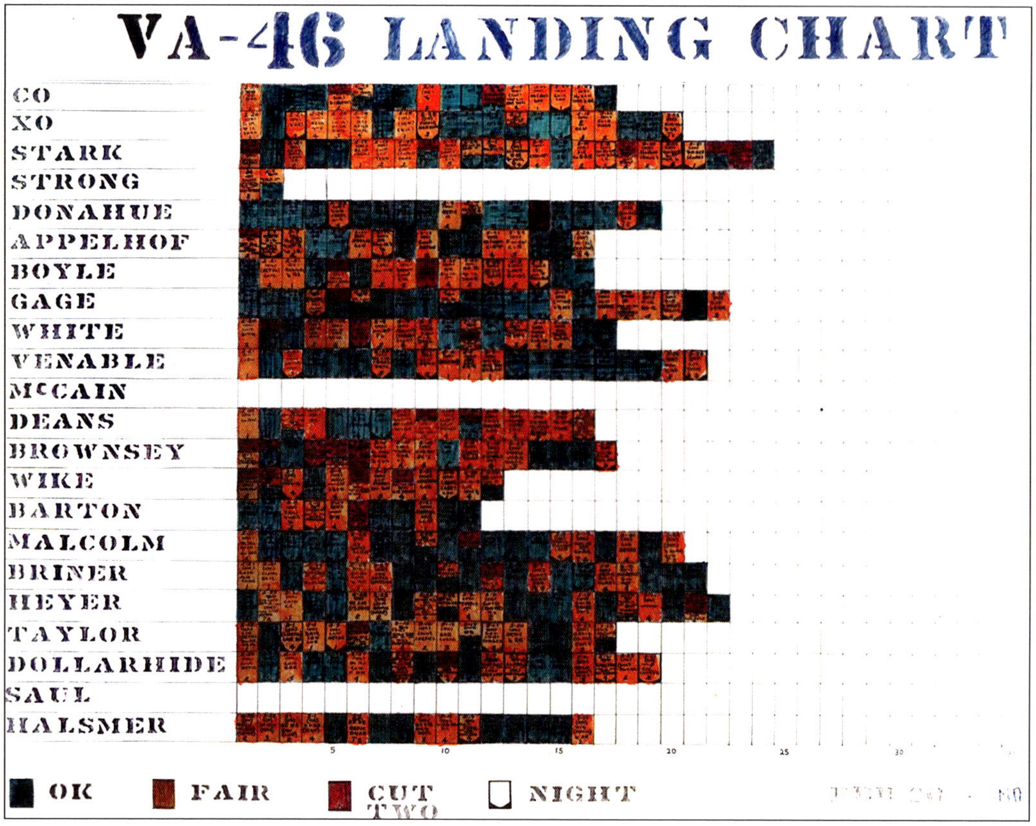

VA-46 flew A-4E Skyhawks in 1967. The names are in order of seniority. Each square includes remarks as well as date and wire, making it a bit cluttered. (Dollarhide)

Paddles Shorthand

In order to debrief (critique) the pilots after landing, LSO's comments are written in a book. Because flight deck action is rapid, a special shorthand developed over the years. After the aircraft number is a grade, and the wire, if a trap. The landing approach is divided into sections beginning with the start (X), to in-the-groove (IG), in-close (IC), and at-the-ramp (AR) The ramp is the portion of the flight deck that slants down to the fantail. Hitting the ramp is very bad. L and R are obviously Left and Right of the centerline (Low is Lo). F means Fast; Slo is Slow because S means Settle (picture a fat hen getting in her nest). P is Power. In addition to these is a batch of more exotic terms. To further refine the terms: an underline emphasizes it, a parentheses means a little. Hence the grades in diminishing order: OK, OK, (OK), Bolter (B with an arrow though it).

A circle around a comment means the pilot was slow to respond to a call. A box indicates no response. These are usually for LU (line up), P (power), and Att (attitude). A HOOK in a box means the pilot forgot to lower the tailhook and owes the LSO a bottle. Two crew aircraft means two bottles as it is a checklist item.

The lens is set so that if a pilot does everything correctly, his hook will catch 3# wire. Therefore, (OK) 2 HiX SIG (FAR): "A fair pass to the two wire, high start to settle in the groove, a little fast at the ramp," is not as good as the ultimate, OK 3.

LSO NATOPS manuals include lists of standard symbols. As the manual itself grew in size and scope, so too did the symbology. The 1964 manual has 47 descriptive symbols, which 40 years later grew to 73 (including NERD: Not Enough Rate of Descent). Grades went from 5 to 11 and added more symbols for ACLS. The 1964 manual retained abbreviations left from the days of paddle passes: CU (cocked up), EG (eased gun), HO (hold off), TAR (turn at ramp), and DFD (dive for deck).

Platform Frivolity

Inevitably, local abbreviations, usually humorous, were created:

- DNKHS = Damn Near Killed Himself
- DNKUA = Damn Near Killed Us All
- HNIWHD = Had No Idea What He Was Doing
- TTH = Talk To Him (chew him out in the ready room)
- HUA = Head Up His Ass
- DOLF= Dog On Linoleum Floor (overshoot start, coming back all the way)
- EA = Elephant's Ass (high and stinky)
- AFU = All "Fouled" Up (surprisingly, AFU is on the standard list)
- FUBAR = "Fouled" Up Beyond All Belief
- OGSH = Only God Saved Him

Greenie Boards

Who made the first board displaying traps and their quality is unknown, but it was such a good device that the idea of the greenie board spread rapidly from Paddles to Paddles. The closest to formal recognition was an article in the U.S. Navy's aviation safety magazine *Approach*.

Having your landing talent, or lack thereof, on public display can be an exercise in leadership. "I think I told you about my XO when we started getting ready for the boat. He insisted on having a greenie board set up in the ready room the very first day. He announced this at an all-officers meeting and I raised my hand and suggested we get a few bounces in before we did that, because none of us had been to the boat since the training command. The XO said, 'What's the matter, afraid of getting embarrassed?' I looked him right in the eye and said, 'No Sir. I wasn't thinking about me.'"[8]

Squadron LSOs were expected to be among the best and usually were, although there were accusations of a Paddles Protective Society influencing grades. "I had a bad tailhook snubber on my Vigilante one fine day and after four hook-skip bolters, a tanking, and three more bolters was sent to DaNang, where the problem was fixed, and we returned to *Kittyhawk*. Next day, as squadron LSO, I was carefully drawing many lines in the small square on the greenie board when my CO looked over my shoulder and said, 'There's no such thing as eight OK passes for one trap! You LSOs are all in cahoots.'"[9]

Call signs have replaced last names on this board of an F/A-18 Hornet squadron. Unknown is whether the board was set up for the requested picture or if the pilots are that good. The dollar bills are "lucky bucks," which are purchased from the LSO party fund for $5, or more, at the beginning of a line period. They allow you to "buy" an upgrade to an OK after a no grade or fair landing (you can't upgrade a cut, bolter, or WO).

Greenie boards also kept track of flights. In a good squadron, pilots fought for traps. A look at the board kept anyone from getting too far ahead of his peers. Another exercise in leadership: Senior officers who pulled rank to bag traps were not popular with junior officers.

Why greenie? The makeup of a board is up to the squadron LSO(s). Sometimes a format was passed down. Thanks to the article in *Approach*, the basics were decided: a series of squares, each representing a trap. If there were multiple passes to get the trap, the square was divided up. The date and wire were shown. A black outline or black corners showed it was at night. Yellow was a fair (OK) pass; white or brown (the color of dog-poo) a no-grade; red, a cut or wave-off; and the sought-after OK was green. Hence, greenie board. A pilot's goal was to have his line be all green. A squadron's goal was to have the entire board OK green.

Early boards were made from paper or cardboard that the LSO drew on and colored with crayons or markers. Permanent boards with pins to hold colored disks (one squadron used beer bottle tops) became normal. Paddles updating the greenie board in the ready room always drew a crowd, . . . and commentary.

Trends

Although greenie boards are a form of recognition, the grades and comments have a more serious purpose. The LSO NATOPS manual states, "Squadron LSOs shall keep current trend data on all squadron pilots . . . at a minimum, Squadron LSOs shall debrief pilot trends prior to each at-sea period during work-ups. On extended deployments, trend debriefs shall be done at least monthly. Pilots shall initial and date the trend sheet each time they are reviewed."

On the platform the writer notes the comments from the controlling LSO in a book. (A handheld PD was tried, but the data could not be entered fast enough.) The book is then taken to squadron ready rooms for individual debriefs before being passed to each squadron LSO who transcribes the data into his own pilot-by-pilot records. Today the data is computerized in an Automated Performance Assessment and Readiness Training System (APARTS). Either way of transcribing the data is not a Paddles' favorite job. From this information, pilot trends are derived, giving the LSO a teaching tool and alerting him to any unsafe habits.

Awards

Recognition is given in the form of an embroidered patch worn on a flight jacket for 100 landings on a particular aircraft carrier, making the aircrew a Centurion. Although becoming a Centurion is an honor, the recognition that means the most is the Top Hook (sometimes called the Golden Hook) Award given at the end of a line or operating period. A Top Hook plaque goes to the individual pilot who has the best landing grade average in the air wing. Another Top Hook award is given to the squadron with the best landing grade average. Competition is fierce.[10]

Other Navies

With the value of the aircraft carrier proven, a handful of other countries got into the business, and with few exceptions, Great Britain provided the ships. Of the ten Colossus class light carriers completed in 1945 and 1946, four went to other nations. Six Majestic class light carriers were authorized and begun during World War II. Five were completed for countries other than the UK (the sixth was scrapped mid-construction).

Anticipating a future independent Canadian Navy, two CVEs during the war were fully manned by Canadians: HMS *Puncher* and HMS *Nabob*. HMS *Warrior* (Colossus class) was loaned to Canada from 1946 to 1948 as HMCS *Warrior*. In 1958 she became *Independencia* in the Argentine navy. Majestic class carriers *Magnificent* and *Powerful* were completed for Canada. *Powerful* was renamed HMCS *Bonaventure* while *Magnificent* kept her name with "HMCS" (Her Majesty's Canadian Ship) added. The pair were fondly known as "Bonnie" and "Maggie" and served until 1957.

Vengeance (Colossus class) was loaned to Australia in 1954 until being sold to Brazil in 1957 where she became *Minais Gerais*. Two Majestic class aircraft carriers also went to Australia: *Terrible* became HMAS *Sydney* in 1948 and *Majestic* the *Melbourne* in 1955. *Sydney*

HMS* Venerable *was known in the Dutch Navy as* Karl Doorman *before going to Argentina in 1968, where she became* 25 de Mayo. *Former USN Skyhawks are on deck.

Foch *and* Clemenceau *rotated on station during the civil war in Lebanon, 1983–1984, with airwings composed of Crusaders, Super-Étendards, Alizés, and helicopters. The triangular pattern is another method of assisting pilots' perception.*

Sao Paulo ***continues in Brazilian service, although the carrier spends much time in the shipyard for repair and maintenance.***

was decommissioned in 1976 and *Melbourne* in 1983. *Sydney* served in Korea.

Two MACShips, *Gadila* and *Macoma,* were operated by Dutch crews under British control during World War II. The Netherlands then briefly operated the CVE HMS *Nairana* 1946–1948 as *Karl Doorman*[11] In 1949 HMS *Venerable* went to Holland and continued the *Karl Doorman* name until 1968, when she joined the Argentine navy as *25 de Mayo.*[12]

25 de Mayo came close to seeing combat during the Malvinas/Falkland brouhaha. She covered the landings and occupation of the islands, but when hostilities began in May 1982 there was not enough WOD to launch her heavily loaded Skyhawks. When the Argentine cruiser *Belgrano* was sunk by torpedo, *25 de Mayo* retreated into port. There was no carrier war in the Falklands.[13]

Lead ship of the class, HMS *Colossus* was completed for France as *Arromanches* in 1951. Two slightly smaller American carriers were transferred as well: USS *Langley* (CVL-27) in 1951 and USS *Belleau Wood* (CVL-24) in 1953. *Langley* became *Lafayette* and *Belleau Wood* translated back to the original battle, *Bois Belleau.* HMS *Biter* became *Dixmude* and was the only escort carrier of the post-war transfers that continued to operate as an aircraft carrier. *Dixmude, Lafayette,* and *Arromanches* all saw combat in Indochina with *Lafayette* and *Arromanches* in the four-day scrap at Suez as well. *Lafayette* was scrapped in 1963, *Bois Belleau* in 1960. *Arromanches* converted to a commando ship in 1968 before decommissioning in 1974. *Dixmude/Biter*'s checkered career lasted 1942–1966.[14]

France built two aircraft carriers of her own, *Clemenceau* (R98) and *Foch* (R99); both were 32,800 tons and 870 feet long. The landing area angled 8 degrees with two catapults and two elevators. *Clemenceau* was active 1961–1997 and *Foch* 1963–2000, then was sold to Brazil and renamed *São Paulo.*

India purchased the incomplete *Hercules* and had her completed in Belfast, Northern Ireland, as *Vikrant* in 1961. *Vikrant* played a significant role during the Indo-Pakistani War of 1971. She had several updates and was able to operate Harriers with a ski-jump. Retired in 1997, *Vikrant* became a museum ship until 2012.

The "Ouija Board" helps keep track of airplanes and equipment on the flight and hangar decks (there is a scale drawing underneath). The cutouts of airplanes, with and without wings folded, are to scale and moved about to show actual location on deck.

Chapter 8

BIG BOMBS, SUPERSONICS AND SUPER CARRIERS

1956–1964

Addressing the need for a large onboard carrier delivery aircraft, the Grumman C-2 Greyhound can carry passengers, cargo, or a combination of the two. Passenger seats are mounted facing the rear for the shock of arrested landings. The ride isn't the most pleasant but for many people it leads to their first trap.

Aircraft carriers kept getting bigger. The carrier-versus-carrier battles of World War II showed the need to be able to strike the enemy and defend yourself simultaneously. Attacks against well defended targets required a mix of airplane types and many of them to destroy a target. The solution was multiple carriers acting as a unit. However, there were disadvantages compared to a large single carrier. A large aircraft carrier could carry and operate many more aircraft. The advent of the angle deck made simultaneous landings and launches possible. Both the U.S. and UK had planned on making carriers larger than any before the end of the war. Gibraltar class CVBs of 45,000 tons were planned for the Royal Navy in 1942, but deferred by 1945 before any steel was cut. In the United States, CV-58, to be named USS *United States*, had its keel laid in 1949. That year was a time of budget cuts and acrimonious debate over the role of the navy. Construction was abruptly stopped and the project was canceled. The ship would have been more than 1,000 feet long with a flush deck and weighed 65,000 tons.

The U.S. Navy's largest and smallest attack aircraft aboard USS* Saratoga *(CVA-60). The Douglas A4D-2 Skyhawk on the catapult has a inert Mk7 nuclear bomb as well as two 300-gallon wing fuel tanks. The Douglas A3D Skywarrior behind carried its bomb in an internal bomb bay. The catapult officer is midway to touching the deck in the signal to fire the cat.

Dawn of the Super Carrier

Carrier use during the Korean War and the established role of carrier-launched nuclear weapons justified the building of a super carrier, a quantum leap over the carriers that fought in World War II and Korea. USS *Forrestal* (CVA-59) had her keel laid in 1952 and was commissioned in 1955. Appropriately named for James V. Forrestal, who had been a naval aviator in World War I and undersecretary, then secretary of the navy, was instrumental in building its size. When the U.S. services were unified, Forrestal continued the fight for battle groups centered on carriers and opposed the Truman administration's severe cutbacks.

England built more carriers, but none larger than HMS *Eagle* (1951) and HMS *Ark Royal* (1955) at 804 feet and 36,800 tons.

The *Forrestal* was a big leap in aircraft carrier size. About a fifth longer than a 27C Essex conversion, 1,048 feet versus 872 feet, the length does not tell the whole story: Her displacement was more than double, 60,100 tons vs. 27,100. More important for flight operations, *Forrestal*'s flight deck had more than double the area, 237 percent. This increase enabled the designers to have three deck edge elevators on the starboard side, which could be used while landing aircraft. (Aircraft had to wait for a break in the landings to be able to taxi to the bow from the two elevators behind the island. On the follow-on Kittyhawk class the position of the island and one of the elevators was swapped so that two elevators could feed the starboard bow catapult at all times. The port-side elevator was also moved aft from forward on the angle to a position that did not foul the deck when lowered.)

Although the touch-down spot for a trap was the same and the length of the CDPs and their spacing was standard, having the wires farther down the deck meant the hook-to-ramp clearance was higher, and therefore safer. More deck forward of the wires made getting airborne after a bolter safer, and the extra clear areas on both sides lent a measure of reassurance to pilots. The postage stamp analogy for carrier size was no longer quite as correct. With few exceptions, until the 1970s all pilots had their first landings on 27C ships and reactions to landing on *Forrestal* and her later sisters were favorable.

I had almost 200 traps, all on 27C carriers, when I was an instructor in the A-4 Skyhawk RAG. During CarQuals on *Kittyhawk*

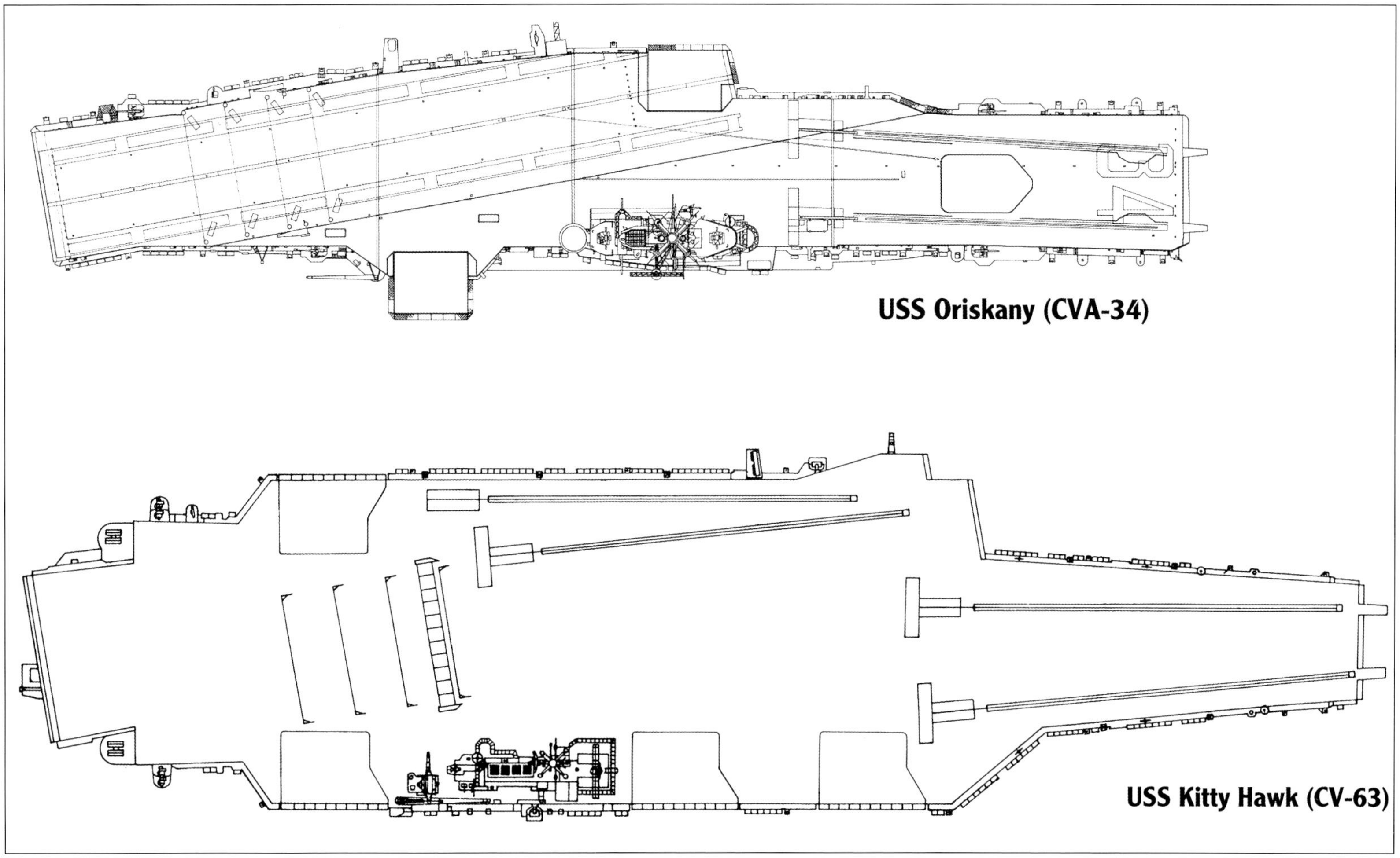

Scale drawings of Essex class 27 Charlie and USS Kitty Hawk. *Overall length is not as significant as the area of the flight deck. With the arrival of the Forrestal class the definition of "big deck" changed.*

(CVA-63) word came down to our temporary ready room that the deck was available and there were no replacement pilots ready to go. So four of us lieutenant instructors fired up A-4Es and went off to bag traps to add to the ship's total (competitive captains loved that). On my first pass I was flying my usual on speed, on center line, centered ball approach when there was all this gray deck below me. Odd, never saw that before. Pulled off some power to land. My grade? TT1 NEPAR (no grade, taxi to 1# wire, not enough power at ramp underlined!)[1]

The platform was no longer close to the stern but moved so that the LSOs would be in the same position relative to the arresting gear. It was also farther from the centerline. Airplanes could be parked just forward of the platform, which in some cases meant bending down to watch the complete runout or bolter. (A-7 Corsairs with engines running were aggravating because their exhaust burned the eyes. Who would trust a teary Paddles?)

A challenge for LSOs of the period was the number of aircraft types he could expect to see. A deployed air wing could have as many as eight types of aircraft, each with unique characteristics. Developments in addition to the angled deck that slashed the U.S. Navy's accident rate included a Navy Safety Center and NATOPS program (Naval Air Training and Operating Procedures Standardization). No longer did individual squadrons do as they thought best. The initiatives met with some initial resistance: One squadron was reputed to have been burning the new NATOPS manuals on the fantail as the carrier left port. But the accident rate dropped dramatically. After all the aircraft types had a manual, the ships and LSOs got them.

Examples of air wing composition:

- *Forrestal* in 1955: full squadrons of FJ-4 Furies, F2H Banshees, AJ Savages, and AD Skyraiders plus detachments of EW Skyraiders, ECM Skyraiders, photo Banshees, and the ship's TF COD
- *Midway* in 1958: full squadrons of F3H Demons, F8U Crusaders, FJ-4 Furies, A3D Skywarriors, AD Skyraiders, plus detachments of WF Trackers, ECM Skyraiders, photo Crusaders, and the ship's TF COD

- *Saratoga* in 1958: full squadrons of F3H Demons, F8U Crusaders, A4D Skyhawks, AD Skyraiders, A3D Skywarriors, plus detachments of F9F-8P photo Cougars, WF Trackers, and the ship's TF COD
- *Enterprise* in 1964 Operation Sea Orbit (around the world cruise): full squadrons of F-8 Crusaders, F-4B Phantoms, A-4C Skyhawks, A-1H Skyraiders, A-5A Vigilantes, plus detachments of E-1Trackers, RF-8 photo Crusaders, and several C-1A CODs

The first LSO manual was issued in October 1963. This revision from one year later has 18 pages. (By comparison, the 2004 LSO NATOPS edition was 89 pages.) The latest edition is digital. Toby Tobin's notes on the back of the photograph that was used read, "For 1300 Yen in 1950, you too could have a tiger on your suit! As suits wore out, 'Old Tiger' was cut off and the lads in the para-loft would sew him on a new suit."

Douglas Skyrays, known as "Fords" from their F4D designation, held both speed and time-to-climb records. Pilots said landing approaches in F4Ds were like sitting on a beach ball.

Don't Know Where to Run

LSO CDR John "Pirate" Nichols had this tale in "The Catwalk" column of *The Hook*:[2] "It was a moonlit night in 1962 as *Shangri-La* (CVA-38) prepared for the 2200 launch. My squadron, the VF-62 Boomerangs (F8U-1Es), and VF-13 Aggressors (F4D-1s) composed the fighter contingent of Air Group 10. The remainder of the air group consisted of VA-46 and -106 (A4D-2s) and VA-176 with its formidable old AD-6 Spads.

"About 10 minutes before launch my trainee and I groped our way aft to the platform, which was attended by ten LSOs, of which six were trainees. Airborne were ten A4Ds, six Spads, four Crusaders, and four Skyrays. The cats fired, the ADs made their deck runs, and silence returned to the flight deck.

"The recovery went smoothly. All four F8Us got aboard on the first pass! As did the Skyhawks. The first three F4Ds trapped as the Spads entered the pattern, and the last Ford called 'ball' with 1,600 pounds of fuel. The approach began badly lined up right and degenerated to low in the groove, settling at the ramp. Wave-off. The Spads delayed their break and the Skyray got an immediate turn downwind. He reported abeam with a fuel state of 1.2 as the ADs began breaking up for landing. His next pass started high in the groove; low, low underlined! 'Burner, burner, wave-off!' The four Spads came aboard and the helo hovering off the starboard side moved closer to the ship.

"Meanwhile, the F4D called the ball on his third pass with 800 pounds and the squadron LSO began putting soothing words on him. The approach was erratic, ending high at the ramp; bolter. On the pilot's next abeam position he had 300 pounds remaining. There had been some debate between the captain and the air boss about using the barricade, but the time had passed for that. The LSO was now faced with a situation we all detested: a desperate pilot in the 'go-for-it' mode.

"Our intrepid Skyray pilot called the ball with a slight tremor in his voice, state zero. Twelve LSOs were certain that under these circumstances the pilot's natural instinct was to have a go at all four wires, so it was certain the controlling LSO was safety-wired to the 'pilot go-for-it mode.' The approach was perfect until two seconds from the ramp, at which time our fearless aviator sucked off a handful of power and dropped the nose. Simultaneously the LSO screamed, the air boss screamed, and the pilot probably screamed while pushing the throttle against the afterburner stops. The burner lit as the hook began a contest with the ramp. The ramp won and the hook point fell into the sea.

Now, the F4D was a spectacular-climbing aircraft in afterburner, especially with only about 50 pounds of fuel. The aircraft climbed straight up above the flight deck. The trainees who had jumped in the net scrambled out just in time to see the flame of the afterburner begin to dim then flicker and go out. The roar of the engine ceased. Again silence returned to the deck. The only sound was the sea rushing past the hull and the curses of the controlling LSO.

The first supersonic Douglas-built Navy jet was the bat-wing F4D-1 Skyray point-defense interceptor. Holder of numerous speed and time-to-climb records, the "Ford" (for F4D) was a unique aircraft for LSOs. (Douglas Aircraft Co.)

Runaway Engine

An honest airplane to bring aboard although back in late winter of 1960, a "Guppy" Skyraider (the radar version with pilot and three crewmembers along for the ride) gave an ensign pilot all that he could handle. The *Randolph* (CVS-15) was conducting around-the-clock anti-sub operations and this guy was finally landing after four and a half hours droning around the night sky. His first approach was OK, but he was waved off for a foul deck. As he set climb power that massive R-3350 motor banged, shot flames out the exhaust, and went to 65 inches of manifold pressure; 57 inches was the absolute limit. Trying to keep it under control, the pilot shot up to 5,000 feet. He'd lost his throttle control. Holding overhead (at an undesired high speed) waiting for the last two Stoofs to land, he looked down to see all the deck lights on because the last S2F had crashed. Forty-five-minute delay. Next his engine slowly rolls back to idle. Banging the throttle back and forth had no effect. He was going down and called the ship to report that he was about to ditch. At 1,000 feet, the %!@#! engine goes back to high power and up they go again.

The pattern repeated before the wreckage was cleared away and it was time to try and bring the Spad back aboard.

For the first pass, the engine set itself somewhere in-between so they were only 50 knots too fast. At the cut, the ensign pulled the mixture control to cut off and headed for the wires. He figured with the attitude the airplane had it would surely hit propeller first so pulled back on the stick hoping to snag a wire. No such luck. He just floated and floated off the end of the deck. With a prayer he shoved the mixture back up. The 3350 caught with a roar and went back to 60 inches. He hauled it around the visual pattern even though it was night, and called the ball with way too little fuel and way too much speed, he was at 180 knots. The LSO took one look at the tail up and nose down attitude and called, "No way, 701, take it around again."

This time the pilot kept it at 200 feet so that the flat pass and G in the turn would keep his speed down. Past abeam the power began to reduce as it had before so it became a race to get on deck before it went to idle. The ship had sped up, so there was 40 knots of wind over the deck. Speed down to 115 and power dropping, on the cut he again chopped the mixture and caught the 2# wire as pretty as can be. (Powell, "Tales from the Platform," *Flight Journal*, April 2004)

A McDonnell F3H Demon refueling from a Douglas A4D Skyhawk carrying a "buddy store" on his centerline rack. The buddy store was versatile and could be carried by aircraft that had bomb racks. The store was self-contained with an air-driven hydraulic pump and 2,000 pounds of jet fuel.

"All eyes focused on the wingtip lights directly above the ship. Then they went out. Twelve LSOs looked at one another and someone said, 'Sheeit, I wouldn't know which way to run.' So he lit a cigarette and we discussed the events of the day. Then we clearly heard the sound of an ejection seat firing somewhere above. It seemed like a long time before eight tons of empty Skyray impacted off the port side, about 100 yards away.

"Now, our thoughts turned from our own survival to the poor devil hanging from a parachute somewhere above us. The pilot, who to this point had all the excitement of a lifetime compressed into about four minutes, began to be concerned about his recovery in the darkness. In order to facilitate his rescue, the Ford driver reached into his G-suit pocket and selected a flare. 'Better to light it now than wait until I'm in the water,' he thought. Feeling the bumpy night end of the flare, he pulled the tab. Holding it above his head, he continued his silent descent toward the black void. After a few moments he began to smell something burning.

"From the LSO platform we observed a white light in the dark sky. The light grew in intensity, becoming nearly as bright as the moon. The parachute was engulfed in flame as the shroud lines and canopy burned spectacularly. About 50 feet above the water the fiery mass accelerated noticeably as the nylon parachute melted. Someone suggested this might be a new way to prevent parachute-pilot entanglement in the water.

"The pilot was rescued expeditiously and returned to *Shangri-La* for his LSO debrief. In all, it was a good night, not a great night."[2]

Aerial Refueling

Besides the angle deck, mirror, and steam catapult, there was another development that significantly changed carrier operations, Aerial Refueling (ARF). Applicable for a wide range of military aviation, the most obvious use was to extend the range of an aircraft. ARF also made it possible for aircraft carrying a heavy load to get airborne from short runways and then take on a full load of fuel for the mission. The navy used air refueling for these purposes but also as a safety factor during landings. In straight-deck days an airplane running out of gas landed and was on deck whether with a trap or going into the barrier. With the angle deck even a decent pass might result in a bolter with the jet flaming out before getting around for another landing attempt. Rigging the barricade saved the airplane, but at the cost of a fouled deck for a long time. ARF provided the option of putting enough fuel in for more tries at the deck.

The fitting for the hose and basket is between the main wheels and permanently installed on this multi-role EKA-3B, which was fitted for jamming enemy radars as well as tanking. Tankers were always the last to recover at night, which placed an extra strain on their pilots because there was no gas available if he had trouble getting aboard.

The first air tankers were AJ Savages with a North American Aviation (NAA)–designed fueling package. With their nuclear delivery role superseded by the A3D, tanking became their main mission. However, the Savage was unpopular on carrier decks due to its size, unreliability, and handling quirks. Douglas Aircraft developed the D-704 refueling pod, which could be hung on an external bomb rack. Because the early jets had barely enough fuel for their own missions, the adaptable Able Dog was drafted. In 1955 the U.S. Navy decreed all future fighters would have refueling probes. Eventually the bantam Skyhawks and huge Whales became the primary tankers on the carriers. Later, A-6 Intruders (including the KA-6 version with a built-in store), A-7s, and S-3s were used. The Corsairs and Vikings carried the buddy store on the left wing, which made taking on gas difficult for RA-5 and F-8, which had their probes on the port side.

For a recovery, there was a duty tanker holding high overhead the ship. When an incoming aircraft was low on fuel (the aircraft was described as "trick or treat"), the tanker was called down to "hawk the deck" and stayed close to the fuel-critical airplane on approach. If the airplane boltered or was waved off a good tanker pilot was positioned left and slightly ahead with the basket extended. In seconds the low-state airplane was taking on fuel.

LSO Darryl "Ace" Jewell

LSO Darryl "Ace" Jewell spent more years on the platform than anyone. He was a superb pilot and LSO. However, he did not suffer fools, no matter what their rank. Acid tongued and outspoken, he did not get regularly promoted which, perversely, allowed him to take assignments that kept him flying and waving.

As a teen Jewell enlisted in the navy and was a gunner in SB2C Helldivers for the end of World War II. His squadron was onboard for *Franklin D. Roosevelt*'s round-the-world cruise where he survived a ramp strike where the SB2C was held on deck by its propeller stuck in the flight deck. He left active duty because "going aboard ship with some crazy ensign was not my thing." Ace did two years of college on the GI Bill so he could join the NavCad program. He earned his pilot's wings in 1950 and was soon in Korea flying F4U-4 Corsairs. Besides 78 combat missions Ace became an LSO. In 1954 he was assigned to the newly reopened NAAS Barin Field[3] as Assistant Special Services (recreation) Officer. There are some nicknames that are not acceptable for pilots, including the presumptuous "Ace." However, in Jewell's case, Ace was for his talent as a baseball pitcher. This sports ability was a problem. He was kept in the meaningless job so he could play and coach; up to five teams at a time. His complaints (over his CO's head) made him a gunnery and CQ instructor where he waved student pilots ashore and at sea.

Ace went back to sea duty in, first, VF-54 as assistant operations and LSO for a WestPac deployment on *Kearsarge*. Another deployment followed flying Cougars on the *Bon Homme Richard*. His third consecutive deployment was on *Hancock*, but both the LSOs in Air Wing 2 had been killed so Ace wound up waving that air wing aboard *Midway*.

When the first mirror was installed it was not stabilized, so during tests Ace or another Paddles spun a crank on the OLS trying to compensate for the ship's motion. Engineers consulted him about the Fresnel lens then in development and may have brought up the idea of a movable light source, which became MOVLAS.

After completing his college degree, Jewell went to the F8U RAG at NAS Moffett. The CO was big on Captains Cup sports competition and kept Ace for three years where he played, coached, flew, conducted FCLP, and went to sea for a week each month. For his own CQ in the Crusader he impressively got the eight traps without refueling.

The Marine air wing at MCAS El Toro had only a single LSO, a trainee, and Jewell was ordered to help the pilots qualify in Crusaders, Phantoms, and Skyhawks.

Despite BuPers promises of a fleet squadron, Ace went to *Ranger* as flight deck officer. He disliked and frequently disagreed with the air boss, which resulted in an unsatisfactory fitness report and reassignment to the shore-based instrument training squadron in Lemoore. Besides his instructional flying, Ace was Paddles Emeritus on the West Coast. He flew with the A-4 RAG, waved FCLP, and went out on CQ detachments where he waved, advised the junior Paddles from all the RAGs (a half-dozen different types of aircraft), and played a mean game of Smoke.[4]

Jewell went across country to AirLant as CVW training where he continued working LSO matters, went on frequent CQ trips, and wrote the first LSO NATOPS manual. His last duty was with a ferry squadron flying 22 different types of aircraft.

Couple of Ace Jewell TINS

While Ace was waving a CarQual session on *Midway*, the captain called the platform and asked why the recovery rate was so poor. Ace shot back, "If you'd put the F-ing wind down the F-ing angle we'd get more traps." "Mr. Jewell report to the bridge!"

Minutes later Ace fouled the deck by walking straight across on his way back to the platform. The other LSO asked how it went. "I lost, five Fs to two."

Another time, Ace was on the platform late one afternoon waving for the Crusader RAG VF-124 off the West Coast. The F-8 "steel dart" was not the easiest aircraft to bring aboard and it had become a long day for Ace and his team on the platform. With frequent fouled decks and a batch of bolters, an ensign replacement pilot was instructed to bingo to NAS Miramar.

After trapping another Crusader, Ace glances past the island and sees a black smoke-trail climbing away to the west. Guessing it was the ensign, he called primary and suggested they contact the errant pilot and find out where he was headed. Responding quickly, air ops gave the ensign no-directional-gyro vectors back to the ship. By now he didn't have enough gas to do anything but fly one pass and, if unsuccessful, eject from the Crusader. Without time to rig the barricade, Ace worked the F-8 on a straight-in

C-130 Biggest Ever Aboard

In 1963 the navy decided to attempt landing a C-130 Hercules aboard an aircraft carrier. The current COD airplane, the Grumman C-1 Trader, was small and had a limited range. Something larger was needed, so a four-engine KC-130F from the Marine Corps was loaned to the test center at Patuxent River. The Marine markings were painted over with navy and the legend "LOOK MA, NO HOOK" was put on the side of the fuselage. Lockheed installed an improved anti-skid system so braking began right at touchdown, and adjusted the nose gear oleo to stiffen the action. With a 132-foot wingspan there was only 15 feet of clearance by the island so a special stripe was painted on USS *Forrestal*'s flight deck.

The pilot, former LSO James H. Flatley III, in 2006, wrote of the event:

They could not find a C-130 crew interested in going to the boat. So, the Naval Air Test Center fingered two fighter pilots, who couldn't even spell 'propeller.'

They gave us the keys to a Marine KC-130. Let there be no question that the flight engineers (ADR-1 E. F. Brennan and ADR-1 Al Sieve) were the key guys in the cockpit, while my co-pilot (LCDR W. W. "Smoke" Stovall) and I just concentrated on flying the aircraft. We had one four-hour familiarization flight with Lockheed's chief test pilot before making exactly 100 test landings on the runway at Patuxent River.

Interestingly, relative to rotations, we were directed not to rotate for takeoff until the wings were forward of the Forrestal's island structure due to concern for the 15 feet of wing tip–to–island

A Lockheed KC-130F bureau number 149798 gets airborne well before the bow after a deck run. After becoming the only carrier-qualified Hercules in the world, BuNo 149798 saw action in Vietnam, Iraq during Operation Desert Storm, Afghanistan, and Iraq again in Operation Iraqi Freedom before retiring to the Naval Aviation Museum in Pensacola, Florida. (Thomason)

Although the C-130 belonged to the U.S. Marines when it arrived at Patuxent River it was repainted with "United States Navy" and the designation "VR-1" for the Navy Transport squadron, which provided the flight engineers. The emblem on the fuselage is for the flight test division of the test center. "Look Ma, No Hook" is only on the right side where the slogan can be seen by observers in and on the* Forrestal's *island. (Thomason)

clearance. In fact, we could have been waving to the captain as we went by the bridge at eye level had we not been saddled with said restriction. Forrestal kept 40 knots over the bow for the duration of the trials, so rotation at 54 knots indicated into 40 knots of lift (sic) was very conservative given the C-130's performance.

Our first approach at a gross weight of 80,000 pounds was made at 79 knots indicated, flying a standard shipboard 3.5-degree glide-slope. Again with 40 knots down the deck. LCDR "Ozzie" Osborne and LT Jerry Daugherty, both Carrier Suitability Project pilots, alternated LSO duties. They would give us a "cut" (to go to full reverse on all four engines) as we crossed the ramp about 10 feet in the air. We stopped in 295 feet on that initial landing, which was short of the fourth and final arresting cable, had the cables been in place on the deck. We were worried about the cables doing a job on the tires given that we were both standing on the brakes at touchdown.

We made four trips to the ship. The first on 30 October 1963 was 42 approaches for 19 T&Gs only due to 50- to 70-knot squalls and a moving deck. Out again on 8, 21, and 22 November for a total of 10 more T&Gs and 21 full-stop landings.

"Smoke" Stovall and I quickly found our way back to the cockpits of our tactical aircraft.

Although the landings were successful, and certainly set an unbreakable record for the largest and heaviest airplane to land on a ship, practical considerations prevented Herks on the Boat from becoming operational: (1) The entire flight deck had to be clear. (2) If the C-130 became unflyable, the only choices were to push it over the side or head for a port with a large enough crane to hoist the airplane off. The new, larger, and longer-range COD, the Grumman C-2 Greyhound, flew a year after these tests. (J. H. Flatley and used with permission)

The Chance Vought F8U/F-8 Crusader was sleek, fast, and somewhat difficult to bring aboard ship. The wing did not go up as usually thought, but rather, the fuselage went down for improved pilot visibility and landing attitude.

"When you're out of F-8s, you're out of fighters," was the saying. Chance Vought's F-8E Crusader was the Navy's first fully operational supersonic aircraft, joining the fleet in 1957. Capable of speeds of Mach 1.8, the Crusader established an enviable record as a potent "MiG Killer" in Vietnam, and scored the last U.S aerial victory in naval aviation history using guns. (Mike Machat)

approach. As he crossed the ramp, Ace screamed, "Cut, you dumb SOB, cut!" The power wheezed out of the J57 as the hapless ensign pulled the throttle past the idle detent and settled onto the 4# wire.

After flight quarters was secured, Ace burst into the crowded ready room. He began a debrief that was louder and fouler than usual. When asked why he was heading west, the ensign replied "I guess my gyro compass was screwed up."

"Then why didn't you #!%!# look up and check your wet compass?"

"Because I couldn't see it. The sun was in my eyes."

PLAT

The first operational PLAT (Pilot Landing Aid Training) optical device was installed in USS *Coral Sea* (CVA 43) in 1961, and by 1963 all U.S. carriers had them and every pilot, and even many non-fliers, on the ship became instant LSOs. With television screens (most think the "T" in PLAT stands for Television) in all the ready rooms, on the bridge, CIC, air ops, and a dozen other locations throughout the ship, suddenly many eyes were watching landings up the glide path. The real LSOs had a continuing struggle explaining why the glide slope on the PLAT was not that accurate, and much was missing from the simple screen image.

Movie cameras were used to film landings and takeoffs from the early days, primarily to aid in accident investigation. Coverage was usually a sailor operating one camera. Most of the footage was unwanted, and that which was had a significant delay in developing before it could be viewed. Television changed that. Not only could a camera with an operator be positioned on the island to record takeoffs and landings, but a small camera[5] could be buried in the flight deck on the centerline past the last wire. PLAT was useful as a training aid. If the LSO wanted to review a particular pass with a pilot he called the PLAT control room and had a particular section of the tape played.

Improvements continued to be made. The TV lens became stabilized with the OLS and low-level light cameras were used. A repeater screen was placed on the LSO platform where it is especially useful for lineup and acquiring aircraft in low visibility. The newest versions are officially Integrated Launch and Recovery Television Surveillance Systems (ILARTS), although the simpler acronym PLAT remains the common term.

Last Combat for British Carriers

In November 1956 two days of devastating attacks by aircraft from HMS *Eagle*, *Albion*, and *Bulwark* and the French FN *Arromanches* and *La Fayette* destroyed more than 200 aircraft of the Egyptian Air Force and established complete air superiority. Three more days of fighting followed, during which the naval aircraft flew in support of the troops on the ground, but the operation had already turned sour. Muddled commanders without clear objectives amid a confused political situation fumbled the chance for a sustainable occupation. Suez saw the first large-scale, vertical envelopment with helicopters from HMS *Ocean* and *Theseus*, now designated as Commando Carriers. Although successful, it was too little and too late. All British and French troops were forced to withdraw. The Suez Crisis "signified the end of Great Britain's role as one of the world's major powers."[6] The value of the angled deck of the Royal Navy carriers was proven as the number of sorties per day far exceeded that of the axial deck French carriers, even with jet aircraft; Sea Venoms, Sea Hawks, and turboprop Wyverns. From 1956 on, no Royal Navy aircraft carrier went into combat and the size of the fleet dwindled.

The carriers based in Aden did support work alongside RAF fighters during the brief action in the Radfan section of that country (1964). Single CVs were a force in presence for the Brunei Rebellion (1962), Kuwait (1961), Tanganyika Army Mutiny (1964), and the Beira Patrol (Rhodesian Independence, 1966). The FAA saw combat in Malaya, but it was commando ships with helicopters only. By the Falklands War, Harrier VTOLs and helos were on the ships. British losses and the length of the Falkland Battle would have been far different if the Royal Navy had had a fully capable aircraft carrier instead of the so-called through-deck cruisers. Argentina had a capable carrier, but their leaders chickened out of using *25 de Mayo* and she sat in port while her air wing operated from shore bases distant from the battle zone. HMS *Hermes* was at Falklands, but in 1971 had been converted to a commando ship and had a ski ramp installed. She never trapped another tailhook aircraft. Plenty of material from the Falklands (Malvinas to the Argentines) for lots of what-ifs.

The landing gear, engines, and aft fuselage have torn off and the fuel tanks exploded as the Cutlass travels up the deck edge before falling into the sea. What is left of the LSO platform is below the flaming F7U. (National Archives)

Wrong-Way Tom Reilly

The F7U Cutlass afterburners were a "hard" light, typical of the era. When the nozzles opened jet fuel sprayed into the hot exhaust and lit with a "whoompf." If there was not a light off, the open nozzle caused a severe loss of thrust.

Moments before the Cutlass crashes into the ramp after a bad approach, LSO Tom Reilly (his paddles still in his hands) dashes to safety across the **Hancock's** ***flight deck. (National Archives)***

Pilots in a squadron new to the Cutlass flew about 25 hours in it before going to USS *Hancock* (CV-19) for carrier qualification. The squadron executive officer was not only low on jet time, but had been flying multi-engine patrol planes. The attitude then was that any naval aviator could fly any navy airplane, so there he was. When the pilot who flew the airplane earlier mentioned the slow burner light, the XO said he didn't need afterburner. You will for a wave-off, the first pilot said. "I have never taken a wave-off in my life," said the exec. He still hasn't.

The Cutlass went low turning in the groove. The controlling LSO was Lieutenant Tom Reilly, who signaled the low and to add power. Already on the backside of the power curve, the executive officer was slow to react and went lower. Reilly frantically waved his arms over his head for a wave-off. Too late. Possibly, the pilot had shoved the throttles past the detent and the nozzles opened, but the burner did not light. The cocked-up Cutlass headed for the LSO platform. Two other LSOs jumped into the safety net and scrambled through a hatch into the ship's hull. The sailor working as the spotter/phone-talker leaped so hard that he went over the net and fell 50 feet into the ocean. Reilly had no choice but to sprint across the flight deck to get away from the crash.

The Cutlass smashed into the ramp and exploded in a fireball. The main landing gear was well below the deck edge. The forward section with the cockpit continued up the deck. Witnesses said it looked as if the pilot were trying to fly, unaware that there was no airplane behind him. The flaming wreckage rolled over the catwalk

VAW AD-5W early warning version of the Skyraider with radome and an expanded cockpit for four crew of VAW-11 in 1958. Adjustment levers to raise and lower are on the back of the mirror.

Navy's classic anti-sub "hunter-killer" team is represented here with the Douglas AD-1 (top) and AD-4W (bottom). Skyraiders operated in concert with early Navy jets like the F2H Banshee and F9F Panther in Korea, and later the A-4 Skyhawk and F-4 Phantom in Vietnam, presenting LSOs of those respective time periods with a wide variety of aircraft. (Douglas Aircraft Co.)

Re-designated in 1962 from AD-6 to A-1H, this factory-fresh Skyraider wears the new overall gull-gray with white undersides color scheme adapted for all carrier-based Navy aircraft in 1956. (Douglas Aircraft Co.)

Developed as a carrier-based anti-sub patrol aircraft in the early 1950s, Grumman's S2F/S-2 Tracker grew into the E-1 Tracer early-warning radar version, and C-1 Trader Carrier On Board (COD) delivery aircraft. S2F-1S pictured here has the Magnetic Anomaly Detector (MAD) boom and surveillance radar extended. The dome on top contains ECM antennas. Tailwheel and tailhook are in their retracted positions. (U.S. Navy)

and into the sea. The executive officer was lost. Seven men were in the port catwalk; miraculously, none had more than minor injuries.

Night Dead-Stick Trap

Gary Starbird[7] was an ensign attached to VAW-II at North Island flying AD-5Ws in 1959–1960, assigned to Det Tango, due to go on a WestPac cruise in *Yorktown* (CVS-10). We were out a few miles from North Island getting all pilots qualified on night carrier landings. ENS Starbird was the last to land. He made a deck-run takeoff and was on his way home.

The LSO got his gear together and was about to board an AD waiting to take him home. I was standing by him when I glanced up at Starbird's aircraft. Fire! A great sheet of fire through the prop. I yelled to the LSO, "The bird's in trouble," as he grabbed his gear and headed back to his station. I didn't see the results of his efforts, but Starbird did not need a cut signal. With all the odds against it ever being done, Starbird did everything exactly right. He made the most beautiful, night, dead stick landing aboard an aircraft carrier you could imagine. Just to make it look better, he didn't blow a tire and picked up the 2# wire. Inspection revealed the engine had blown a cylinder.

I had the privilege of being leading chief of VAW-11 Det Tango onboard *Yorktown* with the greatest group of pilots and men ever. We had no losses of any kind, men or aircraft, and missed only one scheduled flight.[8]

Chapter 9

TONKIN GULF YACHT CLUB

1965–1972

"F-8 Crusaders carrying Sidewinder missiles. The F-8 on the port cat will be first; the deck crew are looking that way and standing clear of the foul line. Starboard catapult will be seconds later. Both jet blast deflectors are raised. As soon as they are lowered the next airplanes will be taxied forward for hookup.

Yankee Station, Tonkin Gulf, Line Backer, Rolling Thunder, Vietnam. These are the places and names that defined carrier aviation to a generation of tailhookers. For eight years the thrust of U.S. naval aviation was in that unhappy war. If you were an American carrier pilot it was certain you would fly missions from Yankee Station on one, two, even three tours of duty. Going to WestPac no longer meant routine flying and liberty in the exotic ports of Japan and Hong Kong; it meant the steady grind of mission after mission. Vietnam was Korea all over again, and three times as long. The enemy had sophisticated air defenses with extensive support from China and the Soviet Union. Political restraints hindered meaningful attacks and frustrated aircrews.

Carriers During the War in Southeast Asia

Even with the risks, for hard-chargers, Vietnam was the ultimate practice of their chosen profession. Frequently heard in the carrier ready rooms, "It might not be much of a war, but it's the only one we got." On the line, a flight a day, frequently two, was the norm. Flight hours and traps built up. Flying at sea is high risk and getting shot at added more zest. Unlike the grunts in-country, you didn't have mud, muck, mosquitoes, monsoon rain, and hellish heat. You landed back aboard, showered, and dined in uniform with real china, silverware, and a white tablecloth. There was plenty to bitch about, but plenty to enjoy. The life of a carrier pilot was good . . . unless you were shot down.

U.S. operations began from Yankee Station (190 km due east of Đồng Hới, at 17° 30′ N and 108° 30′ E) in May 1964. As the war escalated after the Tonkin Gulf incident in August of that year, bombing missions went into North Vietnam proper, and from the spring of 1965 to the end of 1972 (except for the Bombing Pause years 1969–1971 when there were frequently less) there were three carriers on the line. Designated Red, White, and Blue, the ships flew from midnight-to-noon, six-to-six, and noon-to-midnight so there was continuous coverage. The daily schedule was a mix of cyclic operations with various missions and major strikes called Alfas, which had 25 to 30 aircraft striking a single target.

A line period was between 20 and 30 days. Every 6 to 8 days was a stand-down day for one of the ships. A day with no missions. A day to replenish JP for the airplanes, fuel oil for the ship, food for the crew, and most important, ammunition. After a line period the carrier went to ports such as Sasebo, Singapore, or Hong Kong for R&R, but mostly into Cubi Point in the Philippines, where the Rest and Recreation happened after aircraft and ship maintenance was done for the day. The schedule was a rugged one.

At the end of a deployment (never call it a "cruise," love boats make cruises, warships go on deployment!), back in the States, the squadrons returned to their air stations, the carrier her home port, and the cycle begin again with personnel transfers, aircraft replacement, and updates. Then short times at sea in training areas in the Caribbean or Southern California, culminating in an operational readiness inspection (ORI) before a final load out and a return to Yankee Station for another six- to eight-month deployment.

There was plenty of work for LSOs in the Tonkin Gulf. If on cyclic ops there was a launch and recovery every 1-1/2 to 1-3/4 hours. Alfa strikes meant a large number of aircraft to recover, but a longer time before there was a launch. LSOs were no longer assigned to a ship with that as their primary duty, but to each squadron and the CAG staff. The LSOs in an air wing were formed into teams headed by experienced LSOs; at least two with the CAG and Assistant CAG Paddles and, if fortunate, a third or even fourth team. LSOs like to fly. The teams divvied up the schedule either with alternate days or doing half a day so they could fly when not on the platform.

Douglas A-4 Skyhawk from VA-195 in the barricade with a broken left main mount. Getting an airplane clear and the barricade properly stowed takes time, so if possible, the emergency is the last aircraft recovered. Rigging the barricade takes less than 5 minutes. LSOs have to remind pilots that because of the stanchions that hold the barricade up, they will briefly lose sight of the ball in close and to "hold what you have."

In contrast to operational Navy aircraft, a brand-new airplane leaves the factory in a basic color scheme that includes national insignia, "NAVY" titles, and the aircraft's bureau number, or BuNo. Pictured here is a factory-fresh Douglas A4D-1 (A-4B), which became the navy's primary attack aircraft during the Vietnam War. (Douglas Aircraft)

One LSO could manage a recovery solo (the phone-talker wrote the book), but two or more was better. Every launch had an LSO standing by in the event an airplane had to return to the carrier in a hurry. On the announcement "LSO to the platform!" several Paddles sprinted through interior passageways to assist.

The usually clear skies and calm sea meant plenty of chances to train new LSOs. Then, depending on how bad the weather was, or if nighttime, or if the returning airplane was battle damaged, the more experienced LSO took the pickle.

There was a certain pride in a smooth recovery with minimum interval between airplanes, but it was the unusual that went into

USS Kittyhawk (CVA-63) conducting an underway replenishment (UnRep) in 1967 at the height of the Vietnam War. Her deck load is typical for the large carriers in the Tonkin Gulf; two squadrons of F-4 Phantoms and A-4 Skyhawks; single squadrons of E-2 Hawkeyes, A-6 Intruders, RA-5C Vigilantes, and EKA-3 Skywarrior plus a detachment of EA-1 Skyraiders. The sooty, black smoke from the boilers is rising as the ship speed is low and wind is from the port side, but when there is high wind over the deck for recovery, especially if even slightly starboard, "blowing tubes" becomes hazardous (see Chapter Ten).

platform lore. One day the LSOs looked out to see a Skyhawk with no nose behind the A-4 on final. The entire nose section had been blown off just forward of the pilot's feet; there was just a big flat plate. No nose meant no airspeed or AoA indications, but flying by feel the pilot was doing a good job of staying on speed. The A-4, like most navy fighters of the time, had no nosewheel steering; steering on deck was by differential braking. During pull-back after a trap, the nosewheel swiveled backward, but came around again when the A-4 began to move forward, but not always. Sometimes the nosewheel cocked to one side and it required extra power and tapping the brakes to get it straight. This delay was referred to as "sitting in the gear," although a more impolite word was used.

The first A-4 trapped. Everyone knew it would be close. The controlling Paddles raised his arm. The red foul deck light was bright, the talker chanted a litany of "Foul deck, Foul deck!" An LSO stepped away from the wind break to look up the deck. "He's s*** in the gear!" The LSO with the pickle let the damaged Skyhawk come as close as he dared but had to hit the wave-off lights. Seconds later, "He's moving," and the lights went green. The pilot knew he had priority and bent it around in a steep left turn. A hundred yards from the ship, the engine quit; he ejected and was immediately picked up by the plane guard helo.

USS *Intrepid* had been an attack carrier before becoming a CVS and had the latest cats and arresting gear. During Vietnam she made three deployments in her previous role with an air wing made up mostly of Skyhawks with a few Crusaders because of her size. Two of the big deck carriers were on Yankee Station at the same time.

At the end of the last recovery of the day, the LSOs looked up to see an F-4 Phantom with gear down, flaps down, hook down. One of the LSOs called primary, "Boss, we've got a Phantom in the groove."

Following an old tradition, airplanes that land by mistake on a carrier not their own are decorated and sometimes held for ransom (ice cream). When USN airplanes were dark blue, humiliating a mistaken arrival was often routine because officers and chiefs carried liquid, white shoe polish with sponge tips.

Wrong-Way CR Jones

In 1968 an errant, battle-damaged Skyhawk returning to *Intrepid* (CVS(A)-11) wobbled, swerved, and veered at the platform. The assistant and the phone talker both jumped into the safety net and were killed. LSO "CR" Jones dived left onto the flight deck and sustained a 5-inch cut across his shoulder from the bomb sway brace on the crashing A-4.

Watching the PLAT, squadron mates saw Jones lying on deck. First one arm moved and shook. Then the other wiggled, followed by both legs kicking before the camera moved to the crash itself. Not too long after, Jones walked into the ready room and was greeted with gasps of amazement. "We thought you were dead with your back broken when we saw your arms and legs twitching."

"Nah. I just wanted to check everything was working before trying to stand up."

LT Ken Hespe, who was an LSO, had landed just prior to the crash. He ran across the flight deck, grabbed a handheld radio and, still in his flight gear, talked the remaining eight aircraft aboard. There was no mirror, it had been destroyed in the crash.

Remarkably, a request for more information using the Freedom of Information Act (FOIA) made while researching this book was denied because the crash of an A-4 48 years ago was still "classified"!

LSO escapes across the flight deck like Jones' and Reilly's (see Chapter Eight) are one reason the sunken platforms of the 1970s were disliked by Paddles.

"He's probably got battle damage. Take him."

The large, twin-engine Phantom trapped and taxied forward to park behind A-4s and Skyraiders. Walking up the now-quiet flight deck, the pilot had his head down and muttered, "I'll never hear the end of this."

"What's the matter?" his RIO said, "I thought it was a pretty good landing."

"You idiot, we're on the wrong ship." Only then did the backseater look up at the big "11" on the island. The captain posted Marines around the airplane in ten minutes, but it was too late, the wayward Phantom had been suitably decorated as tradition demanded.

Seventeen attack carriers logged 71 Tonkin Gulf cruises 1964–1972, losing 530 aircraft to known or suspected enemy action and 329 operationally. The A-4 bore the brunt of the offensive missions and suffered accordingly, with 282 carrier-based losses, while air wings wrote off 138 Phantoms and 118 Crusaders.

LSOs Ashore, Part 2

In 1965 the USMC area of responsibility was just to the south of Vietnam's DMZ and the Corps' specialized support aviation was needed. The order was given and in just 24 days Seabees and MABS (Marine Air Base Squadron) built a functioning airfield at Chu Lai using AM-2 aluminum mat for the runway. (The Marines jokingly referred to the 1½-inch-thick, specially coated, sturdy panels as their "tin foil" runway.) The initial length was little more than 3,500 feet, so MOREST (Mobile Arresting Gear) was installed to stop landing A-4 Skyhawks. Approaches were flown using a mirror under LSO control. Eventually the mat runway reached 7,800 feet, but soil support problems made half unusable while the problem was fixed on the other half, so use of an LSO continued.

A Marine LSO bringing in a Skyhawk. The jeep with a radio was normally parked 1,000 to 2,000 feet from the end of the runway as an LSO station. Unlike on the ship, the touchdown point was farther from the single cross-deck (runway) pennant. Monsoon rains were a problem because the runway became slick; another reason for arrested landings. (Kirby Schnell)

Grumman S-2E Trackers warming up before flying from USS* Hornet *(CVS-12) in the Sea of Japan April 1969. "Very rough (and cold) weather! We (*Hornet*) were the 'Lead' carrier of a four-carrier strike force sent to the Sea of Japan as a response in force to the North Korean shooting down of one of our VQ EC-121s. We were called off Yankee Station along with* Ranger, Enterprise, *and* Ticonderoga. *Only* Hornet *S-2s were flying, ensuring there was no North Korean or Soviet submarine threat. We had some rough recoveries with that weather; many wave-offs, and several bolters, deck pitching, and of course, the fantail was doing the '27 Charlie Shuffle' all the way into the wires." (Carroll Bains, USS* Hornet *CATTC Officer and COD pilot)

On 1 June the first squadron of A-4s landed in the morning using the MOREST. By 1300 the first strikes were launched using JATO (Jet Assisted Take Off) bottles.[1] The complete installation—mat runways, mirror, MOREST, and Catapult (installed at Chu Lai later)—was a SATS (Short Airfield for Tactical Support).

LSO Kirby Schnell: "As VMA-311 Squadron LSO I spent many hours at the short SATS field. In the early days of ops at Chu Lai there was an LSO on duty to mark JATO ignite points and to recover every aircraft into the MOREST gear. The mirror setup was pretty much like on a carrier: mirror on the pilot's left, glide slope 3 degrees. Some short roll-in, but not much. Bolters required a third step; go to full power, close speed brakes, and raise tail hook to avoid a full-power engagement in the abort gear, which at times was not far down the runway. It was there in case of JATO failures and to keep airplanes from running through the construction area.

"Launches were with partial fuel, full ordnance, and JATO bottles. JATO was punched at 80 knots with a computed speed for burn out and rotation. You held your heading off the cross wind or turned out to sea and jettisoned into the bay (there has to be a mountain of JATO bottles over there!)."[2]

Other Places, Other Crises

The following events outside Vietnam during the 1960s proved the mobility and territorial independence of aircraft carriers:

The U.S. Navy

- 1962, Cuban Missile Crisis 23 October–20 November
- 1967 during the Six Day War, American aircraft carriers deployed to the Mediterranean (including one transiting to Vietnam) and stood by on alert awaiting developments. In June, at a time when the United States was trying to keep a neutral position between Israel and Egypt, the USS *Liberty*, an elaborate state-of-the-art intelligence-gathering ship, was in international waters off the Gaza Strip. Word came to the USS *America* (CVA-66) that the *Liberty* had been attacked by both

planes and ships with the attackers' identity unknown. Planes were armed and preparations made, but none launched. The reasons for a lack of response remain unexplained.

- Less than one year later another intelligence ship brought the carriers into action. In January 1968, the USS *Pueblo* was fired upon, boarded, and captured by the North Korean Navy. USS *Ranger* had completed its second line period on Yankee Station when she was ordered to head north. *Enterprise* was in Sasebo, Japan, at the beginning of her Vietnam deployment and was also sent to Korea.
- 1969, the North Koreans shot down an EC-121 surveillance aircraft and in a repeat of their 1968 experience, *Enterprise* and *Ranger,* along with *Ticonderoga* and *Hornet*, stood by in the Sea of Japan.

The Royal Navy

- 1961, HMS *Centaur* with 807 Squadron Scimitars in July sat off Kuwait for weeks and the Iraqis did not advance.
- 1964, Sea Vixens and Scimitars from various carriers at Aden alongside RAF Hunters during the Radfan Campaign. The Radfan Campaign was a series of British military actions during the Aden Emergency.
- 1964, Tanganyika Army Mutiny, HMS *Centaur* helicopters landed a commando of Royal Marines in Dar-es-Salaam with Sea Vixen fighters ready to go.
- 1966, Lackluster "Beira Patrol" was carried out by HMS *Eagle,* off Lourenco Marques to blockade Rhodesia.
- 1967, Multiple carriers provided air cover for the withdrawal of British forces from Aden.

Advanced Landing at Sea

Early night flying required good visibility, but as techniques and equipment improved, what worked in darkness also worked other times when there was no visibility and "night" became synonymous with "all-weather." So too with carrier approaches.

Finding the Boat

Ships' radar controllers not only directed fighters against incoming enemy but could guide their own airplanes back to the vicinity of the carrier. A homing beacon called YE/ZB was installed on American carriers from the start of World War II. YE/ZB sent out signals in Morse code with a different letter in each of a dozen quadrants. For security the quadrant letters were changed daily. The segmented circles on plotting boards and ready room displays were for the YE/ZB. Flying the YE/ZB was a lesson in practical geometry. Once a pilot heard and identified the letter he knew what quadrant he was in. As he flew closer he crossed into another quadrant that provided an exact heading to "home plate." YE/ZB remained in use until replaced by Tacan (Tactical Aid to Navigation). Tacan is a UHF signal broadcast from the ship and read as bearing and distance in the cockpit. Because having the Tacan on made locating the carrier easy for an enemy, many methods of getting airplanes back to home plate have evolved: vectors from an airborne E-2 Hawkeye, radar and navigation systems in the aircraft themselves, or a smaller ship a set distance from the carrier with its Tacan on, among other usually classified tricks.

Dead Reckoning

Finding the carrier without any homing device was a complex exercise in dead reckoning. By noting heading, speed, and time the position of the airplane could be determined and a course to where the carrier was supposed to be (Position of Intended Movement: PIM) could be calculated. Navy pilots were taught to read wind direction and strength and include wind drift in their calculations. A rotatable disk marked with degrees and scaled lines under a plastic sheet along with an E-6B circular aviation calculator was used to draw the track. The British brass considered this too difficult for one man (probably RAF thinking), which is why the FAA World War II fighters Skua and Fulmar were burdened with a navigator.

To make the plotting board usable in single-pilot aircraft, there was a horizontal slot in the instrument panel, which the plotting board slid in and out of.

James Flatley, fighter squadron commander and ace, manning his Hellcat with his plotting board. A circular slide rule, fondly known as a "whiz wheel," was mounted in the lower right-hand corner of the plotting board. Awkward to carry around, once in the aircraft they slid nicely into a slot in the instrument panel. The British considered the workload and degree of difficulty in finding the way back to the carrier to be so high that their front-line fighter at the start of World War II, the Fairey Fulmar, had a two-man crew, pilot and navigator.

U-2 at Sea

Despite its 3,000-mile range there were places the Lockheed U-2 could not reach, so the CIA established Project Whale Tale to operate the U-2 from aircraft carriers. In August 1963 a U-2 was hoisted aboard USS *Kittyhawk* during the night. At sea the next day, the airplane took off and made a series of approaches to the deck to prove the validity of the concept. Lockheed modified three U-2As into U-2Gs by beefing up the landing gear, installing wing spoilers, and adding a tailhook. Company pilots were trained in T-2 Buckeyes at NAS Pensacola and carrier qualified aboard USS *Lexington* before going aboard USS *Ranger* in March 1964 to carrier qualify in the U-2 off the California coast.

The only operational mission of a carrier-launched U-2 was from USS *Ranger* two months later in the far Pacific checking on French nuclear weapon tests on Mururoa Atoll.

The U-2R was much larger and had foldable wings and an integral tailhook. It was used to qualify five CIA pilots on USS *America* in November 1969.

Lonny "Eagle" McClung was one of the navy LSOs for the program:

During my tour we conducted periodic FCLP to polish the skills required for carrier operations. The U-2 had an approach speed of approximately 70 to 75 knots. From the LSO perspective, the problem was that the jet was a glider with an engine. It did not want to stop flying. The wing was equipped with effective spoilers to kill lift in the descent and landing pattern. Due to the low approach speed, plus the requirement for precise line-up control, the optimum wind over the deck was determined to be approximately 20 knots. This limited the burble induced by the ship's island to enhance line-up control. The glide slope was set for 3 degrees. LSO/Pilot technique was to fly a normal approach and utilize two cuts. A verbal "cut 1" was the signal for the pilot to pull the power to idle. "Cut 2" was to deploy the spoilers and set the landing attitude with slight back pressure on the yoke. LSO technique was to back up the radio call for cuts with activation of the installed cut lights on the Fresnel lens. It was not uncommon to have a blue water "cut 1." Normal aircraft weights were used on the arresting gear.

Once onboard the aircraft could be towed around normally. The U-2 did not have the normal tie-down hard points that U.S. Navy jets do, so the planes were stored on the hangar deck. To put

the plane on the hangar deck, the nose gear was modified so that it rotated 90 degrees. The tail wheel was set on a small dolly that allowed the jet to move sideways. The jet was pushed out on the elevator with one wing extending over the water, and the elevator was lowered, then the jet was pushed sideways into the hangar bay.

Carrier launch of the U-2 was a deck run. Shore-based operations required devices we called "pogos" on the wing. They were shackle-shaped spring devices with rollers on the bottom that held the wing tips up. They allowed the aircraft to taxi without the wing tips dragging the ground. When the U-2 lifted off, the pogos fell off and were retrieved by the ground maintenance crew. For ship deck launch the 20 knots of wind over the deck was enough to give the ailerons some aerodynamic authority. Maintenance personnel held the wing tips up and when the pilot applied power for the launch, they simply let go and the wings had enough aerodynamic authority to control the aircraft during launch. Climb speed was 165 knots with a high thrust-to-weight ratio, so the U-2 had a very steep climb angle.

During my tour, the U-2R was developed. We conducted what would be termed "carrier suitability" on the U-2R. Bill Park was Chief Test Pilot for Lockheed Skunk Works. I took him to Pensacola, VT-4, and got him carrier qualified in the T-2 Buckeye. Next we developed the FCLP procedures, which we found were essentially identical to the U-2G with the shallow glide slope and two cuts. Once we were confident of those procedures, we scheduled testing at Lakehurst to confirm hook/arresting wire engagement. We then took the plane to Wallops Island and did the initial carrier operations on USS *America*. Because of the added wingspan on the U-2R, line up was even more critical. We did not have any other aircraft on the deck during U-2R operations. Procedures and pilot/LSO technique were essentially identical to U-2G operations. No operational missions were conducted during my tour before I detached in 1970.

***The Lockheed U-2's 103-foot wing span reached over the normal foul deck lines but did permit use of the normal arresting gear during shipboard evaluations conducted in November 1969. The long, glider-like wings and high-thrust engine of this later-model U-2R also made the deck run very short. Note the civilian registration number N812X painted on the tail fin. Outrigger "pogos" holding up the wing tips are painted red for optimal visibility during deck operations aboard USS* America.**

Despite careful plotting, misreading the wind, a combat engagement, or the carrier not being where it said it would be meant arriving at a spot with nothing but ocean in sight. Standard procedure then was a square search. The length of each leg was a multiple of how far one could see. A higher altitude meant seeing farther, but even small cumulus clouds could hide ships if one was flying above them. The first leg was the visibility distance followed by a 90 degree turn and that distance again. After the next 90 degree turn, the distance was the first leg plus itself, as is the leg after that. By the next turn the distance is three times the original (visibility) leg; repeat the turn and go the same distance. Keep increasing the length of the leg after every second turn. This continued until you found your carrier, found another carrier, or ran out of gas. "It's called dead reckoning because if you don't reckon right, you're dead."

Looking for Centerline

The mirror eliminated the need to actually see the LSO. However, visual cues for line-up were still necessary. Deck lighting went through many variations; at least there was a centerline and outline of the landing area using dead lights.[3] Tries were made with a correct rectangle and angled-in patterns to provide a false perspective. Shaded, dim white lights on the landing area were attempted to reduce the feeling of descending into a black hole. The entire deck was lighted with red lights so the deck crews could see to perform their duties. "Lighting by Lucifer," was the quip. Red lights are difficult to see from a distance (security consideration) and do not destroy a pilot's night vision.

For a period, the crews that were night flying were briefed in their ready rooms wearing dense, red, filter goggles before going up and outside to the flight deck. There were sort of "light locks" (akin to air locks) before the hatches opening onto the deck; small compartments with red lighting with a door behind from white light and a door in front into the dark. In the airplanes all interior lights were red. Add oxygen and communication hook-ups and analogies to womb security were frequent.

Eventually, it was realized that a visual was no longer necessary for targeting and lights could be white and bright. Well, brighter. They had to remain dim enough that transitions into true darkness could be made without difficulty. For the carrier this meant a series of flood lights mounted on the island shining onto the flight deck. Looking like moonlight, this is what the system is called. The landing area is still outlined but the centerline is improved with a strobe effect leading the eye forward. (Also used as an approach light at most airports. If you watch one working, the slang term "rabbit" is obvious.) Another improvement in lighting is so simple it's a wonder it wasn't thought of much earlier. A row of lights goes straight down from the fantail on the centerline. Because these "drop lights" are 90 degrees from the centerline lights, if on centerline the pilot

A CVN ready for night operations. The ball and datum lights are on rheostats to change their brightness. The landing area is outlined with a rectangle of white lights. The lights on the centerline appear of differing brightness because of the strobe action. The red drop lights are on; because they appear a straight line with the centerline, the airplane is lined up correctly. The waist catapult tracks are apparent because they are shiny and reflecting the evening sky. Pictures that truly show the ship at night do not show much; pictures at dusk or in dim light have to suffice.

A night launch of a Hornet. Afterburners make maintaining night vision an issue of the past. "Moon" lights mounted on the island cover the entire flight deck with a yellowish light that is subdued, but bright enough to cast the shadows in the foreground.

sees a straight line, but if off to one side he sees a "V" pointing toward the center.

Looking for Glide Slope

There weren't any changes to the mirror OLS for night work. The two bars in green for reference and the green lights for cut and red lights for wave-off activated by the pickle were variable to match ambient light conditions. The source light's intensity could also be varied by a rheostat so that the meatball was not too bright and "flare" at night.

Say "Fre-nel"

A marked improvement in equipment became standard in the late 1960s. Called the "Fresnel lens," it replaced the mirror. Not only was the Fresnel lens less susceptible to unwanted reflection and grime buildup, it was visible farther away and had much better definition. Pilots could see movement more quickly and fly a more precise approach.

The Fresnel lens was named for a French physicist who realized that the only part of a lens that did anything was the curved part; all the glass under that was only support and bulk. A Fresnel lens removes all but the curved portion. The appearance is a series of circular ridges. A lens 6 inches at its thickest part can be flattened to less than 1 inch. Fresnel adapted his lens to maritime beacons with the first installed in a lighthouse in 1823.

Modern versions are made of special plastics, can be very thin, and have the look and feel of a vinyl record. Fresnel lenses used on-ship are of the highest quality and mounted in temperature-controlled boxes, but mundane examples are sheet enlargers for reading, fire starters, and automobile taillights. LSO vocabulary shifted from calling the OLS the "mirror" to simply, the "lens."

Typical Fresnel lens (FLOLS) installation. The basic lens box is tilted for hook-to-eye correction for types of aircraft. When the pickle wave-off button is pressed the red vertical lights come on and blink and the inner part of the horizontal datum lights go off. The four green lights at the top are cut lights used to acknowledge control and signal more power when operating without a radio. The smaller red lights are also wave-off lights, which work off a backup electric supply.

Wave-off lights and all the datums are lit in this night test. The glow in the lens is not the ball but interior reflection from the light source. The FLOLS is stabilized +/- 3 degrees of ship's pitch, and +/- 6 degrees of roll. Beyond those limits the ball moves with the ship. It is not stabilized for heave (movement up and down). (Figures from Fresnel Lens Bulletin *1965)*

A reflector sight on a British aircraft carrier. The principle of operation is the same as FLOLS except, to correct for hook-to-ramp clearances, the lenses and datums are moved up and down. While still called Bats, the LSO is on a seat and looks through a sight to verify that airplanes are on glide slope.

The Fresnel lens with five lighted cells had the same reference, cut, and wave-off lights as the mirror, and added a special bottom cell that was red and pulsed to dramatically remind the pilot that he was dangerously low on the glide path. (Old quip: "The LSO kept asking me what color the ball was. If he doesn't know, why is he an LSO?")[4]

The Fresnel Optical Landing System (FLOLS) provides a better method for correcting hook-to-eye distance. Rather than raise or lower the entire mirror assembly, the Fresnel light box could be rolled side to side. This tilted the plane of light.

Because the landing centerline is removed from the roll axis the height of the glide slope could be changed without changing the basic (tilt) angle of the glide path. If a pilot was not on centerline, he saw a centered ball and was above or below the desired glide slope. The neutral (vertical) roll angle was 7½ degrees. Only a few aircraft used roll angles much different from this; A-3, RA-5, and E-2 are examples. The settings for each type are found in the Arresting Gear Bulletin for the particular carrier.

The first production FLOLS was "point" stabilized, which meant the optical display was stable in space at only one point, 2,500 feet astern of the ship. USS *Franklin D. Roosevelt* had an Mk 6 Mod 0 installed in 1960. The Mk 6 MOD1 was tested and evaluated during 1963 and 1964. The MOD1 had "line" stabilization and used a scaled mechanical analog computer to continuously solve the lens position equations. Rather than just a single point, line stabilization stabilized the entire optical beam for ship's pitch and roll. FLOLS became standard on all carriers.[5]

MOVLAS

Battle damage has always been a consideration in aircraft carrier design; catapults on the hangar deck, arresting gear on the bow, for example. In the days of paddles a spot for an LSO to stand could always be found. However, with the advent of optical landing systems (mirror and Fresnel lens), pilots familiar with the old arm-waving signals soon disappeared along with LSOs who were able to wave with paddles. Something was needed to replace a damaged mirror or lens. The solution was a simple arrangement of lights on a frame called Manually Operated Visual Landing Aid System (MOVLAS). The datum lights were the same, but now the meatball did not depend on physics to show the glide slope; the LSO put the ball where he wanted it. A stack of amber lights lit three at a time. Control of the lights was with a lever in a box. The middle position is on glide slope, up is above, and down is below. The pickle is fastened to the lever, so the LSO still has cut and wave-off lights in one hand and a radio handset in the other. The LSO has direct control of the airplane's vertical path as he once did with outstretched arms and paddles. Paddles slang calls the control the "happy stick."

MOVLAS may be located in three places. Station #1 is immediately in front of the FLOLS and utilizes the FLOLS wave-off, datum, and cut light displays. Because the MOVLAS can show any position the LSO wants, its most frequent use is when the sea state has the carrier rolling and pitching beyond FLOLS stabilization limits. The LSO feels and knows the deck's motion, and with skillful manipulation of glide path presentation can safely bring airplanes aboard. Unless told they are flying MOVLAS, pilots should not know the difference.

MOVLAS set up in the number-two position forward of the FLOLS. The exuberant "double hands up" marks the end of the timed event. Rigging the MOVLAS in the various positions, similar to rigging the barricade, has a maximum time allowed to be considered combat ready.

Stations #2 and #3 are independent of the FLOLS and are located on the flight deck port and starboard side, respectively, and connected to the LSO platform. Because the light does not actually show glide path, a caution when the MOVLAS is set up is to leave the lever in the down position when not being used just in case a pilot somehow sees a ball, thinks he is high, and flies into the ocean trying to correct.

Pilot and LSO proficiency in MOVLAS recoveries is required before an air wing is considered operational.

Precise Guidance

CCA is the naval version of a GCA at a shore station. A controller watches radar screens showing line-up and glide slope and gives instructions over the radio. GCA/CCA approaches require extensive training and frequent practice for both controllers and pilots. At sea the controller gives instructions until, "three-quarters of a mile. Call the ball." The pilot then says the usual call sign, aircraft type, fuel state, and ball. If he does not see the ball the response is "Clara" and the controller resumes instructions down to half a mile, instructs to call the ball again, and the pilot either continues under LSO control or, if Clara, executes a missed approach.

The VHF ILS (Instrument Landing System) does not require a human operator. When it came into common use the USAF had it installed at its bases and GCAs gradually disappeared. However, an ILS installation takes up considerable space, not available on a ship,

Naval aviator training as well as jet age carrier qualifications took a giant leap forward with the swept-wing Grumman F9F-8T Cougar. Wearing its standard high-visibility NATOPS white and orange markings, the Cougar operated as a trainer with the post-1962 designation TF-9J, and flew operationally until 1974. (US Navy)

The McDonnell Douglas F-4 Phantom II was the victor in a fly-off competition with the Vought XF8U-3 Super Crusader, winning the coveted production contract with twin-engine reliability and a second crewman to operate increasingly complex onboard tactical systems. More than 5,000 Phantoms were built, and the carrier-based aircraft brought Mach-2 performance to the Navy in 1960. This is a U.S. Marine Corps F-4S. (Mike Machat)

and is not usable when the deck is moving even the slightest. The navy kept its CCA controllers.

A better system was introduced in the 1970s. A very precise radar,[6] of the type used for weapon guidance, locked on the approaching aircraft and fed the information to a computer that was also getting information from the ship's gyros. The computer sent a signal to the pilot showing where he was relative to the glide slope and centerline. An independent receiver was at the controller's station to verify that the sent signal was correct. The controller still had the CCA precision radar to monitor and as a backup. The system is called the Automatic Carrier Landing System (ACLS). Automatic because that is the ultimate goal, a hands-off approach all the way to landing.

When first implemented there were three modes: Mode III was not much different from a CCA; the controller gave instructions. The difference was where he got his information from. In Mode II the pilot flew instruments to keep horizontal (glide path) and vertical (centerline) needles centered. Mode I was fully automatic using the autopilot to fly the airplane.

Night Approach

Your mission is over and it is time to return to "Mother." Deep inside the ship is the Carrier Air Traffic Control Center (CATCC). "This seaborne air control center was operated in perpetual dimness behind a heavy metal hatch. Galaxies of red and amber dial lights surrounded rows of individual radar-repeaters. Faintly lit, wiper-like sweeps crossed greenish, phosphorescent screens illuminating damp, attentive faces. Other profiles formed and faded, from chain-smoked cigarette glows and ebbs. Terse questions begat brief, precise responses."[7]

Your first call is to Marshall Control in CATCC with who you are, where you are, and how much gas you have. Marshall gives you an altitude, Angels, to hold at, Fox Corpen, and an approach clearance time, EAC. The distance on the Tacan bearing, Fox Corpen, is determined by adding 15 NM to your assigned altitude, Angels. You check your nav indicator, if necessary by laying your pen across the needles to estimate the heading, which will get you to your holding place in the sky. You are all alone. If you had a wingman he is headed for his own hold 1,000 feet and 1 mile away from yours. At times like this having an NFO or copilot is comforting, and helpful. Someone to share the load, cross-check, and share the worry.

Holding is almost boring. You fly a racetrack pattern, adjusting turns and legs to cross exactly over the point, noting the time to the second. You can be a bit lazy at first, but as your EAC gets closer the sweep of the second hand becomes more important. Your speed is Vmax endurance, you're not going anywhere, just staying in the air burning as little fuel as possible.

Holding is a time of apprehension. Thoughts of what is to come, what-ifs, run through your head. Time to look around, if there is anything to see. Glorious nights with moonlight bright on the ocean, blinking lights both above and below. Boats, ships, and stars. Other nights when down below is a solid layer of cloud, white with a moon, dark gray without. Knowing that once in the cloud it will be dark, probably rough. Memory of the squadron joker's quip that God can't see below the overcast.

Other nights there is nothing outside the cockpit. Nothing. No light. Nothing until, if lucky, the welcome meatball and deck lights seconds before impact.

EAC time; cross the fix. Flip the speed brakes out; whatever it takes to make your airplane fly at exactly 250 knots descending at exactly 4,000 fpm. Report leaving marshal and if more than 10 seconds off, report that also. Cross-check altitude plus 15 equals distance on the DME. Adjust as needed. At 5,000 feet call "platform" and reduce your sink rate to 2,000 fpm. At 10 miles, slow to 150, lower landing gear, and set flaps to approach configuration. The final controller comes up, "Final bearing. Maintain heading." He gives small heading changes, not in magnetic readings, but degrees of change. "Come left two degrees, you are on centerline." At last, he says, "You're approaching glide path. You are 200 feet below. You are on glide path." You reduce power, move speed brakes, flaps, whatever it takes for final landing configuration. Tailhook? It was down before you even entered holding. Complete the landing checklist by yourself. Better with a crew. The controller continues, "Check landing gear down." You Roger, "Gear down."

"You are on glide path, on centerline." At three miles, "Do not acknowledge further transmissions. Slightly below glide path. Come right two degrees." So he continues. If his voice stops for 30 seconds you will execute a missed approach. "On glide path, on centerline. Three quarters of a milc. Call thc ball."

You look up. There it is. A centered ball, deck lights; a bit hazy but there. You swallow and try to sound cool. "304, Hawk, ball, 2.4." (For multi-crew aircraft, LSOs prefer the pilot to make the ball call. You can tell a lot from those few words.)

Paddles simply says, "Roger ball." Those two words have import. Unspoken is, I have you. You are under my guidance. I will get you aboard. I will keep you safe.

Now it is almost easy. You have trained for this moment for years. Done hundreds of practice landings. Every landing you have

A carrier deck at night is a bewildering whirl of colored lights, dark spaces, and noise so loud you can see it. All the hazards of the day are there but made more lethal by those you cannot see. An FA-18 Hornet with lights on, meaning, ready to launch.

made since primary training has been a carrier landing. Meatball, line up, angle of attack. Meatball, line up, angle of attack. The litany doesn't stop. Tiny corrections. Keyed for any word from the LSO. Concentration in its purest form. You ignore the black around you. You ignore the illusions of tilting, plunging, too high, too low. Meatball, line up, angle of attack. The lights are clearer. You are aware of the huge deck coming up at you. Meatball, line up, angle of attack changes. Meatball, line up, meatball, line up. Try not to twitch the stick. Finally, meatball, meatball, meatball! Make the impact a surprise. He who looks at the deck, shall smite it mightily.

Touchdown. Impact. Best, a great tug against your straps. You thumb the speed brakes in, pull the throttle back. A trap.

Swiftly, lights off, flaps up, follow signals, hook up, throttles, steering, follow director, brakes, taxi, fold wings, clear area. The next airplane is exactly one minute behind.

Into a spot. A director with lighted wands stands in front of you on the dim deck. Flips his thumbs at each other; you are chocked. Rolls his hands over each other; you are chained down. Slashes his hand across his throat; shut down your engine.

You peel your mask off your face. Open the canopy and breathe the most glorious air in the world; wind over the deck on an aircraft carrier speeding over the ocean.

Dark Humor

LSO to new pilots, "Landing at night is the same as landing in the day. Only you can't see anything."

The standard phraseology from the ship's controller after a night bolter or wave-off was, "Climb straight ahead to 1,200 feet. When comfortable, turn downwind, heading xxx." One airplane held its initial heading. The controller reminded the pilot, "Cleared to turn." The pilot's reply, "You said 'when comfortable,' I'm not there yet."

How tense are pilots at night? Some carrier planes have their all-important attitude gyro offset in the instrument panel. After a bolter, when asked about fuel, "Say state," several pilots have responded, "Ask me something on the other side of the panel."

A new pilot in Stoofs (Grumman S-2 Trackers) asked how he would know if he had boltered. His LSO said, "You know how you feel when you've sat on the toilet with the seat up. It's the same thing."

At the very end of 1981 CAPT John Waples had 397 night traps, hot on the heels of all-time champ VADM Bill Martin with 440. CAPT Waples said then he had no goals other than getting at least four more night traps, "So I can say I have over 400." ('Wonder if he made it?)

By now the reader knows that "Roger ball" is the LSO's acknowledgment that the pilot sees the ball. Not an uncommon name, every so often there was an article in base papers about the "real" Roger Ball. LSOs joke that Roger Ball was the first LSO and he had two wives with a son by each. The Mexican wife had Manuel (manual) Ball and the German wife had Otto (auto) Ball.

The saint in charge of landings happens to be a former U.S. naval aviator named Roger Ball. He smacked the back end of the ship one bad navy night and ended up in the spud locker, but they saved his bones and a couple miracles are attributed to them. So he got promoted to saint. That's why every U.S. Navy Landing Signal Officer says "Roger ball" when you tell him who you are and how much fuel you have. He's really praying. [*The Cannibal Queen: A Flight into the Heart of America,* Stephen Coonts]

I was a tired pup and wanted to get it over with. I trapped for the fifth time, went to full power, came back to idle, looked to the right, and raised the hook, and then came over the radio the sweetest, kindest, most wonderful news I have ever gotten in my entire life. The seasoned air boss said, "Congratulations, 102, on one of your many bolters; you actually should have caught a wire, but you got a hook skip (my tailhook jumped over #4 wire). We are going to count that as number six. Your signal bingo to Cecil. Bravo Zulu (well done in navy lingo)." My skipper was standing next to the air boss and told me what happened next. There was a slight pause, and then this distant voice replied, "You mean I don't have to go again?" "No, son, head for home. You've had a long day," answered the air boss.

A USO troop with Bob Hope and songstress Barbara McNair were onboard a carrier in this Tonkin Gulf for a show that night. When McNair heard of this hazardous near miss over the target, she was on the platform, and LSO deBoxtel handed her the radio. When the back-seater called, "Field Goal 603, Vigilante, Ball," she replied, "C'mon home, baby, we're waiting for you."

During an early deployment of the A3D Skywarrior on the *Kittyhawk*, the pilot was having trouble seeing the ball. "Paddles, I see two meatballs."

"Okay, close one eye."

FLASHPOINTS
1973–PRESENT

A Grumman F-14 Tomcat coming aboard. The platform is crowded with visitors wearing cranial helmets, which LSOs do not. The equipment panel is open and a green clear deck light is in its box. Barrel-like containers contain inflatable life rafts.

The signing of the Paris Peace Accords in January 1973 ended the war in Vietnam for the United States. To the fliers of the USAF and U.S. Navy the cease-fire seemed abrupt considering the all-out effort of the preceding months. For a time there were six aircraft carriers in the Tonkin Gulf, the largest task force since World War II. Then the Alfa strikes stopped. Carriers went home for needed overhauls. Those that remained flew reconnaissance missions in Laos and Cambodia and removed the mines they had placed not long before. Combat stopped. POWs came home. Southeast Asia smoldered with minor actions until North Vietnam broke their promises and invaded South Vietnam in 1975. The NVN Army routed the troops of the south. Saigon fell in April and thousands of Vietnamese fled the country, many by sea. USS *Coral Sea* and USS *Hancock* were part of a large task force for Operation Frequent Wind, the evacuation of Saigon. The two carriers were farther out than the other ships and avoided most of the chaos of VNAF pilots flying out to safety. Forty-five Hueys and a Chinook were pushed overboard to make room and many more pilots had to unload their passengers and then ditch their helicopters in the sea.

Last of the individual LSOs

John James "Bug" Roach III may be the last Paddles known for his individual skill and personality. The nature of the waving business has always been evolving and the LSO has gone from one man with paddles to a team operating sophisticated devices. Bug delighted in any new devices that could make recoveries safer. He considered development of new LSOs one of his main goals. He judiciously worked trainees into the team on the platform. He taught, he encouraged, he inspired. The result was a generation of well-qualified LSOs who could brag that they were Bug trained. But, when the going got tough, he was the one with pickle in one hand and radio handset in the other who took control and eased tension with his voice and reputation. Like the fictional Beer Barrel, when you heard Bug controlling, you knew you were in the best of hands.

Bug Roach waved 10 barricade arrestments, 20 single engine approaches, 5 aircraft missing main landing gear, 2 A-4 Skyhawks with major battle damage, the first ever S-3 Viking with an unlocked wing, and used a hand-held radio to talk down 6 aircraft at night with no lens and the landing area lit by the headlights of flight deck tractors. The video is available online of Bug working an A-6 Intruder that had torn one landing gear off earlier, at night, with a wildly pitching deck, into the barricade. It is more dramatic than anything Hollywood could do and an example of how an LSO who has the magic touch sounds.

Roach began by flying F-8 Crusaders during the Vietnam War and made combat cruises with three different air wings on three different 27C class carriers as pilot and Landing Signal Officer. After two separate CAG LSO tours he was recruited for a third air wing that needed an LSO in a hurry.

On one of the first days at sea, Bug was in the "dirty shirt" chow line wearing his leather flight jacket and heard, "Hey you, with the jacket, you can't wear that."

Bug turned. "First off, my name is Bug Roach, not Hey You. I'm wearing this jacket because the Secretary of the navy says I can. Who, may I ask, are you?"

"I'm the XO of this ship. What are you doing here?"

"I am the new LSO and I'm here because nobody else would take the job of waving this air wing onto this boat."

Bug's standard wear on the platform was Oshkosh bib coveralls, white T-shirt (weather permitting), and cowboy boots with fancy metal toes. One night he had on a bow tie. When asked why, he replied that gentlemen dressed for dinner and after the recovery he was going to the dirty shirt wardroom for a burger. He used to leave his float-coat open. Challenged by the ship's safety officer, he explained he took the inflation bladders out anyway, so why bother.

His then-CAG described a remarkable recovery during operations in the Yellow Sea:

The weather late that day was sloppy, low class weather. Low clouds alternating in near zero, zero conditions: fog, low visibility. All of which created between a half mile and a quarter mile visibility and a ceiling of sometimes 50, sometimes 100, feet. During one of the good periods, we sent out two S-3 Vikings to keep an eye on the many Soviet subs in the area. Then the ceilings went down. Weather ashore in Korea was alternating between WOXOF[3] and minimums and we had the two S-3s airborne with no place to land or divert them. The ship's captain wanted to divert them but Bug came to me and said that he could get them aboard. I called the CO and said we wanted to try rather than divert the aircraft. He said that he would give it a try but reserved the right to cancel their approaches at any time.

LSO "Bug" Roach in his domain of the platform with his float-coat nonchalantly open during a visitor's day at sea.

So, down the chute they came. Bug was on the radio telling each of the S-3s that the object of the approach was to get them under the overcast safely, so he called their turns and altitude to get each to the ramp. One at a time they descended, got underneath the overcast at less than 100 feet, and then drove into a visual to the carrier. At that point, Bug directed them up the side of the ship, and called their upwind and downwind turns by telling them when to turn and when to go wings level. He rolled them out in the groove, kept each at the same low altitude until they intercepted the ball, and then quickly worked them from level to the deck. Thanks to that great "Bug" voice and manner, each made a great trap.[2]

After that CAG LSO tour Bug was flying Skyhawks in an adversary squadron at NAS Miramar when Kuwait was invaded. The CAG LSO in his old air wing could not deploy due to his child's illness and Bug raised his hand. During *Ranger*'s deployment to the first Desert War (Desert Storm), he waved airplanes (probably the most senior Paddles ever; he was a full commander), flew combat missions (probably the oldest aviator to do so), and bagged his 1,000th arrested landing.

The Navy League of Central California created a special LSO achievement award, which was to be presented at the next Tailhook convention. Sadly, Roach was killed in a failed ejection from a Skyhawk before that event. The award continues to this day, and is now officially known as the Bug Roach LSO of the Year Award.

No-Hook Landing

During the disastrous, chaotic day that was the fall of Saigon, a United States Navy task force was off the coast of Vietnam for evacuation Operation Frequent Wind. Most of the ships closer in were auxiliaries, many of which had landing platforms for helicopters. The two aircraft carriers were farther out, but even they had recovered so many helicopters that late arrivals were ordered to drop their passengers, depart and ditch, and await their rescue.

A Cessna O-1 Bird Dog light observation airplane flew over USS *Midway* (CVA-41). The Bird Dog had seats for a pilot and an observer. Many had been provided to the Vietnamese air force (VNAF) for use by forward air controllers. The Bird Dog made a couple of passes dropping messages (all of which blew into the sea) before one was stuffed into a leather pistol holster that landed on the deck. The note read, "Can you move the helicopter to the other side, I can land on your runway, I can fly for one hour more, we have enough time to move. Please rescue me! Major Buang, wife, and 5 child."

Midway's captain, Larry Chambers, called for volunteers to move the helicopters crowding the flight deck. If there was no place for them, they were pushed over the side. The value of the discarded helos was $10 million. The CDPs were removed so they did not foul the small wheels of the O-1.

After a first tentative pass, the Bird Dog touched down on the second try, bounced, and stopped halfway up the deck. The ship's crew gathered around, applauded, and cheered as Major Buang climbed out, followed by his children and wife holding their baby.

Space was found to bring the Bird Dog back to the United States as a souvenir of a remarkable event. It is on display at the U.S. Naval Aviation Museum in Pensacola.

Two weeks later during the *Mayaguez* Incident, which was largely a USAF and USMC operation, aircraft from *Coral Sea* made an attack on targets on the Cambodian mainland in what is considered the last battle of the Vietnam War.

A Break in the Action

U.S. aircraft carriers did not see any significant combat for the next 19 years.

While the war in Vietnam was going through its ups and downs, U.S. Navy carriers went to Korea in response to the capture of USS *Pueblo* (January 1968) and the shooting down of a U.S. Navy reconnaissance plane (April 1969).

The Mediterranean has always had its conflicts. U.S. Navy aircraft carriers were off the coast of Lebanon in 1973 during that civil war and in the same year performed a role carriers are uniquely suited for. The United States wanted to replace Israeli A-4 Skyhawks lost during the Yom Kippur War but could not get any countries in Europe or Africa to allow the Skyhawks to land on their way from Lajes in the Azores, so the plain gray A-4s aerial refueled from tankers from USS *John F. Kennedy*, trapped aboard USS *Franklin D. Roosevelt*, spent the night, launched, refueled in the air, this time with tankers off USS *Independence*, and continued on to Israeli bases.

The year 1983 saw a day of strikes against targets in Syria and, back in the balmy Caribbean, a couple days of bombing during the invasion of Grenada, which would have been comical, except men died.

Libya had declared a "Line of Death" across the Gulf of Sidra and had it challenged by American carriers exercising freedom of navigation rights. Opposing F-14 Tomcats cost Libya a pair of Sukoi Su-22s in 1981 and two MiG-23s in 1989. Buttons with "Navy-2, Libya-0" were popular afterward. The four kills were the only American F-14 victories.[1]

In response to a Libyan-backed bombing of a Berlin nightclub, which killed American nationals, an attack on Libya was ordered in 1986. It was an egregious example of interservice rivalry at work. The main bombers were a stream of F-111s that flew from England and around Spain at Gibraltar to avoid flying over land. Multiple air refuelings were needed and crew fatigue a factor. One F-111 was shot down due to unimaginative planning. The entire operation could have, and should have, been done from aircraft

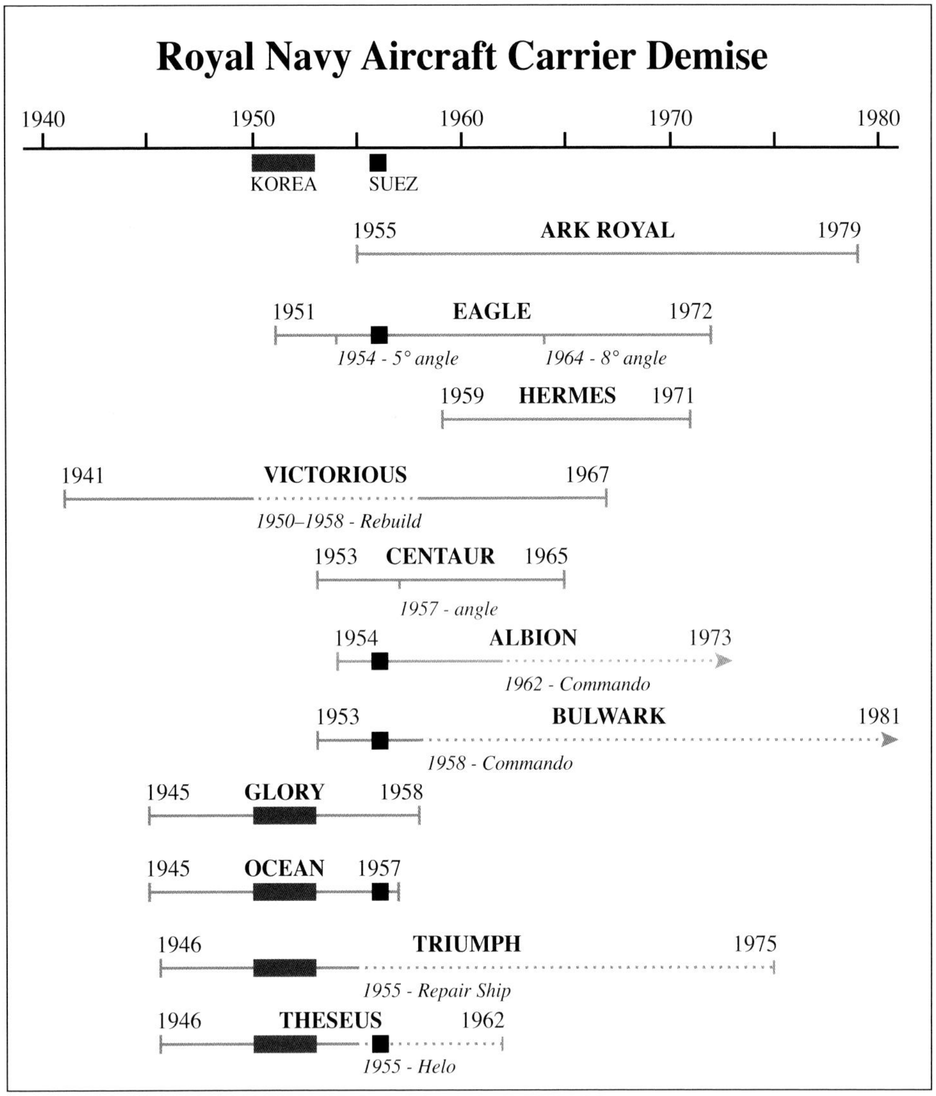

The demise of Royal Navy carriers. (Jacob Powell)

carriers already in position. (Not the first example. Looking forward to 2002 and the campaign in Afghanistan, the situation is the reverse.) In April 1988, there was a brief flurry as part of the Tanker Wars where U.S. Navy carrier aircraft destroyed oil platforms and Iranian warships in retaliation for the sinking of a United States Navy ship.

Swan Song of the Fleet Air Arm

The Royal Navy fleet was changing from the last of the real aircraft carriers to the newly commissioned through-deck cruisers, which may have had the same names as battle-proven ships, but relied on helicopters and VTOL AV-8 Sea Harriers.[4]

The *Ark Royal*'s last commission (RN term for deployment) was stylish and a fitting end. Ark had spent much of the summer on the American East Coast. First down south working out of NS Mayport and using the Florida training ranges before going north to the Norfolk area. When ashore her Gannett squadron was hosted by the E-2 RAG, the Buccaneers shared ramp space with the A-6s at Oceana and the F-4Ks (Phantom FG1) were at home with the F-4Js of VF-101Ark Nimitz pier12

In September 1978, *Ark Royal* sailed into the North Atlantic, crossing the Arctic Circle, for NATO exercise Northern Wedding. Due to a quirk in Royal Navy pay rules, she could not put into the United Kingdom without her crew losing money, so for the farewell visit of the Queen Mother, who had commissioned her in 1955, the Ark stayed at sea off Scotland and the Queen Mother and her entourage were brought out by helicopter for the ceremony.

When the end finally came, the last aircraft launched, a Phantom FG, was crewed by both an FAA and RAF officer.[5] However, the honor of the very last catapult shot was given to the wardroom piano.

The Middle East Mess

The invasion of Kuwait in 1990 set in motion one of the most effective, well planned, and overwhelming military retaliations ever. The campaign against Iraq had well defined goals and reached them quickly. Part of the overkill was no less than seven carriers flying strikes in the four days the war lasted. *Independence* in the Gulf of Oman; *America*, *John F. Kennedy*, and *Saratoga* in the Red Sea; and *Midway*, *Ranger*, and *Franklin D. Roosevelt* in the Persian Gulf.

CVs intermittently were in the area enforcing a No-Fly Zone when not chasing into Afghanistan or while on ill-conceived NATO missions over Bosnia in 1999. In 2003 Iraq was again invaded with debatable justification and a struggle against irregular forces drags on to this day despite the campaign being declared over in 2011.

The galvanizing events of September 2001 sent American forces into Afghanistan.[6] U.S. Navy carriers were quickly in position and launched strikes against Taliban forces, a classic example of the aircraft carriers' mobility and responsiveness.[7] However, the target locations meant a 1,000-mile round trip from the Arabian Sea. Once air bases were established in surrounding countries with USAF squadrons in position, there was no need for navy fliers to continue with the long and demanding missions. Like the 1986 strike into Libya, the wrong service was in action.

The current effort is against the Islamic State (ISIS/ISIL). Once selective bombing was authorized in August 2015 aircraft of Air Wing Eight from USS *George H.W. Bush* (CVN-77) began attacks a

HMS Ark Royal *and USS* Nimitz *(CVN-68) tied up at Pier 12 at Naval Station Norfolk in 1978 before Ark left on her last commission as the Royal Navy's last true aircraft carrier—perhaps (see Epilogue). The road off the pier goes to the air station and aircraft to be hoisted onboard are towed down it. In the old days, pilots landed at the air station and taxied single file all the way to the ship.*

A McDonnell F4K Phantom on Ark Royal. *Omega was chosen for the squadron tail marking as it symbolizes the last; in this case, the last Royal Navy Phantom squadron. The Fresnel lens system, which raised and lowered rather than tilted, is on the edge of the flight deck.*

full week before any land-based aircraft. France's nuclear-powered carrier *Charles de Gaulle* arrived in the fall. According to Barrett Tillman, "The operation (with the typically grandiose name "Inherent Resolve") appears open-ended."[8]

French navy Super Étendards catapulting from the Foch. *The French navy continues in action in the Middle East with the carrier* Charles De Gaulle.

Last of the Oil Burners

Among all the reasons nuclear-powered aircraft carriers are better than conventionally powered ships is one usually forgotten (except by LSOs and pilots): no smoke in the groove. Exhaust smoke from a

USS Carl Vinson *(CVN-70) was commissioned in 1982 and represents the modern U.S. Navy aircraft carrier as used for global force projection in the Gulf Wars and other Mid-East conflicts. This nuclear carrier measures 1,092 feet long and has a combat load displacement of approximately 100,000 tons, yet can reach a cruise speed in excess of 30 knots. (Mike Machat Collection)*

Vigilante at the Ramp

"Vigilantes! The A-5, LSO's nightmare. Seventy feet and 25 tons of screaming steel. Fill out the accident report on the ball call."

"Had a Vigi one night with all the lights out except the starboard wing light. And that looked like a slow approach light. Hairy. I do remember the nights of laughing and scratching that came to an end when the Vigi called the ball with 2.5 and one green light. Wheels down? Yep. Show me a donut. I've got one. Bridge, Paddles, want us to take him? Negative, Paddles, give him the Aldis lamp on the way by. Roger that, 604 you copy? Roger, the next pass we'll have 1.8 if we can make it tight. Roger that. On final put your red flashlight up on the glare shield so we can see you in close. "You look around there's nobody but you and the talker. Talker, see if you can get a hold of ready room 5 and get them to hold the movie." (LSO T. R. Swartz)

Actually, they were not that bad. I waved in the Vigi RAG for three years. Nasty reputation came from the early A-5A. Biggest part of training was to convince pilots it had a stick and throttle like other airplanes and didn't take superman to land well and safely. No one I trained ever broke an airplane at the ship. Although I was waving for one spectacular crash.

Nugget pilot on CarQuals. Gent had an attitude problem and I probably shouldn't have taken him anyway. Pilots new to the Vigilante were teamed with experienced backseaters, RANs, from the RAG staff. "Dr. Volcano" was with this kid. The A-5 did not have ailerons; it had spoilers for roll control. When you called for a lineup correction, you had to watch that the nose tweaked up to compensate for the drag. Day, steady deck, so no excuses. He drifts right, I call, "Come left." Spoilers open, nose comes down and sets up a horrific sink-rate. "Power, power! Wave-off," and I hit the wave of lights. Too late, too slow. The Vigilante slams into the deck and bounces short of the 1# wire and traps on the 4#. At the top of the arc, Dr. Volcano ejects. Rocket-seat worked fine and a good chute, but he lands on the flight deck hard and is dragged into the nose wheel of the airplane he just punched out of.

Went to see him in sickbay (looked like the losing team in a football game), enough bruises for eleven men. His explanation, "I heard the power and wave-off calls and when we hit, I heard the airplane breaking apart."

A centered ball as seen from the RIO's cockpit of an F-14B conducting FCLP at OLF Fentress near NAS Oceana, Virginia. The LSO shack is partly visible behind the canopy frame. The LSO, lens, and painted carrier deck are all positioned as on a carrier. At night, the only lights on are the outline of the landing area. (Mike Machat photo)

The entrance to the LSO school at Naval Air Station Oceana, Virginia. The walkway is painted like a carrier deck. A Bug Roach quote (more like a mantra) is on the sign, "Be one with the ball."

The LSO school logo with the easily translatable motto in fractured Latin.

carrier's burners has been a problem since the very beginning of carrier flying as shown by the various places the stacks were located until coming up through the island became the least bad choice. What came out of the stacks was determined by the ship's engineers. Power changes meant readjusting the fuel-air ratio. Normal stack gas was almost invisible. There were periods of black smoke during changes, but nothing like the filthy mess created by blowing the tubes. That black cloud was not just smoke but loaded with particles of sticky tar.

The tubes run through the boilers where water is made into steam for the turbines. The burning oil covers the tubes with a layer of soot, which had to be cleaned off with blasts of steam or risk tube burn-through. Standard practice was to blow tubes on the mid-watch, midnight to 0400. Al Fullerton commented, "By 2400 Midnight I [chief engineer] always called the air boss before I wrote night orders to make sure flight ops were secured, maintenance had all the aircraft wrapped (openings covered, canopies and panels closed), and the officer of the deck had a good crosswind to blow soot over the starboard side. Cuz I liked airplanes and the air bosun was my drinking buddy. We would get soot on planes parked aft on occasion necessitating me buying him beer.[9]

"The USS *Franklin D. Roosevelt* had a habit of blowing tubes with jets in the pattern. Hardest touch down I ever had was when the 'Roosy Roo' blew tubes with me on short final. Lost sight of the landing area. Paddles turned on the wave-off lights but did not transmit wave-off on the radio. Came out of the smoke to see wave-off lights in close. Caught a wire climbing with full power and was slammed to the deck really hard. A few popped rivets. Ouch."[10]

USS *Kitty Hawk* (CVA-63) was the last conventionally powered aircraft carrier in the U.S. Navy and was decommissioned in May 2009. Her last CO was in a C-2 Greyhound for the last arrested landing on her deck. That trap was number 407,511, a total surpassed only by *Lexington* (CV/CVA/CVT-16) over a 49-year career that began in World War II with 493,028. *Enterprise* (CVN-65) was the only other aircraft carrier to log more than 400,000 traps.[11]

Bringing NAVAIR training into the modern digital age, the McDonnell Douglas (now Boeing) T-45A Goshawk is the current carrier qualifying aircraft for new naval aviators. The T-45 replaced the long-used North American T-2B Buckeye, which served as the backbone of NATOPS for nearly four decades. (U.S. Navy)

Training Ashore

FCLP presents many difficulties as a way to train for night landings. The ideal airfield was away from civilization but not too far from the air base. Being in the boonies meant few, none ideally, locals to complain about the noise late into the night. Any lights except the deck outline detract from the reality of landings at sea. The more buildings in sight, the more distracting the light and the temptation to cheat by flying visually rather than by reference to instruments. Ashore practice is at the mercy of local wind; anything besides down the runway to 10 degrees right is unrealistic. Eventually, airfields used for FCLP had landing-area lights built into the runway and the control tower turned the main runway lights off during practice and on for takeoffs and full stop landings. Before that, kerosene flare pots and battery-powered brick lights simulated the carrier deck. Late wave-offs sometimes blew the lights around and LSOs had to scurry to put them back in place. The flare pots added the excitement of an open flame.

"Chasing those battery-powered lights was part of the deal. I waved A3Ds and it seemed like every time they touched down things had to be reset. Most of the time at NAS Sanford and even NAS Albany the pattern was right-hand, adding to the false reality, but for the most part I always thought that all the variables added to the pilot's ability to learn eye, throttle, and stick requirements. As one parameter changed another was affected. Once they figured out the corrections required and the amount of acceptable change as they entered final, my thought was, the pilots had picked up all they were going to get from FCLPs.

"We usually had one night before a cruise when all the wives, kids, and girlfriends came out to the end of the

A dramatic view of a Landing Signal Officer team watching as a Boeing F/A-18F Super Hornet touches down on the USS* Harry S. Truman *(CVN-75). (USN photo by MC3 K. Wilson)

A complete view of IFOLS. The narrow catwalk runs the length of the flight deck and the white safety curb most of the way. The heavy, black rubber strip in the catwalk seals the catapult tracks when not in use.

A current **[modern?]** *platform (technically the LSO station) with matching consoles on a hydraulic jack. The previous equipment panel is mostly blank and will be removed. A radio speaker for those without a handset is under the blue obstruction light. The wind break still folds down but for airplane clearance, not for LSO visibility. Used CDPs (they can take only a prescribed number of hits) lay on the deck for Paddles to stumble over.*

runway and got to see things up close and personal. They got to make the LSO calls, ask who this Roger guy was, write in the book, and ask their husband for a little more power in the groove. From their perspective it was like a carnival show." [12]

The LSO station could be as little as a portable radio and a folding chair, or two, or a semi-permanent heated and air conditioned shed.

"As a nugget LSO at Oceana I waved the VF-74 "Fords" (Douglas F4D Skyrays) for FCLP and CarQuals. I was qualified enough to wave alone on Friday nights, and took my young wife with me to write a book. She sat in a chair with a flashlight and did her best, amazed and fearless. I quietly told the next pilot in the groove over the trusty ARC-27 radio that he was due for a late wave-off. I eased off to the edge of the runway; Miz B was busy scribbling in the book. I hit the wave-off lights, the pilot lit the afterburner, which, if you recall, exploded mostly outside of the tailpipe, and it blew her over. My thought was, I've done it now, I will be getting the cold shoulder and tongue lashings for a week. She picked herself up and said, "That was the most beautiful thing I've ever witnessed."[13]

Naval air stations themselves had the problems of lights and neighbors, so remote fields (OLF, Outlying Landing Field) were set up. NAS Cecil had OLF Whitehouse in the swamps of the Florida Panhandle until NAS Cecil was closed. NAS Oceana has OLF Fentress in the formerly open farm fields of Virginia Beach; today, urban encroachment is bringing lights and complaints. West Coast naval air stations were often hampered by nighttime marine layers making the field Instrument Flight Rules (IFR) and unusable for FCLP. "NAS Lemoore in the wintertime was famous for its solid fog. Often the base went several days with the weather barely getting up to GCA minimums, forcing FCLP to the desert. NAF El Centro, in the desert, with summertime extreme high temperatures, added the adventure of night crop dusters adjacent to, and occasionally almost under, to the night FCLP pattern. Additionally, bouncing prop planes in those high temperatures (C-1, E-1B) required that after four or five passes, the plane had to go to delta pattern to cool the oil temperature before continuing FCLP." [14] The OLF on San Clemente Island off the coast of Southern California is about as close to a carrier as it gets because it is a small island that drops off to the ocean at the runway ends and is dark. However, getting LSOs and support personnel there is difficult; the one runway is sloped and the Pacific winds bizarre.

According to LSO George Shattuck, "When I started waving, we were based at NAS Moffett Field and used NAAS Crows Landing in the San Joaquin Valley for FCLP. We'd fly a T-28 to Crows to get set up. We had a bunch of flashlights in heavy rubber casings, which we set out to light the deck landing area. After that it was pretty much a lawn chair, radio, and the pickle. We often flew home with that T-28 baggage compartment full of cantaloupes, fresh beans, and lettuce right out of the field. Some of the farmers loved to come watch the ADs fly FCLP. FCLP became a little more sophisticated when we moved to NAS Lemoore with the built-in deck lights and a shack to sit in."[15]

According to LSO Daniel Bo Howe, "We used to go tarpon fishing in Key West in the salt ponds between the runways when the airplanes went in to refuel. Of course the mosquitoes took some of the fun out of it. Because there weren't that many Vigilantes available, it took all night to get a class through a session."[16]

Simulators for Pilots

In the early 1970s, Ling Temco Vought developed a simulator, the Night Carrier Landing Trainer (NCLT):

I did two trips to LTV during the evaluation. It was one primitive lash-up. The screen-dome and cockpit were leftover from a lunar landing simulator. Don't remember what worked and what was pictures; Attitude gyro, directional gyro, airspeed, AOA, maybe RPM. Throttle was a single lever, pretty sure with APC. But the contraption did move and it was dark out. Visuals not too bad for the time. On

An LSO console with an ILARTS picture and information surrounding it on the upper left, a selectable data screen below, lighting controls on the lower right, and communications on the touch screen above.

A Boeing E/F-18G Growler on the lowered elevator and an F/A-18 Super Hornet on the flight deck. Retractable guard stanchions for the elevator are raised. The flight deck is 80 feet above the sea.

Sikorsky H-60s are used as plane guards and normally fly a pattern on the starboard side of the carrier during launches and landings.

deck-in close had big pixels. Ah, but the LSO end; view was same as pilot's on a TV screen; Sony, I think. Sat on a stool. Controls were large rheostats. Took ten turns to change wind 1 knot, direction as bad. Played CCA controller as well. Seem to remember indicators for glide path and centerline deviation. All the while the computer was printing out lines and lines of data for every few seconds of the pass. Made brief attempt at using for debrief, but so many numbers meant nothing. The print outs were part of the contract so I got to take ten pounds of connected paper with feed hole edges home with me. My kids used it to draw on for years.

By the next year, NCLTs, designed for A-7, were up and running at NAS Lemoore and NAS Cecil Field. They were pretty good. Fully functional cockpit, good visuals. Techs tweaked the computer and got RA-5C responses. Because the Vigi did not have one, the HUD was turned off. The LSO station had a correct view plus graphics of glide slope and line up. Even had wave-off and cut lights. Used to take nuggets up for two or three sessions. Used to schedule the first one the night we traveled and made them wear helmets and oxygen masks. After that it was any time and just a headset. They thought I was nuts until after their first real night landings and they realized I had wanted the sim to be as real as possible with fatigue, disorientation, and discomfort.

Like all simulations the NCLT was not perfect, but real enough. Had a CDR on staff who wanted to try it out. He boltered, was waved off, boltered, waved off, or something like that. On fifth or sixth pass, he says, "Okay, I've seen enough."

"'No way,' says I, 'You don't get out until you've got a trap.' Don't remember how many more it took, but when he got out, his khakis were sweat soaked to his waist.

The features of the NCLT were incorporated into the advanced simulators for the aircraft themselves. A training session can now include everything from a catapult shot, to weapons delivery, to approach in bad weather, to a night trap. Pilots training for the ship in FA-18 Hornets fly a couple of day FCLP sessions, four to six at night, and another six in the simulator, which has the advantages of more accurately representing the darkness at sea, varied weather and wind conditions, and problems with aircraft systems. The simulators are so sophisticated that the last session links four simulators together so that the pilots can see the other Hornets flying with them in the day pattern.

Simulator for LSO

The LSO Training Device 2H111 (simulator) was built at the LSO school at NAS Oceana around 1984. Since then it has had a major upgrade approximately every 6–10 years. A fully equipped and functional platform can fit a half dozen trainees while the instructor changes parameters like weather, aircraft type, and WOD from a console behind. Standing on the platform you can see the carrier's island over your left shoulder, and the visuals are so good you would swear the deck is moving under your feet.

The school trains approximately 200 students per year. Roughly 150 go through the two-week Initial Formal Ground Training (IFTG) course, 25–45 already fleet qualified LSOs going to fleet replacement squadrons or the training command get refresher and job specific training, and 6–8 CAG LSOs get the equivalent of a Ph.D. in waving. Additionally, every CVN PCO/PXO and Air Boss/Mini Boss goes through a course, and a half dozen foreign LSOs (France, India, Brazil) take advantage of the only LSO school in the world.

Improvements and Progress

LSOs began as one man standing in the wind with paddles in hand. The mirror exchanged the paddles for a handset and pickle, but still one man. A second handset and pickle was added and a second LSO was on the platform as a backup or trainer or both. New equipment was added, the aircraft grew more sophisticated, and the cost of error became higher. Duties on the platform divided and became specialized to reduce the workload on any one individual. Now it is not an LSO but an LSO team. Training and experience is tracked and there are stages of increasing qualification and authority.

In a fully manned team today the LSO stands on the deck with a clear view aft, the assistant LSO is behind a display console monitoring information as well as watching the landing airplane, a staff-qualified Paddles is behind a second console as overall supervisor, and a deck-status LSO is on deck facing up the deck and into the wind (physically the most uncomfortable position). Today's LSO team also includes an LSO writer, a sailor spotter with binoculars (who has been assisting LSOs since the USS *Langley*), and a phone talker to the primary flight control and the arresting-gear engine rooms.

Three pickles control cut and wave-off lights. The LSO relies on the assistant to select radio frequencies or communicate with important stations on the carrier. The supervisory LSO has the same capabilities on his console. Selections are made on a touch-screen.

The area of the platform is large enough for the LSO team and the usual extras of observing Paddles and inevitable visitors (squadron pilots are encouraged to come watch what goes on). The size of the safety net is commensurately large as well.

The Improved Fresnel Optical Landing System (IFOLS) was tested on board USS *George Washington* (CVN-73) in 1997 and every deploying aircraft carrier since 2004 has had the system. Instead of a lamp, IFOLS uses an LED source, which provides a more visible and better defined meatball. The stabilization system is improved as well.

On today's platforms are a pair of consoles, which extend up to chest height so that the LSOs do not have to look down for the information displayed. On a display screen are horizontal and vertical scales. The vertical shows hook-to-ramp clearance with an index mark for the lens setting, and the horizontal marks the CDP locations and where the airplane will touch down if it is centered on glide path. A moving mark on both is dynamic, using signals from the carrier's inertial system to show ramp clearance and touchdown point as the ship pitches, rolls, and heaves, if the pilot is flying a centered ball.[17]

The newest version of the PLAT is ILARTS (Integrated Launch and Recovery Television Surveillance System). ILARTS also gets an input from the ship's inertial sensors and moves the in-deck camera to stay on the glide slope. In the old days, watching the PLAT with a pitching deck, the image of the airplane moved up and down while the cross-hairs stayed centered. With ILARTS the cross-hairs move up and down and the airplane, if flying a good pass, is centered in the middle. The two old, big dials showing wind direction and speed are now a computer-generated icon of a carrier deck with the wind speed down the angle in the icon and the crosswind component on the side it is from. The wind symbology is in the upper left corner of the left top screen in the LSO's field of view. Line-up is checked on the ILARTS. Large Foul and Clear Deck indicators top that display.

The lower screen is used to view aircraft position around the ship, maps of location and shore divert fields, weather information, pages from arresting gear bulletins, or aircraft and pilot status. Plastic status boards with grease-pencil wielding, backward writers have been replaced with electronic displays available at many locations. For example, if the fuel state of an airplane is changed in the darkened spaces of air ops it is displayed instantly on the bridge, flight deck control, primary flight control, platform, and all ready rooms.

USS** John C. Stennis **(CVN-74), first deployed in 1997, is shown here with operational Navy aircraft of that time period. On the flight deck are Grumman F-14 Tomcat and McDonnell Douglas F/A-18 Hornet fighters, Lockheed S-3A Viking and Grumman E-2C Hawkeye anti-submarine and patrol aircraft, and a lone Grumman EA-6B Prowler ECM aircraft. Note F/A-18 on the fantail at the right painted in Navy Aggressor colors. F-14s on the fantail are parked TOD (Tail Over Deck) while the single F-14 at left is parked TOW (Tail Over Water). (Mike Machat Collection)

Showing the incredible advance in seven decades of Naval Aviation history is this depiction of the "World Famous" Red Rippers (VF-11) flying their first high-performance fighter, the Boeing F4B-1, in formation in low-holding with their current aircraft in 1997, the Grumman F-14B Tomcat. The carriers below are the USS Lexington *(CV-2) and the USS* John C. Stennis *(CVN-74). (National Museum of the United States Navy)*

Unlike air wings in the 1960s, which could have up to nine distinctive types of airplanes, variations of the Boeing F/A-18 Hornet are 90 percent of the airplanes landing aboard and identifying, which at a distance or at night is a problem. Daytime, the Rhino (F/A-18E/F) Hornets have a winking white strobe on the belly. At night, Legacy (F/A-18C/D) Hornets have a normal red rotating beacon, Rhinos have one that nutates three times, and the Growler (EA-18G) Hornets' lights blink in twos. All have red and green navigation lights on the undersides of the wings as well as on the tips, which give LSOs a better sight picture to judge aircraft attitude.

Hornets have some interesting features for carrier operations. The auto-throttles are so good it is rare to see approach lights change from amber, and when they do it is not for long. No more, "he was low and going green," heart stoppers. Catapult shots require the pilot to be hands off; the cat officer will not launch unless the pilot's hand is on the grip on the canopy bow called the "towel rack," and the Super Hornet senses the instant it traps and reduces thrust by 20 percent to save wear and tear.

For CarQuals the plane-guard helicopter is not in sight flying circles to starboard. For normal recoveries they stay in close, but during extended flight operations anywhere within 20 miles is permitted. (Probably a good thing as they can practice helo things instead of endless delta patterns.) There is no break when the helo needs fuel or a crew switch. They land behind the island and hot pump. (Hornet pilots say it's scary if you're in your jet parked on the elevator behind the landing spot.)

The Gospel According to St. Fresnel of the Miraculous Lens

Now that readers have come this far, they will appreciate and understand this description in biblical terms of an approach, wave-off, and a second approach to a trap. Various hints suggest it could have been written by the pilot of several types of airplane, including Stoof, Hoover, or Whale, but it applies to any tailhook pilot. Although the gospel is a bit irreverent, the reality is that there was, and is, a lot of serious praying around the boat. (Note: aircraft external lights are kept off while on the flight deck and only turned on as the signal "ready to launch" or in the event of a brake failure.)

Chapter One, Verses I through VI

I. In the Beginning, God created the heavens, and the Aircraft Carrier, and the seas upon which to float it; and yet there was complete Darkness upon the face of the earth. And, as we traveled, there came to us, as a voice out of the darkness, an angel of the Lord, saying, "On centerline, on glide slope, three quarters of a mile, call the ball." I reflected upon these words, for I was still yet engulfed in complete darkness. With deep feeling and doubt overwhelming my countenance, I glanceth toward my companion at my right hand and saith, "What seeth thou, trusted friend?" and there was a great silence. Gazing in a searching manner and seeing naught, I raised my voice saying, "Clara . . ."

II. And God spoke to me, and He said, "You're low . . . power." As the Lord saith, so shall it be, and I added power; and lo, the ball riseth up onto the bottom of the mirror. But it was a tainted red glow, and surely indicateth of Satan's own influence. And God spoke to me again saying, "Power. Power. Power! Fly the ball." And lo, the ball riseth up and off the top of the lens, and the great darkness was upon me.

III. And the voice of the Angel came to me again, saying, "When comfortable, 1,200 feet, turn downwind." Whereupon I wandered in the darkness, without direction, for surely the ships radar was beset by demons, and there was great confusion cast upon CATCC, and there was a great silence in which there was no comfort to be found. Even my Tacan needle spinneth, and lo, there was chaos; my trusted companion weepeth quietly unto himself and from close behind I heard weeping and gnashing of teeth of our flock. There was a great turmoil within my cockpit for a multitude of serpents had crept therein.

IV. And though we wandered, as if by Providence I found myself within that Holy Corridor, and at 1,200 feet, among my brethren seeking refuge; and the voice of the Angel of the Lord came to me again, asking of me my needles, and I raised my voice saying, "Up and centered," and the voice answered, "Roger, fly your needles." I reflected upon these words, and I raised my voice in prayer, for though my gyro indicateth it not, surely my aircraft hath been turned upside down. Verily, as Beelzebub surely wrestled with me, a voice, that of my trusted companion, saith to me calmly, "Friend, fly thy needles, and find comfort in the Lord." And lo, with deep trembling in my heart, I did, and He guideth me to centered glide slope and centerline, though I know not how it came to be.

V. And out of the great darkness, God spoke to me again saying, "Roger ball" for now I had faith. And though the ball began to rise at the in-close position, my right hand was full of the Spirit, and it squeeketh off power and as in a great miracle my plane stoppeth upon the flight deck, for it hath caught the four wire, which God in his infinite wisdom hath placed 30 feet further down the flight deck than the three wire.

VI. And thus bathed in a golden radiance from above, our pilgrimage was at an end, and my spirit was truly reborn. And as I basked in the rapture, God spoketh to me one final time, and He saith, "Lights out on deck."

Arresting Gear Limits

"In late 1975 during CarQuals on the Franklin D. Roosevelt, an F-4J broke a wire and was lost over the side. We came aboard in summer of 1976 with F-4N Phantoms for workups/deployment. The aftermath of the mishap was a limit on max engaging speed. Seem to recall the speed was 126 knots. That resulted in a procedure that unless there was an SPN-10 radar closure rate of 126 or less we were waved off. No SPN-10, no trap. Produced a number of otherwise unnecessary wave-offs when the SPN-10 could not produce a number even with a lot of wind over the deck."[18]

Trapping heavy airplanes with high approach speeds in low wind and two-blocking the gear was always a worry. (Two-block meant there was no more movement available in the arresting gear engine and damage was likely.) LSOs had to be wary of dropped noses, control issues due to lack of power, and other errors that added those last extra knots of speed.

The latest evolution of arresting gear is Advanced Recovery Control (ARC), which "Replaces lever, gear, pulley, and CAM assembly with solid state electronics and hydraulic actuators to provide valve actuator control for the Constant Run Out Valve (CROV)"[19] In other words, there is a limiter/relief sensor, which changes the controlling pressure before the engine is two-blocked.

EPILOGUE

A replica of the first airplane to land on a ship, the Ely-Curtiss Pusher, could have taken off from the fantail, climbed a hundred feet, and then landed before reaching the bow of USS* George W. Bush *(CVN-77). Builder, pilot, LSO Bob Coolbaugh, wanted to try, but the navy said no so he settled for a trip on the deck to commemorate the 100th anniversary of U.S. naval aviation.

Thanks to CDR Bryan "RJ" Roberts, director of the LSO school, I spent two glorious days on USS *George Washington* (CVN-73) in April 2016 watching how LSOs work these days. It had been 32 years since I had been to sea and another 10 before that since I did any waving. I was flown out in a C-2 Greyhound COD (as noisy and uncomfortable as I remember, but airliners can't land on ships) and was given a fancy certificate making me an Honorary Tailhooker, much to my amusement. Although much has changed, much has not. People remain the most important factor of all. The sheer amount of physical labor is staggering. Not just on the flight deck, but on all decks where men and women do all the jobs that make such a complex operation possible.

The Paddles I met (yes, they still call themselves that) were all friendly, enthusiastic, and patient in explaining to this old guy what they were doing. Spirit in the ready rooms was as high as ever.

Back in the introduction I equivocated on male pronouns for LSOs. Since then, women have certainly earned their place in navy cockpits as well as on the platform. I realized how far they have come when I watched LT Leslie "Dirty" Garcia, the OIC of the AirPac F/A-18 FRS Detachment in action. (Her callsign is from an incident early in her Hornet training when she had to fly a long distance with landing gear and flaps extended, i.e., "dirty.") Her, and the team's, performance was superb on a day with rain, high winds, a pitching deck, and missing wires.

Captains' Power

In addition to commanding 5,000 men and women and being responsible for a billion dollars' worth of machinery, captains of aircraft carriers control the world around them.

TINS, a group of VIPs were having their pictures taken with the CO on the bridge. The photographer asked if they could move to the other side of the bridge because the light was better. Rather than walk 80 feet, the captain called, "Helmsman, left standard rudder," and turned the ship around.

TINS, the CarQual period, was drawing to a close and several pilots still needed more night landings. The landing pattern was busy all through to night and into the dawn. As the sun came up, the LSO called on the radio for all aircraft to turn off their lights. The squawk box from the bridge buzzed and the captain said, "I will tell you when the sun rises."

Airplane lights came back on and the pilots continued getting "night" traps.

Your author (with glasses) and CDR "RJ" Roberts on the platform. This photo-op did not interrupt the concentration of the LSO team.

Airplanes are moved around the deck by human muscle. Here in 1943 a Dauntless is being pushed up the deck.

No matter what they were doing before the call "Rig the barricade!" all hands on the flight deck (cat and arresting gear crews, fuelers, crash crewmen) turn out to manhandle the heavy barricade into position.

A young plane captain lugging a hydraulic service unit and tie-down chains to his assigned aircraft. Cranial helmets are hot and snug, goggles bite into your face, flotation vests are heavy and not vented, and most work days are 18 hours long.

Crystal Ball

It is expected in a book like this to speculate on the future, so here goes. There are new acronyms for aircraft-carrying ships. My experience and this history is about CATOBAR (Catapult Assisted Take-Off [Barrier] Arrested Recovery). Today only three nations operate CATOBAR ships: United States CVNs, France's *Charles De Gaulle*, and Brazil's *São Paulo*.

Although Harriers were successful during the Falklands-Malvinas combat they did not have to fly long distances with heavy ordnance loads, an ability that vertical takeoff and landing, VTOL, aircraft lack. Short takeoffs using thrust vectoring and a "ski-jump" are STOVL, which allows aircraft to carry a larger payload as compared to during VTOL.

STOBAR is conventional, rather than STOVL, aircraft launching using a ski-jump to assist take-off but needing arresting gear to land on the ship. STOBAR is simpler than CATOBAR, but it works only with aircraft that have a high thrust-to-weight ratio. Russian, Indian, and Chinese carriers use STOBAR.

Former Soviet carriers have been sold at bargain prices and are in a variety of conditions (one is a museum/amusement park). India and China have active building programs. Great Britain is building HMS *Queen Elizabeth* and has a second planned. They alternate between STOVL, STOBAR, and even CATOBAR.

There will always be a need for mobile airpower at sea in whatever form.

A Centennial

Naval aviation is more than a century old. How much more depends on how you count and what you consider the beginning. To the U.S. Navy, 100 years was in 2011. LSOs, Paddles, and Bats won't hit the century mark until 2022. Who knows what aircraft carriers will look like by then?

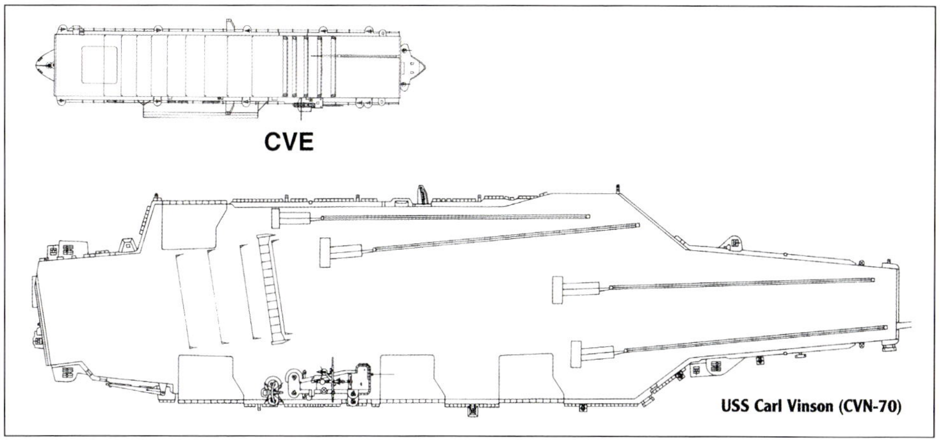

This is the final slide in my presentation to new LSOs. I tell them, next time at sea, stand by the island and look aft, that is the size of the carriers your predecessors flew and waved on.

American aircraft carriers at NAS North Island. Top to foreground: USS Carl Vinson *(CVN-70), USS* Nimitz *(CVN-68), and USS* Ronald Reagan *(CVN-76). The* Reagan *is tied up in the same spot USS* Langley *(CV-1) was tied up in 1922 (compare to the photo of North Island in Chapter 1). The dock area for the other two is landfill in what was once the Spanish Bight.*

Lockheed Martin X-35, seen here over Edwards AFB, was the successful proof-of-concept prototype for the Navy's revolutionary new F-35C Lightning II, and very possibly the last manned fighter aircraft that future LSOs will bring aboard a carrier. The aircraft is currently scheduled to enter service in 2018, and is designed to operate from new digital-age super carriers such as the USS Gerald R. Ford *(CVN-78) in the future. (Mike Machat)*

GLOSSARY

ACLS: Automatic Carrier Landing System

Auto Throttles: Automatic Power Compensation (APC)

Bagger: pilot who is out to *bag* traps, i.e., get as many as possible

Barricade/Barrier: similar words, but different uses. The barrier was 3 feet high and always in place on straight-deck carriers. Its purpose was to stop any airplanes that missed all the wires (10–12) before they crashed into the pack of airplanes parked forward. The barricade is used on angle decks when an airplane must be trapped. It is specially rigged and flight deck crews compete to get it up fast. Both will damage the landing airplane.

Bingo: both verb and adjective. Not the game played in churches and fire halls, but to divert to a shore base from the ship

Bolter: when the tailhook does not catch a wire. Jets go to full power on touchdown to be ready for a bolter and takeoff again. There were no bolters on straight-decks.

Bounce: a touch-and-go landing carrier style. FCLP was called "bounce drill"

Break: the hard turn entering the landing pattern

CarQual: acronym for the full Carrier Qualify, abbreviated CQ. A series of launches and landings at the ship with no mission except to get landings. Usually for pilots new to the airplane type or who have not seen the back end of the boat for some time.

Catapult: "accelerators" in Royal Navy terms

CDP: Cross-deck pennant, the wires that go across the deck for the arresting gear

Clara: "I do not see the ball," short from "Clarify" or a possible TINS

CO: commanding officer, casually "the skipper"

COD: Carrier Onboard Delivery aircraft. C-1s, cargo/passenger versions of the sub-hunter S2F (*Stoof*), along with the A-1 Skyraider, were the last airplanes in the U.S. Navy that were *cut* to a landing.

Cut: chop the airplane's engine to idle and fly to a landing. Mandatory for all aircraft until angle decks were in use; thereafter only aircraft with reciprocating engines required the cut.

Cut Lights: Green lights on OLS to replace Paddles' signal of left arm dropped down, right arm slashed across the throat. After recips went away, still used for other signals.

CV: "C" for Cruiser; "V" in USN designations is from the French *voler*, meaning to fly. "Z" for lighter-than-air is based on Zeppelin and "H" obviously is for helicopter. nb, V, Z, H in squadron designations.

Det: short for detachment. A group taken from a larger unit for some special function. Dets formed for a limited time.

Dirty Shirt Wardroom: wardroom set aside for meals while wearing flight suits or flight deck clothing

Ensign/Nugget: Ens is the lowest navy officer rank. Nugget is a navy or Marine pilot on his first assignment. Both imply a naiveté and inexperience in carrier operations.

FAA: Fleet Air Arm. British naval aviation. The status of the term changed over time.

Fam: familiarization, usually about a first flight in an airplane type, i.e., Fam-1

Fantail: the aft section of an open deck on a ship. On a CV an extension of the hangar deck and far below the ramp. Called "the spud locker" from the time when bins of potatoes were stored there.

Flying boats and floatplanes: flying boats have a hull, float planes have pontoons.

Glide slope: The correct angle for descent to landing. The aircraft is not gliding, but using power.

Gouge: good information, Brit term was *Gen*. Frequently indicating a short cut or summary

Homeplate: also "mother," the carrier one flies from

JP: Jet Propellant (fuel), closer to diesel than gasoline, formulated for turbine engines. Types of JP are numbered. JP-4 was created for use on CVs where the tanks are kept full with sea water to avoid combustible vapor. (The JP is lighter and floats.)

Net, Safety: made of metal mesh, there is one below all platforms for LSOs to jump down, roll, and run to safety when an airplane is about to smash the platform. The far edge is 8 feet away from the platform and there were times when a nervous observer, when signaled into the net, jumped completely across it and into the water 60 feet below.

Observers: British term for navigators

OIC: Officer in Charge

Pickle: hand-control with buttons to turn on the *wave-off* or *cut* lights. In his other hand an LSO holds a radio handset.

Plane-guard: helicopter that stays close to the ship during landings and takeoffs to haul aviators out of the sea. The job used to be done by escort ships (*Small Boys*).

Quals: see CarQual

RAG: old term for today's Fleet Replacement Squadron, FRS, where newly-winged aviators are trained in a specific type of airplane

Ramp: the down sloping aft portion of the flight deck. Airplanes hit the ramp with varying degrees of severity, none of which are acceptable.

Recips: piston-powered aircraft

RN: Royal Navy

Tactical aircraft: basically, airplanes that flew off CVs. Unlike the air force, which calls all sorts of aircraft fighters, the U.S. Navy differentiates between fighters, attack, reconnaissance, torpedo, dive bomber, ECM, and ASW roles. TacAir includes them all.

Touch and Go (T&G): To land and take off again immediately, usually for training

Trap: an arrested landing; ashore or afloat

Two Block: flags on a ship's yardarm are used for signaling. Half-mast is standby for a maneuver. Begin the maneuver when the flag(s) are hoisted all the way up with the pulleys (blocks) together.

USAAC/USAAF/USAF: The American air force over the years; U.S. Army Air Corps (1939); U.S. Army Air Forces (1942); and United States Air Force (1947)

Wave-off: mandatory go around, the signal not to land. (With paddles, the LSO waved both arms over his head. With lens or mirror; red, flashing lights activated by the *pickle*.)

Wind over deck (WOD): combination of natural wind and ship's speed

Wire: a braided steel cable stretched across the deck (also called CDP, Cross-Deck Pennant) connected to pulleys and an engine that slows tailhook airplanes to a stop. Wires are numbered from the stern forward, i.e., 1# is closest to the stern; 4# on modern ships, 12# or so in the old days were the last available.

XO: eXecutive Officer, second in command of a ship or squadron; casually "Exec"

ENDNOTES

Prologue

1 Norman Polmar, *Aircraft Carriers*

2 The guns were the world's largest until World War II Japanese battleships. They also did not work on *Furious*. When the one remaining 18-incher fired the shock was bad enough to move steel structure and shear rivets.

3 Young, *Rutland of Jutland*, as quoted in *Two Block Fox*

4 Polmar, *op. cit.*

5 The Japanese navy had an observer on *Furious* at the same time. One must speculate whether Chevalier met him.

6 Report to SecNav, quoted in *Two Block Fox*

Chapter One

1 Winston Churchill is credited with inventing the term "seaplane" as he considered "hydroaeroplane" cumbersome.

2 *Hermes* career was short. In October 1914 after a mission carrying aircraft to France she was torpedoed by a U-boat on the return leg. Her name was soon used again.

3 The Japanese merchant vessel *Wakamiya Maru* had been made a seaplane carrier in 1912 with the addition of crude, canvas hangars and additional cranes. Because of attacks by her Maurice Farman seaplanes on the German enclave at Tsingtao, China, in Sept. 1914, she is credited as the first carrier in combat.

4 The claim was that *Eagle* was named in appreciation of the United States entering the war. However, there had already been 14 ships of the Royal Navy with that name

6 Origin of calling the aft end of the landing deck the ramp?

7 When Ely landed aboard *Pennsylvania* he had a tailwind. If the ship had been underway it is likely the turbulence from the superstructure would have made his airplane uncontrollable.

8 A slipway at the stern for seaplanes to taxi on to that could then be raised out of the sea to the level of an opening in the hangar deck and rolled off; was eliminated early in the design process.

9 She became renowned across the navy for her engine room instruments, which were displayed only in Spanish and in metric units.

10 Working with *Argus* in Sept. 1927 *Hermes* aircraft attacked Chinese pirates in their stronghold in Bias Bay northeast of Hong Kong.

11 Dan Linton website, *The Evolution of the Aircraft Carrier*

12 What one of her first crew members called her

13 A new regulation required that only rated aviators could hold an aviation command. Reeves was one of several senior officers who underwent Naval Aviation Observer (NAO) training.

14 *Naval Aviation News* May 1973

15 Four of the original names became aircraft carriers: *Lexington*, *Saratoga*, *Ranger* and *Constellation*. Construction of the *United States* was started then canceled. *Constitution*, "Old Ironsides," was not used as the famous sailing frigate was in commission, and still is.

16 Lexington's turbo-electric propulsion system was powerful enough to supplement the city of Tacoma, Washington's electrical supply during a drought in late 1929.

17 Saratoga was a target ship for atomic bomb tests at Bikini Atoll in January 1946. She survived the first blast, but the second put her on the bottom. She was recently opened to a limited number of recreational scuba divers.

18 *Naval Aviation News* Oct. 1962

Chapter Two

1. The Fox flag means flying. "Two-block" is to commence the event the signal flag represents by moving the flag all the way to the pulley, the block. Melhorn used the phrase as the title of his American carrier early history.

2 3,000 aircraft, 67,000 personnel

3 Maybe. Only one source could be found with this statement.

4 Many photographs and movies taken of the launch of the Pearl Harbor attack were taken on *Akagi*, the small and portside island, making identification obvious. The island on the left occasionally causes some to wonder if the photographs were printed backward.

5 As quoted in "Cat Shots in the Dark" by LCDR George Cornelius, USN, in *Flying*, July 1952. Price was a Vice Admiral and Chief of Naval Air Training at the time of the interview.

6 A dead light is a light that is set into the deck; important on a carrier in that it did not stick up.

7 Cornelius *op. cit.*

Chapter Three

1 The IJN was an early exponent of multi-carrier groups operating together to get many airplanes airborne at a time. Contrary to a popular Western notion, the inspiration did not come from the line-up of Royal Navy carriers during the Coronation Fleet Review for King George VI as that was not until 1937.

2 Allied code names were assigned to Japanese aircraft to make remembering them simpler. Male first names were used for fighters; females for bombers and other types. The responsible U.S. Army Air Corps officer's Tennessee background was reflected in such names as Zeke, Claude, Irving, Topsy, and Nell.

3 D'Oyly-Hughes failed to launch any aircraft to form a combat air patrol around the carrier group, reportedly to give the aircrews a rest. The previous commander always had some aircraft in the air. Had he done so, *Glorious* might have been able to spot incoming threats, or have been

able to either turn and run or fight. No aircraft were even on the deck for a quick launch. Nor did he order zig-zagging. Tales of a personal vendetta making him in a rush to return to Scapa Flow abounded.

4 Naval Squadron 802 was reconstituted and Eric "Winkle" Brown became one of its pilots. 802 also was unlucky enough to have three ships sunk while it was aboard: *Glorious, Audacity*, and *Avenger*

5 Lieutenant Commander Lumley Lyster was based at Taranto in 1917, so was familiar with Taranto and its environs, knowledge that he put to good use. He was also instrumental in earlier plans and had been CO of *Illustrious*. Ironically, he had been decorated with the "Order of the Crown of Italy" by the Italians for his World War I service.

6 World naval ships forums

7 Edgar Mikronis, ANA *Wings of Gold*, Summer 2002

Chapter Four

1 Barrett Tillman, "The Indispensible Man," *The HOOK*, Fall 1982

2 Stanley Brand, (ex) SubLT (A) RNVR, correspondence with author 2003

3 *ibid*

4 *ibid*

5 John W. Lambert, *Wildcats Over Casablanca*

6 *Barracuda Pilot*, Dunstan Hadley, Airlife Publishing

7 Stanley Brand, (ex) SubLT (A) RNVR, correspondence with author 2003

8 *ibid*

9 *ibid*

10 *ibid*

11 *ibid*

12 *ibid*

13 *ibid*

14 Naval tradition, sometimes with ceremony. Certificates made with "the blessing of Neptunus Rex and Aurora Borealis"

Chapter Five

1 Barrett Tillman, "The Indispensible Man," *The Hook,* Fall 1982

2 *ibid*

3 *NavNews* 1 Oct 1945, ref Lindsey letter 7 July 1962

4 Mark Peattie, *Sunburst*

5 Tillman *op. cit.*

6 Orchard Place was also where the Douglas Company built the first DC-4s (military C-54) and in later years grew into Chicago's major airport and one of the busiest in the world. The original name is why the airline identifier is ORD.

7 CAPT Charles E. Roemer, "Carrier Task Force X-Lake Michigan," *Foundation*, Fall 1983

8 Barrett Tillman, "The Indispensible Man," *The Hook,* Winter 1982

9 Unclassified and Miscellaneous Ships (IX)

10 Roemer *op. cit.*

11 Roemer *op. cit.*

12 There were scattered examples of LSO who were not pilots; half a dozen AVT officers waved and there was one case of a ship's surgeon.

13 A future fighter ace and Medal of Honor winner

14 Tillman *op. cit.*

15 Jim Mulquin, letter, *Wings of Gold* magazine

16 Thomas McKelvey Cleaver, *Fabled Fifteen*

17 The huge fly-past of 450 varied aircraft dubbed "Operation Airshow" was conducted beneath a low ceiling. Chris Cagle, CO VF-88 at the time and later VADM, said it was the scariest thing he ever did in aviation. Not much, if any, coordination with B-29s and other USAAF aircraft. Flying in formation was full-throttle then throttle-to-idle with numerous near misses.

Chapter Six

1 Barreett Tillman, "Downsizing," *The HOOK*, Summer 1996

2 A P2V-3C did get 182 "traps" on arresting gear set up on shore with the view to landing on a ship. Unlike takeoffs, which could be offset, arrestments had to be on centerline and the 100-foot wingspan of the Neptune did not allow safe clearance of the island.

3 Although considered a major setback for the USN, cancellation of the *United States* may have proved beneficial in the long run as the funds for it were used to modernize existing aircraft carriers. Additionally, it would have been finished too late for the Korean War and the strategic bombing mission had been superseded.

4 The later and widely produced F4H/F-4 was officially the Phantom II.

5 The Pirate was a conventional design adapted to use the low-powered and notoriously unreliable J-34 jet engine. In order to boost performance an afterburner was added to the F6U. However, the enlarged fuselage caused lateral stability problems, which resulted in a redesigned tail with extra fins on the stabilizer. After flying briefly in a development squadron, all the remaining airframes went to training schools for student mechanics.

6 Navy aviator identified only as "Screws" on the Internet

7 Affectionate (?) term for the big-bellied, splay-legged Avenger. Twenty years later the Grumman F-14 Tomcat received the same sobriquet.

8 John Jenista in *The Hook*, Fall 1991

9 *Naval Aviation 1910–1995*, Navy Historical Center, Roy Grossnick 1996

10 Abridged from the *Mariner Miracle*, Captain Wynn F. Foster, Win 91 *HOOK*

11 Fred Blechman, *The HOOK* Win 1997

12 Bob Atherton in *Flight Journal* April 2004

13 LCDR Opie, USN, Assistant Naval Attaché in London, wrote a report on Taranto in 1940 based on Royal Navy experience.

14 Robin Lindsey letter 7 July 1962

15 Tillman, *op. cit.*

16 Jack Thomas, MACShip, LSO letter to author

17 The last operational Seafire was the MK 47 with Griffon engine and contra-rotating propellers, barely recognizable as a Spitfire. Mk 47s saw service in Korea. An Mk 47 was *t*he last of the 22,000 aircraft built under the Spitfire/Seafire program.

Chapter Seven

1 Officially Ship Characteristics Board Programs, SCB or simply Program, e.g., SCB-27A or Program 27C.

2 Wheel-less jets landed on a series of inflated rubber bags filling most of the landing area. The jets were then hoisted onto a cradle for moving about

the deck and for the catapult shot. Both the American and British navy flew trials with the concept proving wildly impracticable.

3 Dosé had not yet flown a jet off the boat, nor had he ever trapped on an angled deck. He began a series of bounce drills; in all, he logged 78 field carrier landings before going to the ship.

4 Gerard P. O'Rourke, *Night Fighters over Korea*

5 AoA could also be used to determine best climb, maximum endurance, optimum turn rate, and indication of an impending stall.

6 French AoA indicators had a selector for air speed, which USN models did not.

7 Jerry Houston, F-8 Web

8 Roy "Shadow" Stafford, *The Hook*, Spring 2014

9 Powell, *The Hook*, Spring 2014

10 An F-8 Crusader squadron kept an incentive jar of *Atomic Fireball* candies in the ready room. A pilot who flew an OK pass was rewarded with a Fireball.

11 Admiral who in early World War II lost a fleet and was lost himself.

12 Correctly, *Veinticinco de Mayo*

13 *Independencia* went into reserve by 1969, as *25 de Mayo* was then in service.

14 HMS *Biter* was built in the United States and escorted Atlantic convoys until damaged by the explosion of a torpedo from one of her own airplanes that had gone over the side. While in the shipyard she had a fire and was not repaired until being returned to the United States, after which she went immediately to France as *Dixmude* in late 1945. As a small deck, *Dixmude* saw limited duty in Indochina in 1947–1948 before becoming an aviation transport vessel. From 1960 the hulk was used as a base accommodation ship. In 1966 the ex-*Biter*, ex-*Dixmude* was returned to the U.S. Navy and sunk as a target.

Chapter Eight

1 Yup, it was me.

2 CDR John B. "Pirate" Nichols III, USN (Ret), "The Catwalk," *The Hook*, Summer 1989

3 Known as "Bloody Barin" from 1944 for 40 fatal accidents in two years.

4 Card game similar to Rummy, but with all the cards (*papes*) renamed. e.g., 3 of clubs = *puppy feet trey*. Less about winning than penalizing for wrong words.

5 A two-camera installation was normal, 40 feet apart, so one was always available. There is no indication which is in use.

6 Sylvia Ellis, *Dictionary of Anglo-American Relations*

7 Starbird eventually had more than 1,000 traps

8 Leo Dewey, Letter, *The Hook* Spring 1990

Chapter Nine

1 Correctly the bottles are rockets, not jets.

2 Kirby Schnell, e-mail to author, 2016

3 A dead light is a light that is set into the deck. Important on a carrier in that they do not stick up. The PLAT camera is in a dead light fitting.

4 One interesting experiment was the "super ball" with the middle made three cells wide. It gave the pilot trend information as he departed from centered ball. After trials super ball was not put into use.

5 Gregory W. Dyczko, *OLA History*

6 The radar is so precise that small reflectors were fastened to the airplane, usually on a landing gear door, so the radar looked at exactly the same spot. A similar reflector on a pole was mounted at the far aft corner of the flight deck to calibrate the ship's antenna.

7 Jerry Houston, *Fight to Fly*

Chapter Ten

1 The Iranians used F-14s in the war with Iraq; apparently with some success.

2 Ernest E. Christensen, RADM, USN (ret) blog input 1984

3 Aerology report for "indefinite ceiling zero feet sky obscured zero visibility in fog." Therefore, also the name of the back bar at O'Clubs, at least Lemoore and Miramar's. "No flying, let's go to the O'Club."

4 Commonly called "Shars"

5 By this time fully half the flight crews were RAF officers although there was no question of jurisdiction as there was in the 1930s.

6 Afghanistan has historically been "The Graveyard of Empires." There is no evidence that current efforts will change that grim description.

7 The nuclear-powered aircraft carrier USS *Harry S. Truman* (CVN-75) and the ships in her battle group were preparing to get underway from Norfolk, Virginia, for an extended deployment to the Mid East two weeks before Christmas in 2002. Just as the lines were cast off, this announcement was made throughout the ship on the 1-MC announcing system, "Peace on Earth to all men of good will. All others, Stand By."

8 Tillman, *On Wave and Wing: A Century of Aircraft Carriers*

9 Al Fullerton, Cheng JFK, e-mail to author, 2016

10 LSO "*Eagle*" McClung, e-mail to author, 2015

11 *Lexington* was decommissioned in 1991, *Enterprise* was taken out of service in 2014, but because of bureaucratic machinations will not be officially decommissioned for two more years.

12 LSO Bob "the Kid" Kuhlke, e-mail to author, 2015

13 LSO T. R. Swartz, e-mail to author, 2015

14 opcit. McClung

15 LSO George Shattuck, e-mail to author, 2015

16 LSO Daniel Bo Howe, e-mail to author, 2015

17 Current Paddles use the term "Gucci" for devices that use the latest in technology.

18 LSO Eagle McClung, e-mail to author, 2016

19 ARC training presentation April 2009

INDEX

An appropriate closing picture: blue sky, wood platform, good view of the equipment box, and the LSO dramatically leaning to will the challenging RA-5C Vigilante into the wires. Author speculated on the squadron (RVAH-6) and guessed at the year (1967, USS Ranger*) by equipment and clothing. After sending the photo to his navy friends, Lonny "Eagle" McClung shot back, "Hey, that was me!" Small world.*

FLYING WINGS & RADICAL THINGS: Northrop's Secret Aerospace Projects & Concepts 1939–1994 *Tony Chong* John K. "Jack" Northrop and the company he founded in 1939, Northrop Aircraft, Inc., will be forever linked with the giant futuristic Flying Wings of the 1940s. Here for the first time is the untold story of Northrop's rare, unique, and formerly super-secret aircraft and spacecraft of the future. Featuring stunning original factory artwork, technical drawings, and never-before-seen photographs, this book shows an amazing array of radical high-performance aircraft concepts from Jack Northrop and his team of brilliant and innovative engineers. Much of this material has only recently been declassified. Hardbound, 10 x 10, 192 pages, 361 b/w and 70 color photos. ***Item # SP229***

A COMPLETE HISTORY OF U.S. COMBAT AIRCRAFT FLY-OFF COMPETITIONS *Erik Simonsen* Many advanced and now legendary aircraft have been designed, built, and flown in every generation of aviation development. Focusing on the Cold War era, this book shows readers how crucial fly-off competitions have been to the development of America's military air arsenal. This book explains in detail how fly-off competitions are conducted, and it shows what both competing aircraft designs looked like during their trials, and what the losing aircraft would have looked like in operational markings had it actually won. Hardbound, 10 x 10, 228 pages, 395 color and 156 b/w photos. ***Item # SP227***

WORLD'S FASTEST SINGLE-ENGINE JET AIRCRAFT: Convair's F-106 Delta Dart Interceptor *Col. Doug Barbier, USAF (Ret.)* This book provides an insightful and in-depth look at the sixth member of the Air Force "Century Series" family of supersonic fighters. From initial concept through early flight test and development and into operational service, every facet of the F-106's career is examined. Hardbound, 10 x 10 inches, 240 pages, 350 photos. ***Item # SP237***

CLEAR THE DECK! Aircraft Carrier Accidents of World War II *Cory Graff* Using photos from the National Archives and museums, Graff examines the amazing Naval aviation actions that took place during WWII. The photos in this edition are black and white. Softbound, 8-1/2 x 8-1/2 inches, 132 pages, 207 b/w photos. ***Item # SP119***

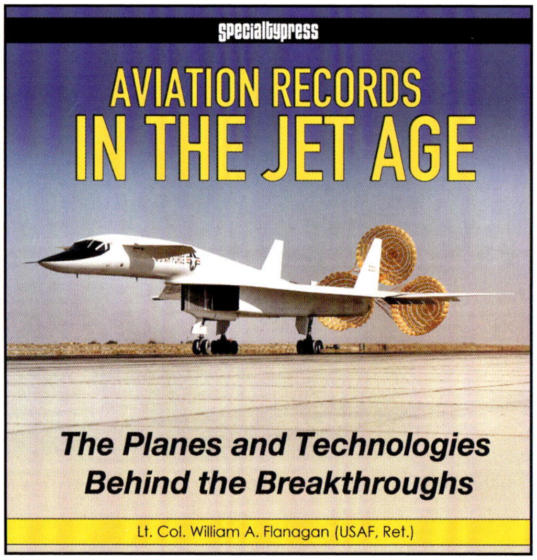

AVIATION RECORDS IN THE JET AGE: The Planes and Technologies Behind the Conquests *William A. Flanagan* Explains in detailed and easy-to-understand terms how specific advances in aircraft design such as powerplants, aerodynamics, flight control systems, instrumentation, and life-support systems led to ever-improved record-breaking aircraft. Hardbound, 10 x 10 inches, 160 pages, 300 b/w and color photos. ***Item # SP230S***

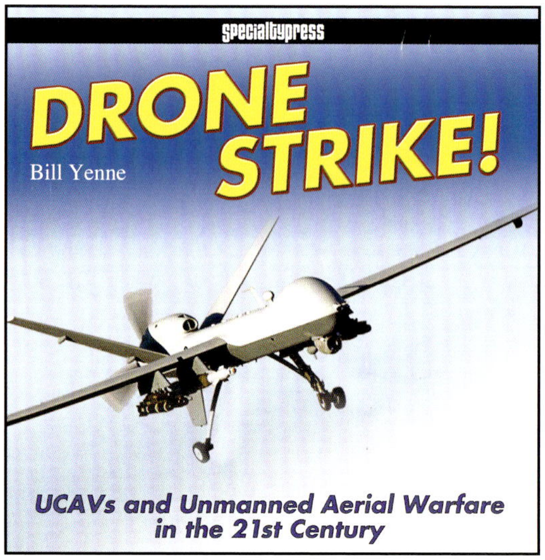

DRONE STRIKE!: UCAVs and Aerial Warfare in the 21st Century *Bill Yenne* Takes you from the end of the 20th Century through today's latest technical wonders, covering such amazing unmanned aircraft capabilities as aerial refueling and landing aboard aircraft carriers even more accurately than manned aircraft. Hardbound, 10 x 10 inches, 160 pages, 300 b/w and color photos. ***Item # SP238S***

Specialty Press, 838 Lake Street South, Forest Lake, MN. Phone 800-895-4585 & 651-277-1400 Fax: 651-277-1203
www.specialtypress.com
Crécy Publishing Ltd., 1a Ringway Trading Estate, Shadowmoss Road, Manchester, M22 5LH, England. Phone: 44 161 499 0024 Fax: 44 161 499 0298
www.crecy.co.uk